# PENANG
## 500 Early Postcards

This book is dedicated to the memory of my parents
Mr. Cheah Kim Yeam
(1904–1987)
and
Madam Ooi Gaik Phuan
(1907–1992)

© Editions Didier Millet, 2012
EDITIONS DIDIER MILLET
25, Jalan Pudu Lama, 50200 Kuala Lumpur, Malaysia
Tel: 03-2031 3805 Fax: 03-2031 6298
E-mail: edmbooks@edmbooks.com.my

www.edmbooks.com

First published 2012

Editions Didier Millet Pte Ltd
121, Telok Ayer Street, #03-01, Singapore 068590
Tel: 65-6324 9260 Fax: 65-6324 9261
E-mail:edm@edmbooks.com.sg

Colour separation by
PICA DIGITAL SINGAPORE

Printed in Singapore by
TIEN WAH PRESS

ISBN: 978-967-10617-1-8

*Front cover:* CLOCK TOWER, PENANG, c. 1910.
The pyramid-roofed lighthouse is on the right, and the Queen Victoria Memorial Clock Tower
can be seen on the left. The domed building in the centre is that of the Hongkong and Shanghai
Bank (HSBC).

*Back cover:* UNTITLED [NYONYAS], c. 1910. Penang *nyonyas* shown clad in traditional attire.

*Opposite:* No. 208 PENANG, BISHOPSTREET, c. 1905.

# PENANG
## 500 Early Postcards

Cheah Jin Seng

EDITIONS
DIDIER
MILLET

No. 78. The Esplanade, Penang

No. 58. Clock Tower.

CHINESE TEMPLE, PITT STREET, PENANG

# CONTENTS

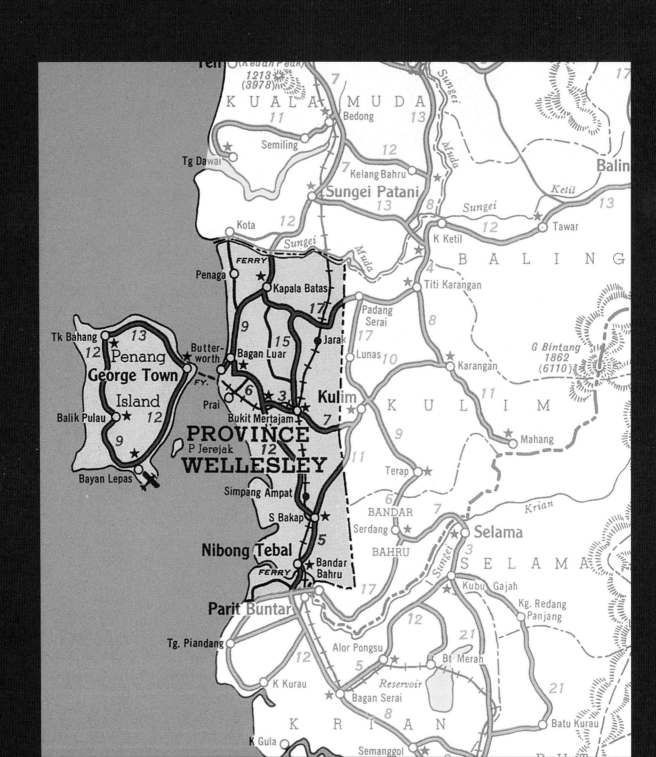

This excellent collection of rare picture postcards captures vividly Penang's social and economic history from the late 19th to the mid-20th century. It is a veritable labour of love, gathered over many years.

Penang was once the transhipment centre for northern Malaya and an intermediate feeder port for ships trading in India, Sumatra, Java, Siam and Burma. Among the postcards in the collection are several depicting scenes reminiscent of Joseph Conrad's novels: the hustle and bustle of Penang's commercial waterfront, stevedores unloading goods from ship to warehouse, and steamers anchored in the harbour, their large funnels belching smoke. Other photographic vignettes reflect the cultural heritage and social life of the different ethnic communities during Penang's colonial era. There are images too of scenic sites such as Penang Hill and the Botanic Gardens, and of narrow streets, wet markets, bazaars, mosques, temples, churches and schools.

As a social historian, I find the most fascinating postcards to be those which reveal bygone scenes that have since disappeared on the island. In the collection we find pictures of the grand Runnymede Hotel, which ceased business in 1941, and of the water-filled moat around Fort Cornwallis which was filled in during the 1920s. There are images of the electric trams and trolley buses which ran through the city streets and of the rickshaws, their pullers and their Jinricksha Department that were once such an unmissable part of everyday life. Long gone too are the racecourse located right in the heart of the city on Macalister Road, before it relocated to Bukit Gantong in 1939, and the majestic Quadrangle, a complex comprising the Governor's Office and other Government Buildings which stood at Weld Quay until bombed by Allied warplanes in 1945.

These postcards are a wonderful artistic record of Penang's unique past and progress as northern Malaya's commercial centre and "The Pearl of the Orient".

Dr Cheah Boon Kheng                                    OCTOBER 2012

*Opposite:* DETAIL OF MAP
OF BRITISH MALAYA, C. 1950

# HISTORY of PENANG and its PICTURE POSTCARDS

Postcard featuring postage stamps used in Penang, which was part of the Straits Settlements.

A portrait of photographer Ernst August Kaulfuss (1861–1908).

In my earlier book, *Malaya: 500 Early Postcards* (2008), I described and published about 95 early picture postcards (ppcs) of Penang. For this book, I have extended the number of Penang ppcs to 500. Penang was, like Singapore, a regional entrepôt in the 19th century, and played an important role in British expansion in Southeast Asia; this is reflected in the number of ppcs of Penang. In fact, Penang has nearly as many pre-World War II ppcs as Singapore.[2]

Every serious collector of Penang ppcs has cards that other collectors do not have as no collection is ever complete! This book exhibits some ppcs not published previously. The ppcs in this book are shown at roughly their original size and in their original colour.

## Brief history of Penang

Penang is located in the northwest of Peninsular Malaysia by the Straits of Malacca. It consists of two parts – Penang Island and Seberang Perai (formerly known as Province Wellesley) on the mainland of the Malay Peninsula.[7] Kedah lies to the north and east, and Perak to the south.

Penang has a land area of 1,048 square kilometres and a population of 1.56 million (2010) comprising Chinese (43%), Malays and other natives (41%), Indians (10%), and others (6%).[124] The capital of Penang is George Town.

Penang, famously known as "The Pearl of the Orient", was originally part of the Kedah Sultanate. It was taken over by Captain Francis Light (1740–1794),[8] on behalf of the British East India Company (EIC), on 11 August 1786.[37] His success in taking possession of Penang is highly praised in British historical accounts: "Pinang, like Singapore, owes its existence as a British possession mainly to the statesmanlike foresight, energy, and diplomatic resourcefulness of one man…Francis Light."[9] On 3 July 1786, a treaty ceding Penang to the British was signed between Francis Light and the Sultan of Kedah. Light landed at Point Pinaggar (the present Esplanade) on 15 July and, on 11 August 1786, took formal possession of the island, officially designated as Prince of Wales Island.[9] At the time of its cession, the population of Penang comprised only 158 Malay settlers.[123]

Light died from malaria on 21 October 1794 and was laid to rest at the Protestant cemetery on Northam Road (now Jalan Sultan Ahmad Shah).[8] His eldest son, Colonel William Light, became the founder of Adelaide in 1836 and the first surveyor general of South Australia.[9,11]

In 1886, in commemoration of the centenary of Light's founding of Penang, the Municipal Council of Penang erected a memorial to him in the style of a Grecian rotunda in front of St George's Church in George Town (*see Chapter 5*).

When Penang celebrated its 150th anniversary in 1936, the Municipal Council commissioned a life-sized bronze statue of Francis Light [1]. As there was no contemporary portrait of him, the statue was based on a portrait of his son, Colonel William Light.[12] The statue was unveiled on 3 October 1939 by Sir Shenton Thomas [2], the governor of the Straits Settlements (SS), at Fort Cornwallis (at the site of the present amphitheatre in the fort).[13,14] It was later moved to the grounds of the Penang High Court and moved several more times before finally moving back to its original location in Fort Cornwallis in 2003, after the fort was restored and opened as a tourist attraction.

As a result of their common heritage, Penang and Adelaide became twin cities in December 1973,[12] following meetings between the Chief Minister of Penang, Dr Lim Chong Eu, and the Premier of South Australia, Don Dunstan.[12]

Penang enjoyed rapid development following its takeover by Francis Light. One of the main reasons for its speedy progress was Penang's strategic location on the trading routes of Europe and Asia [3-4]. At the same time, the tin and rubber boom of the 19th century led to an influx of migrant workers from China and India and, consequently, brisk expansion of the port of Penang.[15,16]

Mail from Penang began c. 1806. In 1826, Penang merged with Malacca and Singapore to form the SS.[7] Postage stamps of the SS were first issued in 1867. Penang, as part of this administrative unit, used SS postage stamps (see page 8, top left; [5-6]). In 1867, the SS became a Crown Colony.[7]

During World War II (1939–1945), Penang was invaded by the Japanese, on 19 December 1941. The Japanese Occupation lasted till 3 September 1945. Even during that tumultuous era, ppcs were produced (albeit very few). These were sent by collectors (top and bottom right; [7-8]).

On 1 February 1948, Penang became part of the Federation of Malaya; this was followed by independence along with the rest of Malaya on 31 August 1957. On 16 September 1963, Penang became a part of Malaysia.[7]

On 7 July 2008, George Town and Malacca were officially recognised by the United Nations Educational, Scientific and Cultural Organization (UNESCO) as World Heritage sites. These two cities are described as reflecting "a mixture of influences which have created a unique architecture, culture and townscape without parallel anywhere in East and Southeast Asia".[7,122]

Today's Penang is a testimony of Francis Light's foresightedness. A British account wrote this in tribute to him: "The debt which the Empire owes to Light is second only to that which it readily acknowledges as the due of Raffles…But however ignorant the British public as a whole may be of Light's great services, Pinang people are not likely to forget them."[9]

## Publishers and Photographers

The earliest ppc in the SS was published in 1897 by German photographer Gustave Richard Lambert (G.R. Lambert). He opened his photographic studio in Singapore in 1867 but left the SS in 1885, leaving the studio to the care of Alexander Koch in 1885. When Koch retired in Europe in 1905, he left the studio to the care of H.T. Jensen of the Parisian photographic studio, Reutlingers.[9] Lambert's studio was ultimately wound up during World War I in 1918. Both Koch and Jensen should be duly credited for many of G.R. Lambert's ppcs, but this is often forgotten![2]

In Penang, the earliest ppc known was sent on 9 May 1898 [9-10], and produced by the German photographer and publisher, Ernst August Kaulfuss, more often known as A. Kaulfuss (see page 8, bottom left; 1861–1908).[18]

Kaulfuss was a pioneer of early ppcs and photographs of Penang, and his early ppcs of Penang are rare. They consist of real photographic vignettes of scenery and people of Penang and Sumatra (photomontages).[19] These photographic images, such as those shown in [2] and [4], were arranged artistically on a ppc, and are in black and white, deep grey or sepia [11-14].

Kaulfuss was the first established European photographer in Penang,[9] and had a studio on Farquhar Street. He travelled widely and published many ppcs of Malaya,[1] however, he did not enter Singapore, perhaps due to an agreement with Lambert (Lambert published ppcs of Malaya up to Kedah but did not cover Penang)[1,2].

The picture side of [8], showing Penang's Eastern and Oriental Hotel. This ppc is dated 1943.

The address side of [7]. This ppc was printed by the Japanese Syonan Army Inspection Team.

The address side of [24]. The sender used a "Deutsches Reich" stamp. Stamps used in Germany from 1900 to 1944 were captioned as such.

The picture side of [37], a Christmas greeting card to Rev. Pykett and Mrs Pykett. The ppc shows a Japanese shrine, and is the earliest incoming ppc in my collection; it was sent to Penang on 23 December 1898.

Following his death in Penang in 1908 he was buried at the Western Road Cemetery.[18]

Kaulfuss's photomontages date from c. 1898 to 1900 [9; 11-14]. Many of his ppcs of Penang are in colour, and these are shown extensively in the later chapters of this book. Kaulfuss himself occasionally appeared in his ppcs [38]. Besides being the most prolific publisher of pre-war Penang ppcs, he also published the "Greetings from Penang" ppc series (c. 1900–1905) [29-36]. These are similar to Lambert's "Greetings from Singapore" ppcs.

Charles Kleingrothe's ppcs of Penang were produced slightly later (c. 1900–1905). His ppcs are visibly sharper, more colourful and better composed than those of Kaulfuss's photomontages. Kleingrothe's ppcs are equally scarce, and are shown in [15] to [24].

Little is known of Kleingrothe except that, like Kaulfuss, he too was German, and that around 1888 he was the manager of Lambert's branch studio in Deli, Sumatra. Within a year, he had opened his own photo studio in partnership with Herman Stafhell and, by 1898, he had established his independent studio in Medan, Sumatra. He operated his studio till c. 1916 when his business succumbed to the economic downturn of World War I (1914–1918). His fate after the closure of his business in Sumatra remains unknown.[20]

Kleingrothe's ppcs of Penang are very distinct in appearance, and are mostly dated 1900 (the date appears after the name of the publisher) [17-20; 22], although a few are undated [21; 23-24].

Tan Chin Kim (1882–1948) [25], a Penangite, was also a pioneer photographer and publisher of Penang ppcs.[16] A chance meeting in 2009 with his last surviving child, Tan Ah Yeang, who is now in her 90s,[21] provided information on the man himself and the founding of Federal Rubber Stamp Company (FRS).[16] As he was a civil servant (he was an accountant with the Immigration Department), he was not allowed to operate a private company. He founded FRS in c. 1910, and left the business operations to his brothers, Tan Chin Hean and Tan Chin Thye, as well as other relatives.[21] FRS had offices in Penang (Beach Street), Ipoh, Kuala Lumpur and Singapore. The Singapore and Straits Directory of 1916[22] listed the FRS at 168, 170 and 172 High Street, Kuala Lumpur, and at Kuala Lumpur Railway Station.[22] Numerous ppcs of Penang and Malaya were published by FRS from c. 1910 to c. 1940, of which [25] and [27] are examples of these ppcs. FRS closed in c. 1940.

Nikko Studio, a Japanese photographic studio, produced ppcs of Penang with beautiful and subtle hues [28]. Not much is known of this studio, except that in 1916 its proprietor was K.S. Okaniwa and its address was 21 Penang Road.[22] It operated from c. 1910 to 1940.

A number of real ppcs have unknown photographers or publishers. It is estimated that among pre-war Penang ppcs, about 30 percent were taken or published by unnamed photographers or publishers. An example of such a ppc is a rare ppc of Lim Eu Toh, taken in 1904 [26]; its photographer is unknown. Lim Eu Toh was the president of the Penang Chinese Chamber of Commerce (1918–1925),[23] and an elected member of the Municipal Commission in 1906.[13]

The earliest known ppc to reach Penang was on 26 December 1898 (below left; [37]). This postcard of a Japanese shrine was sent as a Christmas greeting card to Reverend and Mrs Pykett of the Anglo-Chinese School in Penang by their pupil, S.N. Tanida (bottom left). The ppc was sent from Singapore on 23 December 1898 and arrived in Penang on 26 December 1898.

Other photographers and publishers of Penang ppcs include Arestore, A.M.I., Cooperative Agency, British Empire Series, K.M. Mahmed Esoof, M.J., S.M. Manicum, Pritchard & Co., Penang Photo Store, Raphael Tuck & Sons, Straits Photo, T.C.B., Straits Photo, Valentine & William, Waterlow & Sons, etc.

**[1]**
UNTITLED [STATUE OF FRANCIS LIGHT].

*Cancellation:* Nil
*Back:* Divided
*Publisher:* Not stated

The bronze statue of Francis Light unveiled in 1939. Originally it showed Light holding a sword in his left hand. During the Japanese Occupation (1939–1945), the sword was melted down to make weapons.[121] In 2003, the statue was returned to its original location at the entrance of Fort Cornwallis. Date: c. 1973. [Collection of Dr Toh Kok Thye.]

**[2]**
H.E. SIR THOMAS SHENTON WHITELEGGE THOMAS, GOVERNOR OF THE STRAITS SETTLEMENTS, 1936–

*Cancellation:* Nil
*Back:* Divided
*Publisher:* Not stated

A photographic ppc dated c. 1940 of Sir Shenton Thomas, governor of the Straits Settlements (SS; 1936–1942). It was he who unveiled the statue of Francis Light at Fort Cornwallis in 1939.

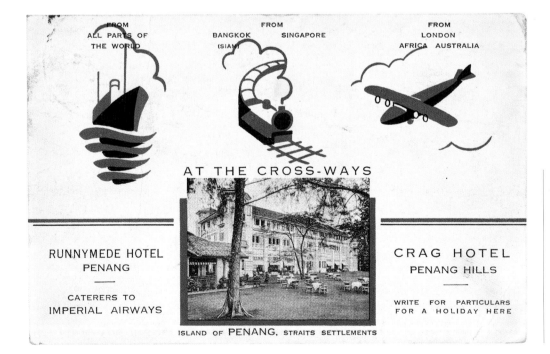

**[3]**

UNTITLED [GERMAN MAP].

*Cancellation:* Nil
*Back:* Undivided
*Publisher:* Not stated

A ppc of a German map showing the location of Penang at the crossroads of shipping and commerce between Europe and Asia. Penang is about five degrees north of the Equator. This ppc is unusual as it is serrated on three sides, and could be part of a larger map. Date: c. 1900.

**[4]**

AT THE CROSS-WAYS/ISLAND OF PENANG, STRAITS SETTLEMENTS

*Cancellation:* PENANG/8 JU/1935
*Back:* Divided
*Publisher:* Not stated

The photograph in the centre is of the Runnymede Hotel on Northam Road (now Jalan Sultan Ahmad Shah). One was able to travel to Penang "from all parts of the world" by ship (*left*), by rail "from Bangkok (Siam)/Singapore" (*centre*), and by air "from London/Africa/Australia" (*right*). Date: c. 1930.

**[5]**

**VIEW OF MUNICIPAL OFFICE/PENANG**

*Cancellation:* Nil
*Back:* Divided
*Publisher:* The Federal Rubber Stamp Co.
Kuala Lumpur.

Penang, being part of the SS, used stamps of the SS. This ppc shows the stamps of the SS that were issued during the reign of King Edward VII (r. 1901–1910), between 1904 and 1906. In the centre is a picture of the Municipal Offices building at the Esplanade; on the left is the Royal Standard of King Edward VII; and on the right is a map showing the SS. The stamps and Royal Standard are embossed on the ppc.

**[6]**

**MALAYA–BORNEO EXHIBITION.**

*Cancellation:* Nil
*Back:* Divided
*Publisher:* Not stated

A real photographic ppc of the "Malaya–Borneo Exhibition". The Malaya–Borneo Exhibition was held from March to April 1922 to commemorate the visit of the Prince of Wales to Singapore. The Prince, the future King Edward VIII, visited Singapore, Penang, Kuala Lumpur and Borneo. Stamps of the SS and some Malayan States were overprinted "Malaya–Borneo Exhibition" for the visit.

**[7]**

UNTITLED [QUEEN VICTORIA MEMORIAL CLOCK TOWER].

*Cancellation:* Nil
*Back:* Divided
*Publisher:* Syonan Army Inspection Team

A real photographic ppc, dated c. 1942, of the Queen Victoria Memorial Clock Tower at King Edward Place. The Government Buildings on the right were still intact at this time (they were later bombed by Allied planes in 1945).

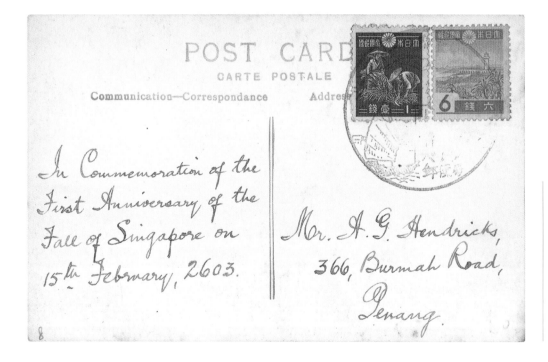

**[8]**

REVERSE OF [7].

*Cancellation:* Not clear
*Front:* The E & O Hotel, Penang
*Publisher:* Not stated

The address side of a photographic ppc of the Eastern & Oriental Hotel in Penang (*see page 9, top right*) sent by a collector to himself using 1¢ and 6¢ Japanese stamps tied by a large violet cancellation commemorating the "First Anniversary of the Fall of Singapore on 15 February 2603" (1943).

**[9]**

**PENANG**

*Cancellation:* PENANG/9 May/1898
*Front:* Undivided
*Publisher:* A. Kaulfuss

The earliest known ppc of Penang was sent on 9 May 1898. It depicts three small real photographic images of Weld Quay, a Malay lady and a rickshaw. The images are surrounded by foliage. The photographer's name, "A. Kaulfuss", is stated near the bottom centre of the ppc.

**[10]**

**REVERSE OF [9].**

*Cancellation:* PENANG/9 May/1898
*Back:* Undivided
*Publisher:* A. Kaulfuss

The address side of [9]; this ppc was sent from Penang to Austria, and franked with a Queen Victoria 3¢ stamp, which is tied by a single ring circular date stamp (cds) "PENANG/MY 9/1898". The Singapore transit cancellation is below the stamp.

[11]

PINANG.

*Cancellation:* PENANG/DE 10/98
*Back:* Undivided
*Publisher:* A. Kaulfuss

An early photomontage by A. Kaulfuss. The Ayer Itam Intake is depicted above, while a Karo (Batak) house is depicted below.[5] Ferns adorn the perimeter of the photos. Once again, the photographer's name is stated under the foliage borders. This postcard was sent on 10 December 1898 from Penang to Austria.

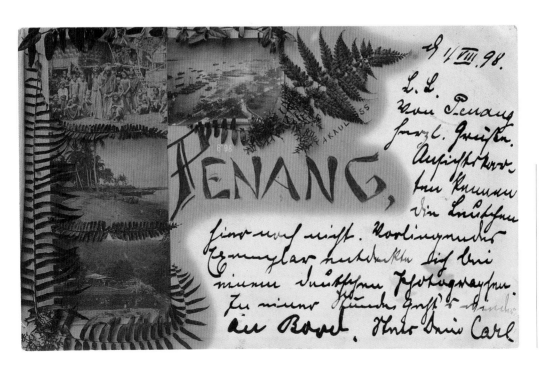

[12]

PENANG,

*Cancellation:* Singapore/AU 3/98
*Back:* Undivided
*Publisher:* A. Kaulfuss

An unusual photomontage ppc by Kaulfuss. It is in a dark blackish tone and depicts four views: a village (*top left*) and Weld Quay (*top right*); a beach (*centre*) and the Botanic Gardens (*bottom*). The photographic images are also bordered by ferns, and the photographer's name, "A. Kaulfuss", is stated above the word "Penang". This ppc was written on "I/VIII.98", and sent to Germany in 1898.

**[13]**

UNTITLED [PENANG].

*Cancellation:* PENANG/AP 28/99
*Back:* Undivided
*Publisher:* A. Kaulfuss

The images in this combination print or photomontage ppc by Kaulfuss consist of a bullock cart (*left*), a riverine scene (*centre*), and a rickshaw and its puller (*right*). The images are adorned by foliage and the tone of the ppc is dark. This ppc was sent from Penang to Trieste, Austria.

**[14]**

UNTITLED [PENANG].

*Cancellation:* PENANG/DE 15/1899
*Back:* Undivided
*Publisher:* A. Kaulfuss

The combination photographs (in light grey tone) in this photomontage ppc consist of a rural scene (*left*), the Ayer Itam Intake (*right*) and a group of Malays (*bottom*). This ppc is dated 15 December 1899, and sent from Penang to Germany.

[15]
PENANG.

*Cancellation:* 1903
*Back:* Undivided
*Publisher:* Phot. Kleingrothe, Deli Sumatra, 1900

A Charles Kleingrothe ppc in greyish blue tone. The photomontages comprise an Indian man (*left*), members of a *peranakan* family (*centre*), the Penang waterfront (*right*), and Light Street (*bottom*). The borders are adorned with flowers and foliage.

[16]
PENANG.

*Cancellation:* PENANG/DE 1/1903
*Back:* Undivided
*Publisher:* Phot. Kleingrothe, Deli Sumatra, 1900.

This grey-blue toned ppc depicts, from left to right: Batak women, tobacco plantation titled "Jonge Tabak", and a dead tiger. The top border and margin of the views are adorned with foliage.

**[17]**
PENANG.

*Cancellation:* Penang/date unclear
*Back:* Undivided
*Publisher:* Phot. Kleingrothe, Deli
Sumatra, 1900.

This ppc, by Kleingrothe, is also in a
grey-blue tone and depicts, from left:
a Malay lady dressed in a kimono, the
waterfall in the Waterfall Gardens (Botanic
Gardens), and a monkey. The borders
are also adorned with foliage. This ppc
was written in March 1903 on board the
S.S. "Banca".

**[18]**
PENANG.

*Cancellation:* Nil
*Back:* Undivided
*Publisher:* Phot. Kleingrothe, Deli
Sumatra, 1900.

As with [16], this Kleingrothe ppc has
labels in both English and Dutch. It
features, from left to right: A Tamil
lady; a view titled "Riviergezicht In Het
Gebergte", meaning "River View in the
Mountains"; and "Waterworks at the
Botanical Gardens". The image of the
Tamil lady is bordered with stylised
peacock feathers.

**[19]**

PENANG.

*Cancellation:* PENANG/DE 26/1903
*Back:* Undivided
*Publisher:* Phot. Kleingrothe, Deli Sumatra, 1900. (I have a similar ppc but without the word "Harbour".)

This ppc is also bluish, and the photograph in the middle is of the Penang Harbour, as viewed from Weld Quay. The lefthand image is of a Malay girl, while the righthand image is of an Orang Utan. Next to the postcard title "Penang" is written "Xmas, 1903". Seahorse designs adorn the margins of the photographs.

**[20]**

PENANG.

*Cancellation:* Nil
*Back:* Undivided
*Publisher:* Phot. Kleingrothe, Deli Sumatra, 1900.

A Kleingrothe ppc of Penang in a grey-blue tone. The central panel shows "Farquar Street", while to its left is an image of three Indians, possibly priests. The oval portrait on the right appears to be of a Malay lady. The borders of the images are adorned with lotus leaves.

**[21]**

**PENANG.**

*Cancellation:* Nil
*Back:* Undivided
*Publisher:* Phot. Kleingrothe,
Deli Sumatra.

The Penang Club forms the central view of this ppc. The lefthand image depicts a wealthy-looking Chinese man, while the righthand image is of an Indian boy wearing a modesty disc. All the views have decorative borders, and the ppc is toned in blue.

**[22]**

**PENANG.**

*Cancellation:* Singapore/1903
*Back:* Divided
*Publisher:* Phot. Kleingrothe, Deli Sumatra/1900.

This azure ppc by Kleingrothe depicts the "Oriental Hotel" (Eastern and Oriental Hotel) in the centre. To its left is a Malay girl, while the righthand view is of a Sumatran man. The decorative borders include a vase of palm leaves. This ppc is dated 21 February 1903, and was sent from Singapore to Holland.

[23]
PENANG.

*Cancellation:* Nil
*Back:* Undivided
*Publisher:* Phot. Kleingrothe,
Deli Sumatra.

A sepia ppc of Kleingrothe depicting a Tamil lady at the top, Fort Cornwallis ("Fort") at the bottom, and a gharry with its driver and a white horse. All views have decorative borders of flowers and leaves.

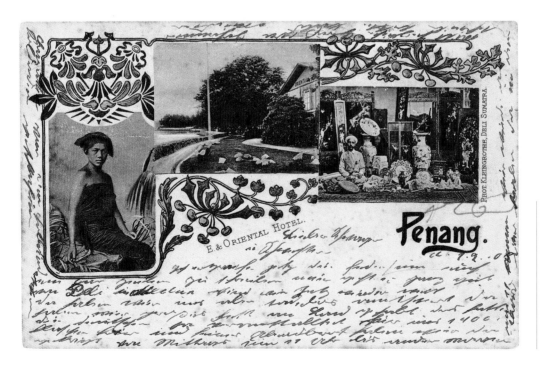

[24]
PENANG.

*Cancellation:* 2/2/1903
*Back:* Undivided
*Publisher:* Phot. Kleingrothe,
Deli Sumatra

This Kleingrothe ppc in dark azure or grey tone has three views: "E & Oriental Hotel" in the centre, a Batak woman on the left, and a man selling porcelain on the right. The three views are decorated with floral margins.

**[25]**

UNTITLED [PORTRAIT OF TAN CHIN KIM].

*Cancellation:* Nil
*Back:* Divided
*Publisher:* Not stated; attributed to Tan Chin Kim of the Federal Rubber Stamp Co. (FRS)

A portrait of Tan Chin Kim (1882–1948). He was the man behind the FRS. (c. 1910–1940). Being a civil servant, he was not allowed to list his name as the founder and proprietor of the company. Date: c. 1935.

[Collection of Madam Tan Ah Yeang.]

**[26]**

LIM EU TOH, PENANG JAN, 1904

*Cancellation:* PENANG/JY 21/1904
*Back:* Undivided
*Publisher:* Not stated

This ppc was sent by Lim Eu Toh himself to his friend in Berlin, Germany. Straits-born and English-educated, Lim Eu Toh was 33 years old when this photograph was taken. He served as the president of the Penang Chinese Chamber of Commerce from 1918 to 1925.[13]

342 - Fire Station and Jinricksha Office, Penang.

**[27]**
**342 – FIRE STATION AND JINRICKSHA OFFICE, PENANG.**

*Cancellation:* Nil
*Back:* Divided
*Publisher:* Federal Rubber Stamp Co., Penang, Kuala Lumpur & Ipoh

The fire station and Jinricksha Office stood along Penang Road. The building with the tower is the fire station; to its left is the Jinricksha Office (its name is clearly visible below the gable). This ppc by the Federal Rubber Stamp Co. is uncommon; it shows fine details. Date: c. 1910.

A 11 - Sungei Penang, Penang.

**[28]**
**A11 – SUNGEI PENANG, PENANG.**

*Cancellation:* Nil
*Back:* Divided
*Publisher:* Made by Nikko Studio, Penang, SS. Printed in Saxony.

This is an early Nikko Studio ppc. It is a typical colour ppc from this studio as it has subtle yet bright colours that are well balanced, producing a pleasant composition. Here, many Chinese sailing junks are shown along the banks of the Penang River. Date: c. 1910.

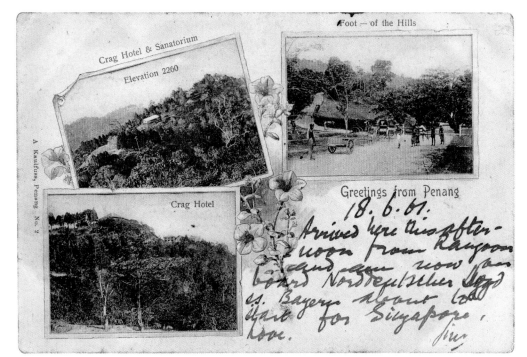

**[29]**

**GREETINGS FROM PENANG.**

*Cancellation:* PENANG/JU 19/1901; it was sent from Penang to England

*Back:* Undivided

*Publisher:* A. Kaulfuss, Penang No. 2

This is a very early ppc by Kaulfuss. It is a triview ppc showing the "Crag Hotel & Sanatorium/Elevation 2260", "Crag Hotel", and "Foot – of the Hills". The ppc was written on 18 June 1901 and states the sender's aims to depart for Singapore after arriving from Rangoon in Burma.

**[30]**

**GREETINGS FROM PENANG.**

*Cancellation:* SINGAPORE/DE 28/1902

*Back:* Undivided

*Publisher:* A. Kaulfuss, Penang, No. 8

Another ppc from Kaulfuss's "Greetings from Penang" series. This ppc, which was sent from Penang to England, was written on 26 December 1902. Kaulfuss was a highly regarded and well travelled photographer. He served as the Sultan of Kedah's photographer. Here, an elephant is shown bearing a howdah (seat or carriage on an elephant) and a European man.

Malay Beauties.

Tamil.

Greetings from Penang.

[31]

GREETINGS FROM PENANG.

*Cancellation:* Nil
*Back:* Undivided
*Publisher:* A. Kaulfuss, Penang, No. 4

This ppc, with beautifully coloured vignettes, depicts three "Malay beauties" and a "Tamil" (although "Sikh" might be more accurate). The views are in soft colours and decorated with flowers at the borders. A black and white version of this ppc also exists.

Greetings from Penang

[32]

GREETINGS FROM PENANG

*Cancellation:* Nil
*Back:* Undivided
*Publisher:* Not stated but likely to be A. Kaulfuss

This black and white ppc features a group of Indian musicians with various musical instruments. Kaulfuss was known to possess a unique collection of photographs of the Malay Peninsula.[9]

**[33]**

**GREETINGS FROM PENANG**

*Cancellation:* Singapore; date not clear
*Back:* Undivided
*Publisher:* A. Kaulfuss, Penang, No. 3

Another ppc of this series with foliage-designed vignette depicting the "Waterfall" (*left*), "The gardens" (*centre*), and "Siamese Pagoda" (*right*). The three views are adorned with leaves and flowers above and palm leaves below. This ppc was written at the Adelphi Hotel, Singapore (*top left*) and dated 18 January 1902 (*top right*). This ppc was sent from Singapore to England.

**[34]**

**GREETINGS FROM PENANG.**

*Cancellation:* PENANG/1907
*Back:* Divided
*Publisher:* A. Kaulfuss, Penang

This is almost a mirror image of [33], but more lightly shaded, and the three views are slightly smaller. The foliage adornments are also slightly smaller. This ppc was sent from Penang to Quebec in Canada.

A. Kaulfuss, Penang. No. 26.

Greetings
from Penang.

DEC 26th 02

Arrived here to-
day, leaving for
Singapore. tomorrow

Kindest regards
to all from

Chas Hudson

[35]
GREETINGS FROM PENANG.

*Cancellation:* PENANG/DE 27/1902
*Back:* Undivided
*Publisher:* A. Kaulfuss, Penang, No. 26

A black and white rustic scene showing a Malay kampong with huts, coconut palms and a group of people, possibly a family. This ppc was written on 26 December 1902, and sent from Penang to Scotland.

Greetings from Penang

[36]
GREETINGS FROM PENANG

*Cancellation:* PENANG/27 MR/1903
*Back:* Undivided
*Publisher:* Not stated, but likely to be
A. Kaulfuss

This sepia real photographic ppc depicts two Indian men (and a child holding a decorative item) peddling various merchandise.

**[37]**

UNTITLED [CHRISTMAS CARD].

*Cancellation:* SINGAPORE/DE 23/98
*Back:* Undivided
*Publisher:* Not stated

This is the address side of the Christmas ppc sent to Rev. G.F. Pykett (1864–1932) and his wife by S.N. Tanida (*see page 10*). It was posted to Penang on 23 December 1898 and arrived on 26 December 1898 (its cds is on the left of the postage stamp). Reverend Pykett was the founder of the Anglo-Chinese School (later renamed Methodist Boys' School) in Penang. Pykett Avenue and Pykett Lane were named after him.

**[38]**

No. 92. WATERFALL GARDEN.

*Cancellation:* Nil
*Back:* Divided
*Publisher:* A. Kaulfuss, Penang

The most interesting part of this ppc is that the European man dressed in white and wearing a white topee is photographer A. Kaulfuss himself.[18] Kaulfuss sometimes appeared in his own photographs. Born in Silesia, Central Europe, in 1861, he passed away in Penang in 1908, and was buried there.[18]

# The HARBOUR

The establishment of Penang as a port-town following Francis Light's takeover of the island from the Sultanate of Kedah in 1786, drew merchants with prior trading links to the island, and later, an influx of migrant workers. It also stimulated Penang's trading activities with various parts of South and Southeast Asia.[126] The island became an entrepôt: a hub for "redistribution and exchange of goods and articles between the India–China route and Southeast Asian trade network."[126]

After the British EIC took control of Singapore in 1819, Penang's port was relegated to serving the northern Straits of Malacca and functioning as a "feeder" to Singapore, which had become the main port of the SS.[125] Towards the end of the 19th century however, Penang's role as a regional entrepôt exchange became fully developed, which led it to enjoy a marked expansion in trade.[125] Penang was eventually declared a free port (a port where goods in transit are exempted from customs duty) in 1872. Its free port status was withdrawn in 1967.[26]

The magisterial illustrated book, *Twentieth Century Impressions of British Malaya* (1908) describes Penang Harbour as "the great transhipment centre for the northern part of the Malay Peninsula and Sumatra".[9] Visually, little has changed in the last 100 years: as a traveller enters Penang Harbour and approaches land, he is greeted by a magnificent panoramic view of Penang (*bottom right*). Other panoramic photographs of Penang Harbour are shown in [39] and [40]. Early views of Penang Harbour are further shown in [41], [42] and [43]; while [44] and [45] are slightly later views, c. 1908.

Penang Harbour consists of the north harbour and south harbour. The north harbour [46] is deeper than the south harbour [47-48]; hence larger vessels use the north harbour, while small vessels use the south harbour.

Prior to World War II, Penang Harbour was crowded with ships of all sizes and shapes, from large ocean-going steamers with tall funnels [49-52] to smaller *tongkang*, prahus, *twakow*, junks and sampans [53-57].

Penang Island is separated from its hinterland, Seberang Perai (formerly known as Province Wellesley; PW), by a channel approximately 3.2 kilometres wide at its narrowest point. People and goods were transported from Penang to Butterworth (in PW) by sampans and other small boats. The first regular ferry service between Penang and PW was started by Quah Beng Kee (1872–1952)[23] and his brothers in 1894, under the name of Beng Brothers.[28] Their ferry service used small launches to transport people and goods from Kedah Pier (Fort Pier) [57-58] in George Town to Mitchell's Pier (*top right*) (now known as Bagan Tuan Kechil Pier) at Butterworth.[28] In 1924, the ferry service was taken over by the Penang Harbour Board. By the end of 1925, the ferry service carried motor vehicles. Initially, the service used the Church Street Ghaut Wharf but this was later replaced by the Church Street Pier [59-60]. Church Street Pier was also known as Ferry Pier.[29]

The Federated Malay States Railway (FMSR) Jetty [61-63] was built in 1901. At 644 feet (196 metres), it was

Ferries and other boats transported people and goods from Mitchell's Pier in Butterworth, Province Wellesley to Kedah Pier in Penang.[28] Date: c. 1930.

*Opposite*:
Swettenham Pier in December 1941. By this stage of the Japanese invasion of Malaya, Penang was virtually cut off from the rest of the Peninsula. The goods are stacked up, waiting for freight steamers that rarely came by due to World War II.

*Below*:
A panoramic view of the Penang Harbour. On the right is the Kedah (Fort) Pier, and next to it are the Fort Cornwallis Lighthouse, and the Queen Victoria Memorial Clock Tower. Weld Quay is on the left.

Penang. Panoramic View.

An albumen photograph of Swettenham Pier. The General Post Office building is on the right, c. 1900.

Transporting elephants by lighters or *tongkang*. Swettenham Pier, c. 1900.

the longest jetty along Weld Quay.[5] The ferry steamers that transported passengers and goods arriving from Butterworth to George Town, used to dock here. The FMSR Jetty was replaced with the Pengkalan Raja Tun Uda (Penang Ferry Terminal) in the 1960s.

The most iconic building along Weld Quay (Pengkalan Weld) is the FMS Railway (FMSR) Station building [63-70]. The name "Railway Station" is a misnomer as it has neither a railway platform nor any trains! Built between 1905 and 1908, the FMSR Station building is presently used by the Royal Malaysian Customs Department, Penang, hence its present name: Wisma Kastam Pulau Pinang (Penang Customs Building). Opposite the former FMSR Station is Wisma Yeap Chor Ee [63-64], built by Yeap Chor Ee, the founder of Ban Hin Lee Bank,[23] which later became part of today's CIMB banking group.

Swettenham Pier (SP) (*top left*; [71-82]), named after Sir Frank Swettenham, governor of the SS (1901–1904), was built in 1903, and opened in 1905. Built at a cost of $600,000, the pier was replete with external berthage of 183 metres. The following ppcs depict SP's fascinating past: four early views of SP [71-72], jetty sheds and godowns surrounding SP for the storage of goods [73-74], the arrival of Indian immigrants [75], and departure of pilgrims for Jeddah [76]. It was also the transhipment centre for tin from Malaya and southern Thailand [77-78], and tobacco from Malaya and Sumatra [79-81]. Even elephants were exported at SP (*below left*; [82])!

Victoria Pier [83-90], named after Queen Victoria (r. 1837–1901), was built between 1885 and 1888.[5] It was used by stevedores and small launches when ocean liners anchored nearby the roads. This pier was demolished in the late 1950s.

Weld Quay (WQ) was named after Sir Frederick Weld, governor of the SS from 1880 to 1887. It stretches from SP to Prangin Road Ghaut. The major piers and jetties of Penang Harbour, including SP, are situated here. Weld Quay was the preferred site for British and European trading headquarters and godowns (warehouses).

The SP end of WQ are shown from [91] to [98]. In [91] Boustead & Co., the Town Club and the General Post Office can be seen on the left of the ppc. The Boustead & Co. building housed many insurance, shipping and estate agencies, including the Asia Petroleum Co.[22] In [93], the Government Buildings are shown on the right and the godowns on the left. The Government Buildings no longer exist as they were destroyed by Allied bombers in 1945. Early views of WQ looking towards and from the General Post Office are shown in [95] and [96]; while [97] and [98] present two further views of early WQ.

The Government Buildings and merchant houses are further depicted from [99] to [102]. The row of buildings stretched from Boustead & Co. to the FMSR Station building and, beyond that, to Wisma Yeap Chor Ee.

Until World War II, WQ was a bustling hub full of small boats and ships. Day and night, labourers toiled loading and unloading goods [103-108].

The Clan Jetties (CJs) [109-110] are situated at the southern end of WQ. These have been in existence since the 19th century, and were named after the surnames of the Chinese communities. There were seven CJs along WQ, including those of the Chew, Koay, Lee, and Lim clans.[33] Today, six remain. The jetties' timber houses are linked by wooden pathways on piles sunk into the sea. The jetty communities still continue fishing, stevedoring, and cross-channel ferrying.[30]

The Sungai Pinang or Penang River (*See Chapter 1* [28]; [111-112]) lies to the southwest of WQ. It was used as a waterway by Acehnese, Malay and Indian traders. The upper reaches of the Pinang River were also where industries such as tin smelting, were located. Among the companies involved in tin smelting was the Eastern Smelting Co. which, during its early years, transported tin upriver by barge.[5]

**[39]**

**No. 1. Panorama of Penang Landing**

*Cancellation:* PENANG/1908
*Back:* Divided
*Publisher:* A. Kaulfuss, Penang

A multiview colour ppc depicting a panorama of Penang Harbour (*top*), "Landing Pier" (*below left*), "Post Office" (*below centre*), and "Beach Str." (*below right*). This panorama of Penang is earlier than that on page 31 (*bottom right*) as the Queen Victoria Memorial Clock Tower, which was completed in 1897, is not visible in this ppc. This may be the first photograph of Penang Harbour taken by A. Kaulfuss.

**[40]**

**Panorama of Penang**

*Cancellation:* PENANG/DE 27/1902
*Back:* Undivided
*Publisher:* A. Kaulfuss, Penang No. 1

This ppc is similar to [39] except that this is in black and white, and the decorative borders around the views are different from [39]. This ppc was mailed in 1902 and sent from Penang to France.

**[41]**

UNTITLED [PENANG HARBOUR].

*Cancellation:* PENANG/AP 26/1900
*Back:* Undivided
*Publisher:* A. Kaulfuss, Penang.

A real photographic ppc of Penang Harbour in c. 1895. It shows the flagpost of Fort Cornwallis on the right, and in front of it, Kedah Pier (Fort Pier). On the left are the Government Buildings and in front of them, the goods shed of the future Swettenham Pier (it would be built in 1903). Written on the top left is "Penang/25.IV.1900".

Penang.

**[42]**

PENANG.

*Cancellation:* 1903
*Back:* Undivided
*Publisher:* Not stated

A slightly later view of Penang Harbour than that shown in **[41]**. It is also a closer view of the Government Buildings. Victoria Pier, completed in 1888, is on the left while Kedah Pier is on the right. Date: c. 1895.

No. 73. Penang wharf.

**[43]**

**NO. 73. PENANG WHARF.**

*Cancellation:* Nil
*Back:* Undivided
*Publisher:* Not stated

The Queen Victoria Memorial Clock Tower can clearly be seen in this ppc; Swettenham Pier is in front of the Government Buildings. A lone sampan is in the foreground. Until Swettenham Pier was built in 1903, there was no wharfage accommodation for large vessels.[9]

Penang from the Harbour

**[44]**

**PENANG FROM THE HARBOUR.**

*Cancellation:* PENANG/JY 22/1909
*Back:* Divided
*Publisher:* Co-operative Agency, S.S./ No. 10

The clock tower of the FMSR Station building (built in 1908) is seen on the left, while the dome of the Hong Kong and Shanghai Bank (HSBC) building, which was built in the Neo-Classical style in 1906, is just visible on the left of the clock tower. This building was destroyed in World War II and replaced with a new structure in 1948 in the late Art Deco style.[131] This ppc was sent from Penang to Ohio in America.

No. 204 Penang Harbour.

[45]

**No. 204 Penang Harbour.**

*Cancellation:* PENANG/JU 9/1909
*Back:* Divided
*Publisher:* A. Kaulfuss, Penang.

A large steamship in the centre is contrasted against a small sampan in the foreground. Penang was once "the great transhipment centre" for northern Malaya, and Sumatra. Except for boats of the French maritime company, Messageries Maritimes, all mail boats from the East called at Penang Harbour, where they would remain for at least six to eight hours.[9]

No. 97 Penang from North.

[46]

**No. 97 Penang from North.**

*Cancellation:* PENANG/25 MR/1911
*Back:* Divided
*Publisher:* A. Kaulfuss, Penang.

The north harbour is deeper than the south; hence till today, larger vessels enter Penang Harbour from the north, which could be "navigated safely in any state of the tide by vessels drawing 27 feet (8.2 metres) of water".[9] On the right, the flagpost of Fort Cornwallis can be seen, and next to it is the Queen Victoria Memorial Clock Tower. Many large ocean-going vessels are depicted lining the harbour in this ppc.

No. 115 Penang Harbour (South).

**[47]**

**No. 115 Penang Harbour (South).**

*Cancellation:* PENANG/DE 17/1909
*Back:* Divided
*Publisher:* A. Kaulfuss, Penang.

Only smaller vessels entered Penang Harbour using this route as, at 18 feet 6 inches (5.7 metres) at low water, it is shallower than the north harbour. A 1908 source stated that there were a staff of "five competent pilots at the port".[9] These pilots had their own launches and met all vessels at either the north or south harbours.[9] Two steamers can be seen in the foreground and behind them are many smaller vessels.

PENANG. SOUTHERN PORT.

**[48]**

**Penang/Southern Port.**

*Cancellation:* Nil
*Back:* Divided
*Publisher:* Raphael Tuck & Sons.
  Penang, Series I.

This is a typical ppc published by Raphael Tuck & Sons in London. It is a painting in watercolour rather than a photograph. The southern port was used by many Chinese junks, as they were of shallow draught. Date: c. 1910.

Penang. Harbour.

18.9.04.

[49]

PENANG, HARBOUR.

*Cancellation:* Penang/1904
*Back:* Undivided
*Publisher:* Not stated

This real photographic ppc dated c. 1900 shows two ocean-going steamers with funnels, and boats in the foreground. The steamers are decorated with small flags. This ppc was written on 18 September 1904.

Harbour, Penang

[50]

HARBOUR, PENANG.

*Cancellation:* 1912 (details not clear)
*Back:* Divided
*Publisher:* Not stated; printed in Germany

This ppc captures an era when large steamers dominated the seas. Swettenham Pier can be seen at the back of the steamers, and the Queen Victoria Memorial Clock Tower is visible in the background, at the centre of the ppc. Ships were directed around the harbour by means of beacons, Wigham and other kinds of buoys, as well as the Muka Head, Rimau Island and Fort Cornwallis lighthouses.[9] Date: c. 1910.

**[51 ]**

UNTITLED [STEAMERS AT PENANG HARBOUR].

*Cancellation:* 1924
*Back:* Divided
*Publisher:* Not stated

Another real photographic ppc showing two steamers at Penang Harbour. The FMSR Station building is visible in the background, on the right. Date: c. 1920.

**[52]**

356. B.I. LINES. S. B./TAI TEN. PENANG.

*Cancellation:* 1928
*Back:* Divided
*Publisher:* Not stated

A real photographic ppc focusing on a large ocean-going liner with three funnels. This ppc was written on board the S.S. *Takliwa* on 9 December 1928. The S.S. *Takliwa* was a cargo liner built in 1924 for the British India Steam Navigation Company, and was used as a troopship during World War II before being converted into a hospital ship in 1945. She ended her service in October that same year when she ran aground at Indira Point, Great Nicobar, Indonesia while repatriating former prisoners of war from Hong Kong to Madras.[132]

Harbour, Penang.

**[53]**

**HARBOUR, PENANG.**

*Cancellation:* Nil
*Back:* Divided
*Publisher:* Not stated; printed in Germany

A colour ppc that captures the lifestyle and economics of Penang Harbour in c. 1910. It shows a lighter or *tongkang* loaded with sacks of perhaps rice. In the distance are a few steamers and sampans.

No. 65, Chinese Harbour, Penang

**[54]**

**No. 65, CHINESE HARBOUR, PENANG**

*Cancellation:* Nil
*Back:* Divided
*Publisher:* A. Kaulfuss, Penang.

The harbour is crowded with *tongkang*. Most have tall masts with lowered sails. A 1908 account stated that Penang was not a "producing or consuming place" and that its exports and imports were largely insignificant.[9] It did, however, establish itself as a distribution centre to and from the Federated Malay States (FMS) and "Siamese Malaya", and to and from the Dutch East Indies, as well as served as an intermediate feeder for trade with India.[9]
Date: c. 1910.

NO. 217    TYPICAL TONGKUNGS OF PENANG

**[55]**

**No. 217 Typical Tongkungs of Penang**

*Cancellation:* Nil
*Back:* Divided
*Publisher:* Printed in England

This c. 1920 real photographic ppc depicts several *tongkang* anchored alongside the wharf with their sails half lowered. Goods are being loaded and unloaded.

No. 714.    PENANG HARBOUR, WITH CHINESE SAILING BOAT IN THE CENTRE, PENANG

**[56]**

**No. 714 Penang Harbour, with Chinese Sailing Boat in the Centre, Penang.**

*Cancellation:* Nil
*Back:* Divided
*Publisher:* Not stated; printed in England

A busy scene of motor boats (*foreground*), a junk and ocean-going steamers (*background*) at the Penang Harbour c. 1930. The business of the vessels was intertwined as the large merchant vessels relied on *tongkang* and sampans to transport goods and people to the jetties.[9] This ppc is tinted with subtle colours.

No. 78. The Esplanade, Penang

**[57]**

**No. 78. The Esplanade, Penang**

*Cancellation:* Nil
*Back:* Divided
*Publisher:* A. Kaulfuss, Penang.

Two sampans are seen rowing away from Kedah Pier (in front of Fort Cornwallis) in the foreground. Sampans and *tongkang* were the workhorses of Penang Harbour, plying the waters to transport goods and people continuously and efficiently. This colour ppc is dated c. 1910.

Esplande Road, Penang.

**[58]**

**Esplanade Road, Penang.**

*Cancellation:* Penang/1919
*Back:* Divided
*Publisher:* K.M. Mahmed Esoof, Penang. No. 3067

A colour ppc showing Esplanade Road, c. 1910, as its main feature. The Kedah Pier (Fort Pier) is on the left, beside Fort Cornwallis.[28] The Fort Cornwallis Lighthouse is at the back with a red roof.

**[59]**

**Church Street, Pier, Penang.**

*Cancellation:* Nil
*Back:* Divided
*Publisher:* Not stated

This real photographic ppc depicts the everyday happenings at the Church Street Pier. Built between 1897 and 1898 for $48,889,[9] this pier was extremely busy and invariably chaotic. In 1924, the Penang Harbour Board took over operations of the Straits Steamship Co. Ltd (this company acquired Eastern Shipping Co Ltd, which had earlier bought over Quah Beng Kee's Guan Lee Hin Steamship Company).[28] The harbour board ran a ferry service from this pier to Butterworth, carrying passengers and motor vehicles. Date: c. 1930.

**[60]**

**No. 171 Church Street Pier, Penang**

*Cancellation:* Nil
*Back:* Divided
*Publisher:* Not stated; printed in England

Another real photographic ppc, dated c. 1930, of Church Street Pier. At the back of the jetty are large rectangular boxes housing the hoisting gear for the gangway. The FMSR Station building clock tower can be seen at the back. [Collection of Dr Toh Kok Thye.]

No. 171                    CHURCH STREET PIER, PENANG

[61]

**NO. 5 – PENANG. F.M.S. PIER & OFFICES**

*Cancellation:* PENANG/No. 20/1909
*Back:* Divided
*Publisher:* T.C.B. Penang

As travellers to Penang approached the FMSR Jetty, they were greeted by the sight of the imposing FMSR Station building and its magnificent clock tower. This colour ppc dated c. 1905 was written on 20 November 1909 and sent from Penang to Paris.

F.M.S. RAILWAY BUILDINGS & PIER, PENANG.

[62]

**F.M.S. RAILWAY BUILDINGS & PIER, PENANG.**

*Cancellation:* Nil
*Back:* Undivided
*Publisher:* No. 8. The Federal Rubber
　　　　　Stamp Co., Penang,
　　　　　K. Lumpur and Ipoh

Another angle of the FMSR Station building and Pier. The building and clock tower can be seen on the left side of the ppc. The FMS Pier was long, measuring 644 feet (196.3 metres).[5] This sepia ppc is dated c. 1900.

2981 F.M.S. RAILWAYS STATION, PENANG.

**[63]**

**2981 F.M.S. RAILWAYS STATION, PENANG.**

*Cancellation:* Penang/1929
*Back:* Divided
*Publisher:* Not stated

A real photographic ppc showing the railway jetty (*left, foreground*), and the FMSR Station building in the centre. At its left is Wisma Yeap Chor Ee. Both buildings are located on China Street Ghaut. The FMSR Station building was often called "the only railway station without a rail" and, as such, operated more as an administrative centre. It had offices, a ticketing booth and a Railway Restaurant with bar and grill.[82]
Date: c. 1930.

**[64]**

**No. 136 CLOCK TOWER,
F.M.S. RAILWAYS, PENANG**

*Cancellation:* Nil
*Back:* Divided
*Publisher:* Not stated; printed in England

This ppc is worth a thousand words, and depicts the bustling Penang Harbour in its heyday. The view was probably taken from Victoria Pier. The buildings shown, from left to right, are: Wisma Yeap Chor Ee; the FMSR Station building and clock tower; the Paterson, Simons & Co. building; and the Borneo Co. Ltd. building. The Borneo Co. Ltd was one of the leading export, import and agency businesses in this region, and also had offices in Singapore, Siam, Java and Borneo.[9]

No. 136      CLOCK TOWER, F.M.S. RAILWAYS, PENANG

F. M. S. R'way Station Buildings, Penang

**[65]**
**F.M.S. R'WAY STATION BUILDINGS, PENANG**

*Cancellation:* Nil
*Back:* Divided
*Publisher:* Co-operative Agency S.S./
No. 21

The FMSR Station building and clock tower stand majestically in this 1920 colour ppc. In the foreground are many sampans and *tongkang* at Weld Quay. As with [64], the pier is congested with lighters or *tongkang*, evidence of Penang's status as a thriving harbour and port town. To the right of the FMSR Station building is the Paterson, Simons & Co. building. The company commenced business in Penang in 1902, after taking over the business operations of Hallifax & Co., importers, exporters and general merchants. Paterson, Simons & Co. operated from Weld Quay, and engaged in business of a varied nature, but had a special branch concentrated on tin and coal.[9]

46

366 - Federated Malay States Railway Buildings, Penang.

**[66]**
**366 – FEDERATED MALAY STATES/ RAILWAY BUILDINGS, PENANG.**

*Cancellation:* Nil
*Back:* Divided
*Publisher:* Federal Rubber Stamp Co.,
Penang, Kuala Lumpur & Ipoh

The centre of the third level of the FMSR Station building is inscribed in appliquéd poster "M.R.1907", indicating the date of completion of this building. Its construction signified the completion of the FMS Railway,[82] which served as a reliable and effective means of transporting tin and crops from the Federated Malay States for export.[82] In the foreground of this ppc is a temporary shed. Date: c. 1910.

[67]
F.M.S. RAILWAY BUILDINGS, PENANG

*Cancellation:* 31 MY/1921
*Back:* Divided
*Publisher:* Raphael Tuck & Sons "Super Glosso" Series

As the FMSR Station did not have a railway track, passengers who wanted to take the train had to buy their tickets here, walk to the Railway Jetty, and board the Railway Ferry Steamers to Butterworth to board their train. The ferry ride was included in the fares to and from Penang. Date: c. 1910.

[68]
F.M.S. RAILWAY BUILDINGS, PENANG

*Cancellation:* PENANG/20 AU/1914
*Back:* Divided
*Publisher:* Not stated; printed in Germany

Tram lines are visible in the foreground, c. 1910; a steam tramway service was recorded to have begun in Penang as early as the 1880s. In its early years, the system functioned more as a light railway, consisting of a single metre-gauge line that serviced the Weld Quay Jetty–Ayer Itam Road route.[87]

[69]

**LANDING GOODS AT WELD QUAY, PENANG**

*Cancellation:* Nil
*Back:* Divided
*Publisher:* M.J., Penang.

A real photographic ppc dated c. 1910. The time (as shown on the clock tower) is 11.10 am, and scores of workers unload sacks of goods from lighters (*tongkang*) at Weld Quay. The FMSR Station building and clock tower provide a nice background.

[70]

**PRY PIER./PRY STATION./A 48 – STATION BUILDING, PENANG.**

*Cancellation:* PENANG/23 AP/1916
*Back:* Divided
*Publisher:* Made by Nikko Studio, Penang, S.S. Printed in Saxony.

A triview ppc showing the pier and railway station in Seberang Perai (Province Wellesley), or Prai, and the FMSR Station building and clock tower in Penang. This ppc has fine, subtle colour tinting, typical of Nikko Studio's ppc.

No. 69. Penang wharf and Harbour

**[71]**

**No. 69. Penang wharf and Harbour**

*Cancellation:* Penang, 1909
*Back:* Divided
*Publisher:* A. Kaulfuss, Penang

An early view of Swettenham Pier, c. 1905. In the left and centre of the foreground, construction work is taking place; while on the right is a godown (warehouse or goods store).

Swettenham Pier, Penang

**[72]**

**Swettenham Pier, Penang**

*Cancellation:* 1909
*Back:* Divided
*Publisher:* Not stated; printed in Germany

Several *tongkang* or lighters can be seen in the foreground, while cranes can be seen busy loading and unloading goods in the background. The construction of Swettenham Pier began in 1889 and was completed in 1904, at a cost of $636,332.[9]
Date: c. 1910.

Swettenham Pier, Penang.

[73]
SWETTENHAM PIER, PENANG.

Cancellation: PENANG/1912
*Back:* Divided
*Publisher:* Not stated; printed in Germany

A colour ppc of Swettenham Pier c. 1910; it shows the Queen Victoria Memorial Clock Tower in the centre, and the FMS Goods Sheds (built in 1907)[1] on the right. On the left, two locomotives can be seen pulling steam trams.

Loading Cargo by Bullock Carts, Penang

[74]
LOADING CARGO BY BULLOCK CARTS, PENANG

*Cancellation:* Nil
*Back:* Divided
*Publisher:* Not stated

Besides steam trams, bullock carts were also used to transport goods. This colour ppc, c. 1905, depicts Indian workers loading goods unto bullock carts. These godowns were built near Swettenham Pier and, as they were newly built (in comparison with the goods shed that adjoined the pier), had a more modern look to them.[9]

**[75]**

**ARRIVAL OF IMIGRANT COOLIES, PENANG**

*Cancellation:* Nil
*Back:* Divided
*Publisher:* Not stated

The above caption is printed on the back of this ppc. Indian migrant workers landed in Penang to work in the rubber estates and railways of Malaya.
Date: c. 1910.

Jeddah Boat, Penang.

**[76]**

**JEDDAH BOAT, PENANG.**

*Cancellation:* Nil
*Back:* Divided
*Publisher:* Not stated; No. 35. A. Beach Street, Penang

A steamer with a large funnel is shown berthed at Swettenham Pier. Pilgrims from Malaya and Sumatra departed for Jeddah at this pier. Penang was once a transport hub for people from the Malay archipelago to travel to Jeddah to perform the hajj. This lucrative business was interrupted by World War II, but resumed after that. It took 13 days to reach Jeddah. Travel to Jeddah by ship was slowly phased out with the growing popularity of air travel in the 1960s and the establishment of the Pilgrim Management Fund (Lembaga Urusan Tabung Haji) in 1969.[135] Date: c. 1910.

No. 109 Sweattenham Pier.

[77]

NO. 109 SWEATTENHAM PIER.

*Cancellation:* Nil
*Back:* Divided
*Publisher:* A. Kaulfuss, Penang.

A colour ppc, c. 1910, of large ocean-going steamers berthed at Swettenham Pier. Port workers can be seen loading goods from the steamer onto tram carts (*foreground*). Tram lines ran along the pier, enabling easy transportation of goods.

Tin Slabs for shipment, Penang.

[78]

TIN SLABS FOR SHIPMENT, PENANG.

*Cancellation:* Nil
*Back:* Divided
*Publisher:* The Federal Rubber Stamp Co., Kuala Lumpur, Ipoh, Penang & Singapore.

Tin slabs are shown being hoisted onto a steamer (*left*) for export; on the right is the pier's godown. A European man, in white and wearing a topee, supervises the process. A 1908 account stated that Penang was the transhipment centre for tin, gambier, pepper, copra, gutta-percha, gum copal, tapioca, and rubber.[9] This real photographic ppc is dated c. 1930.

171a    Penang.    Shipping Tobacco by Norddeutscher Lloyd.

**[79]**

**171a PENANG. SHIPPING TOBACCO BY NORDDEUTSCHER LLOYD.**

*Cancellation:* PENANG/30 JY/1912
*Back:* Divided
*Publisher:* A. Kaulfuss, Penang;
    printed in Germany

Tobacco bales shown being loaded onto a ship owned by the German shipping company, Norddeutscher Lloyd. This company was founded in 1857, and operated successfully until interruptions during World War I (1914–1918) and World War II (1939–1945). In 1970, it merged with the Hamburg America Line to form HAPAG–Lloyd.[31] Date: 1910.

Shipping Tobacco by Norddeutscher Lloyd, Penang

**[80]**

**SHIPPING TOBACCO BY NORDDEUTSCHER LLOYD, PENANG**

*Cancellation:* Nil
*Back:* Divided
*Publisher:* Not stated

European supervisors watch bales of tobacco being loaded onto the ship on the left. Tobacco grown in Malaya and Sumatra was exported via Swettenham Pier. Date: c. 1910.

Norddeutscher Lloyd loading Tobacco, Penang.

**[81]**

**NORDDEUTSCHER LLOYD LOADING TOBACCO, PENANG.**

*Cancellation:* PENANG/20 JY/1912
*Back:* Divided
*Publisher:* Not stated; printed in Germany

A busy scene at Swettenham Pier is depicted in this colour ppc, dated c. 1910. Tobacco bales are being loaded into a Norddeutscher Lloyd steam ship (*right*). Swettenham Pier provided the wharfage accommodation larger vessels needed; it had an external berthage of 600 feet (183 metres). A large liner or two ordinary steamers could berth alongside the front of the pier. The inner face of the southern portion of the pier could also accommodate a small steamer.[9]

**[82]**

**UNTITLED [HOISTING AN ELEPHANT].**

*Cancellation:* Nil
*Back:* Divided
*Publisher:* Not stated

Elephants were transported by ship. This real photographic ppc depicts an elephant being hoisted onto a ship for export; while three more elephants await their turn at the back of the pier. A large group of workers and Europeans (in white with topees) watch the delicate procedure.

**[83]**

**PENANG./VICTORIA PIER.**

*Cancellation:* PENANG/20 JU/1919
*Back:* Divided
*Publisher:* Raphael Tuck & Sons "Oilette"
    Postcard No. 8962

A beautiful ppc in watercolour, dated
c. 1910, showing Victoria Pier in the
foreground and the FMSR Station
building and clock tower in the centre
background. Victoria Pier, which was a
covered jetty,[9] was next to Swettenham
Pier. Here, people are shown waiting for
their turn to board boats functioning as
water taxis.

**[84]**

**NO. 14. LANDING PIER, PENANG**

*Cancellation:* Penang/1907
*Back:* Divided
*Publisher:* A. Kaulfuss, Penang.

This colour ppc, dated c. 1905, depicts
Indian migrants who have just arrived
at Victoria Pier. Sampans are waiting
to pick up the next passengers. In the
background are lighters (*tongkang*).
This ppc was written on 8 March 1907.

9. Victoria Pier, Penang, S.S.

**[85]**
**9. VICTORIA PIER, PENANG, S.S.**

*Cancellation:* Penang/27 FB/1921
*Back:* Divided
*Publisher:* Raphael Tuck & Sons/"Sepia Platemarked"/Postcard 768

A sepia ppc depicting the scenery as it was in c. 1910. Lighters (*tongkang*) can be seen in the foreground, while Victoria Pier is in the centre, and the clock tower of the FMSR Station building is in the background. The construction of Victoria Pier began in 1885, and was completed in 1888, at a cost of $38,697.[9]

Government Wharve's Godowns, Penang.

**[86]**
**GOVERNMENT WHARVE'S GODOWNS, PENANG.**

*Cancellation:* Nil
*Back:* Divided
*Publisher:* Not stated; printed in Germany

Victoria Pier, with pointed roof and landing steps in the centre (*right*), is shown in this colour ppc dated c. 1910. The godowns are on the left. Many lighters or *tongkang* are moored in front of the godowns.

Victoria Pier, ·Penang

**[87]**

**VICTORIA PIER, PENANG**

*Cancellation:* Nil
*Back:* Divided
*Publisher:* Not stated

Victoria Pier with its distinct pointed roof (*centre*) is shown in this c. 1910 colour ppc. The buildings on the right are the godowns. A flat-bottomed *tongkang* with three boatmen can be seen in the foreground. It must have taken great skill to steer a boat of this size.

Victoria Pier, Penang.

**[88]**

**VICTORIA PIER, PENANG.**

*Cancellation:* Penang/2 AP/1914
*Back:* Divided
*Publisher:* S.M. Manicum, Penang/No. 21

View of Victoria Pier from Swettenham Pier. Sampans are concentrated next to the landing steps of the pier (*centre*). The clock tower of the FMSR Station building is in the background. Victoria Pier is no longer in existence. Date: c. 1910.

Penang. Passenger Zatty.

**[89]**
**PENANG. PASSENGER ZATTY.**

*Cancellation:* Nil
*Back:* Divided
*Publisher:* Co-operative Agency, S.S./
No. 7

Victoria Pier was a passenger jetty. When ocean liners anchored nearby, boatmen would use their small launches and sampans to ferry passengers to Victoria Pier. The landing steps of the jetty are clearly visible, and sampans are seen approaching it. This real photographic ppc is dated c. 1910.

No17    Landing Place, Penang

**[90]**
**NO. 17 LANDING PLACE, PENANG**

*Cancellation:* Penang/DE 14/1920
*Back:* Divided
*Publisher:* P.L.I. De Silva, E & O Hotel

A close-up of Victoria Pier on approaching it from the sea. Chinese *tongkang* with tall masts and sails can be seen on the left. The clock tower of the FMSR Station building is in the centre.
Date: c. 1910.

**[91]**

**GENERAL-POST-OFFICE.**

*Cancellation:* 1904; details not clear
*Back:* Undivided
*Publisher:* Not stated

A real photographic ppc of Weld Quay at the end of Swettenham Pier. Victoria Pier and the Government Wharf is sited on the right. Opposite them are the General Post Office, Town Club and the Boustead & Co. building. In the foreground, workers are loading goods from sampans onto bullock carts. Date: c. 1900.

**[92]**

**PENANG.**

*Cancellation:* PENANG/AP 22/1903
*Back:* Undivided
*Publisher:* Not stated

An early ppc, c. 1898, showing part of Victoria Pier on the right. In front of the pier, a horse-drawn tram passes. Opposite the pier stands the stately General Post Office building (its name is clearly visible at the top of the first floor below the roof). A bullock cart in the foreground contrasts with the horse-drawn tram behind it.

Jetty Sheds & Govt: Offices, Penang.

60

**[93]**

**JETTY SHEDS & GOVT: OFFICES, PENANG.**

*Cancellation:* Nil
*Back:* Divided
*Publisher:* Not stated

Jetty sheds or godowns stand on the left, with the Government Buildings opposite. The Government Buildings no longer exist as they were destroyed by Allied bombing in 1945. Tram tracks can be seen along the road on Weld Quay. Date: c. 1900.

Penang. Weed Quay.

**[94]**

**PENANG. WEED QUAY.**

*Cancellation:* PENANG/MR 20/1907
*Back:* Undivided
*Publisher:* Not stated

The building on the right is Boustead & Co. It stood at No. 1, Weld Quay. A steam tram in front of the building bears the name "Penang Tramways". Penang Steam Tramways Ltd belonged to Kerr Stuart, manufacturers of steam tramway engines from England.[87] Date: c. 1900.

**[95]**

PENANG.

*Cancellation:* Nil
*Back:* Undivided
*Publisher:* Straits Photo Co., Penang,
No. 6.

A view of Weld Quay looking towards the General Post Office (gable-roofed building at the end of the quay). Next to it is Boustead & Co., at No. 1 Weld Quay. Workers can be seen resting at the quayside, while others are loading and unloading goods onto the small boats (*right*). One of the names used to refer to Weld Quay was "Kitengi Teru", meaning "Street of Company Godowns" in Tamil.[82]
Date: c. 1900.

**[96]**

WELD QUAI./PENANG.

*Cancellation:* Nil
*Back:* Undivided
*Publisher:* A. Kaulfuss, Penang/No. 39.

A view of Weld Quay from the General Post Office. The first building (*far right*) is the Town Club. Next to it is Boustead & Co., a three-storey building with "a balustraded roof parapet with spherical finials".[30] A steam tram is in the centre of the road while boats and workers can be seen by the quayside. The merchant offices as well as the godowns on Weld Quay were built on reclaimed land and were first occupied in 1893. Boustead & Co. imported a variety of goods, chiefly cotton, piece goods and hardware.[9]
Date: c. 1900.

Nr. 6. Weld Quay, Penang.

**[97]**

**No. 6. Weld Quay, Penang.**

*Cancellation:* Nil
*Back:* Divided
*Publisher:* (Sold by) S.K. Md. Yusoff & Co.

This c. 1905 sepia ppc depicts life at Weld Quay. Workers can be seen loading and unloading goods to waiting horse carts along the quay. Weld Quay was the result of aggressive land reclamation work during Sir Frederick Weld's tenure as governor of the SS in the 1880s.[82] Reclamation works began in 1883 and were completed in 1889, costing $526,107.[9]

Weld Quay, Penang

**[98]**

**Weld Quay, Penang**

*Cancellation:* Nil
*Back:* Divided
*Publisher:* Not stated; printed in Germany

A black and white ppc, dated c. 1905, depicting construction works at Weld Quay; a piling pylon (*foreground*) and a steam roller (*centre*) are visible. Other than Boustead & Co., an English firm, many of the merchant firms that set up operations at Weld Quay were German, including Schmidt, Kuestermann & Co., and Behn, Meyer & Co.[9,82]

PIER PENANG

**[99]**
**PIER PENANG**

*Cancellation:* Nil
*Back:* Undivided
*Publisher:* C.H. 451, Copyright

The building on the right was the old General Post Office (its name is visible between the top floor windows on its lefthand side). The building was subsequently demolished. Today, the General Post Office is housed in a new government building, the Bangunan Tuanku Syed Putra, built in 1961.
Date: c. 1900.

No. 39. Weld Quai, Penang

**[100]**
**NO. 39. WELD QUAI, PENANG**

*Cancellation:* Nil
*Back:* Divided
*Publisher:* A. Kaulfuss, Penang.

A colour ppc, dated c. 1900, showing the commercial buildings on Weld Quay. On the far right is Behn, Meyer & Co., followed by Schiffmann, Heer & Co. The former held the local agencies for shipping lines such as Norddeutscher Lloyd and the Hamburg-America line, as well as mostly German insurance companies, and also exported raw sugar procured from Province Wellesley and Perak. The latter were extensive importers of almost everything in demand in the region, principally piece and cotton goods, ready-made clothing, hardware and ironware. They were also exporters of rubber, tapioca, wolfram and other goods.[9]

Commercial Offices, Penang

**[101]**

**COMMERCIAL OFFICES, PENANG**

*Cancellation:* Penang/1915
*Back:* Divided
*Publisher:* Co-operative Agency, S.S./
No. 12

A colour ppc dated c. 1915 captures
the port industry in Weld Quay. The
commercial firms, from right to left, are:
Boustead & Co., Schmidt, Kuestermann &
Co. and Sturzenegger & Co., Behn Meyer
& Co.,[5] and the Eastern & Pacific Trading
Co. Ltd.[22]

Weld Quay, Penang

**[102]**

**WELD QUAY, PENANG**

*Cancellation:* Nil, but written on 10.10.04
*Back:* Divided
*Publisher:* Not stated

A similar view to **[101]** but a closer angle.
Just visible on the far left of the row of
merchant houses is Behr & Co., standing
at No. 5 Weld Quay. This colour ppc is
dated c. 1910.

No. 70. Chinese junks. Penang harbour.

**[103]**

**No. 70. Chinese junks. Penang harbour.**

*Cancellation:* Nil
*Back:* Divided
*Publisher:* A. Kaulfuss, Penang

The hustle and bustle of life in Weld Quay is caught in this c. 1905 sepia ppc. The freestanding building on the left housed Paterson, Simons & Co., importers and exporters. Its godowns were developed by Phuah Hin Leong, who rented the building to the company.[82] The office building stood at No. 9, Weld Quay.[22]

Nº 14. Weld Quay, Penang.

**[104]**

**No. 14. Weld Quay, Penang.**

*Cancellation:* Nil
*Back:* Divided
*Publisher:* P.L.I. De Silva, E & O. Hotel./
 Printed in England

A sepia ppc depicting low tide at Weld Quay; the boat in the foreground appears to be on the land, possibly due to it being low tide. Workers can be seen unloading goods. Weld Quay is a coastal road stretching from Swettenham Pier to Prangin Road Ghaut; and it is here that the major piers and jetties of Penang Harbour are situated.

No. 66.  Scene on Weld Quay.  Penang.

**[105]**
No. 66. Scene on Weld Quay, Penang.

*Cancellation:* Nil
*Back:* Undivided
*Publisher:* A. Kaulfuss, Penang.

This sepia ppc encapsulates the everyday scene at Weld Quay. In order to move between the quayside and the boats, workers walk along planks while carrying heavy sacks. Date: c. 1900.

Native Junks in Harbour, Penang

**[106]**
Native Junks in Harbour, Penang

*Cancellation:* Nil
*Back:* Divided
*Publisher:* M.J. Penang.

A sepia ppc dated c. 1910. Lighters or *tongkang* are moored alongside Weld Quay. The FMSR Station building clock tower can be seen on the right.

Weld Quay, Penang.

**[107]**
**WELD QUAY, PENANG.**

*Cancellation:* Nil
*Back:* Divided
*Publisher:* Not stated

A real photographic ppc showing, in the foreground, two labourers unloading goods from a boat. They walk precariously on a narrow plank while carrying heavy chests. Victoria Pier is in the background. Date: c. 1940.

Tin Exporting Trem Goverment wharf Penang.

**[108]**
**TIN EXPORTING TREM GOVERMENT WHARF PENANG.**

*Cancellation:* Nil
*Back:* Divided
*Publisher:* Not stated

A real photographic ppc showing Indian workers carrying tin ingots in Weld Quay. Tin was the main export of Malaya at the time. Boustead & Co. even had their own refinery to produce their own brand of tin, called "Boustead tin".[9] Date: c. 1940.

Chinese Bamboo Pier in the Sea, Penang

**[109]**

**CHINESE BAMBOO PIER IN THE SEA, PENANG**

*Cancellation:* Nil
*Back:* Divided
*Publisher:* M.J. Penang.

An early view of the beginning of the clan jetties along the southern end of Weld Quay. A small boat can be seen moored in the foreground; a long bamboo pier is in the middle with many sampans moored along it. A lone attap building is visible beyond the pier. Clan jetties were basically villages built on stilts over water. They were established more than a century ago and housed descendants of a common clan. There were originally seven clan jetties: Lim, Chew, Tan, Yeoh, Lee, Koay, and Ong. Today, six remain. Chew Jetty is the jetty with the largest community.[82] This sepia ppc is dated c. 1910.

Village in the sea, Penang.

**[110]**

**VILLAGE IN THE SEA, PENANG.**

*Cancellation:* Nil
*Back:* Divided
*Publisher:* The Federal Rubber Stamp Co., Kuala Lumpur, Ipoh, Penang & Singapore.

A clan jetty in Weld Quay. These attap-thatched houses were built along plank pathways on stilts sunk into the seabed. Although this habitat is often romanticised, the people who lived here did so out of necessity. The migrants came from poverty-ridden China in the 19th century and found work here as stevedores and cross-channel ferry boatmen. This real photographic ppc dates from c. 1930.

364 - Sungei Pinang, Penang.

**[111]**

**364 – SUNGEI PINANG, PENANG.**

*Cancellation:* 18 MY 1912
*Back:* Divided
*Publisher:* Federal Rubber Stamp Co.,
                Penang, Kuala Lumpur & Ipoh

A serene scene of the Penang River,
c. 1910. The mouth of the river flows
into the South Channel of the Straits
of Malacca, and was used by sampans,
lighters and barges.

Sunger Penang River, Penang

**[112]**

**SUNGOR PENANG RIVER, PENANG**

*Cancellation:* Nil
*Back:* Divided
*Publisher:* Not stated

A beautifully coloured ppc, c. 1910, of a
riverine settlement near the mouth of the
Penang River. A European-style bungalow
can be seen on the right while smaller
dwellings are on both sides of the river.

Esplanade, Penang.

# COLONIAL PENANG

One of Penang's attractions is its colonial architecture. George Town, the capital of Penang, has been described as constituting a "unique and cultural townscape without parallel anywhere in East and Southeast Asia".[122] Although during World War II several important government buildings were destroyed by bombing, the government of Penang has done a commendable job of preserving many of the colonial-era buildings that survived.

## Fort Cornwallis

Fort Cornwallis (FC) [113-120] is perhaps the oldest building in Penang; and marks Francis Light's landing place. It was named after Charles Cornwallis, First Marquess Cornwallis and governor-general of India in 1786.[9,37]

The fort is situated at the end of the Esplanade adjacent to the Queen Victoria Memorial Clock Tower, which is next to Weld Quay [113; 115-116]. In 1786, the FC was just a *nibong* (palm trunk) stockade with no permanent structures. When Indian convict labourers arrived in Penang, Light had the fort rebuilt with bricks.[82] During Colonel Robert Townsend Farquhar's tenure as lieutenant governor of Penang (1804–1805), he commissioned the reinforcement of the fort with a new battery.[82] The fort once had a moat surrounding it [113-116], but it had to be filled during the 1920s due to a malaria outbreak.[37]

The fort was gazetted as a historic site on 8 September 1977, and underwent restoration works in 2000. Today, only the chapel and gunpowder magazine remain of the many civic stuctures that originally stood in the fort.[30]

Fort Point Lighthouse or Pinang Harbour Lighthouse (today's Fort Cornwallis Lighthouse) (*below right*; [117-119]), was constructed in 1882. The lighthouse, which is 21 metres tall,[9,134,135] is the second oldest lighthouse in

Malaysia after Malacca's Tanjung Tuan Lighthouse.[37] The British Union Jack used to be flown from the lighthouse's flagstaff on significant occasions, such as whenever the governor descended from his residence on Penang Hill.

## The Esplanade

The Esplanade (TE; [121-127]) refers to the rectangular Padang Kota Lama (a large field, commonly known as the Padang, on which football, cricket and other games are played), and also the promenade along the sea front.[9] This section of the text discusses the promenade while the other parts of TE are discussed separately in this chapter. The Esplanade looking towards FC is shown in [121] to [123], while [124] to [126] show TE looking towards the Municipal Building and the Cenotaph. The road that separates TE from the Padang is known today as Jalan Tun Syed Sheh Barakbah.

## The Cenotaph

The Cenotaph [127-129] (or Penang War Memorial), is situated at TE facing the Municipal Offices building.

Cenotaphs were built in many British colonial cities and towns[15] to commemorate the devastating losses suffered by the British during World War I (1914–1918).[40] On 11 November 1928, the 10th anniversary of Armistice Day, the foundation stone of the Penang Cenotaph was laid by Resident Councillor Meadows Frost.[40] The Cenotaph was unveiled a year later by the resident councillor in an elaborate ceremony.[41]

The Cenotaph suffered damage during the Japanese Occupation of World War II (1939–1945); it was further damaged during the Allied bombing of Penang (bombs meant for Port Swettenham landed on the Cenotaph instead). A new Cenotaph was designed for free by Messrs

The address side of [113]. This ppc is an example of Raphael Tuck's "Oilette" series. It debuted in 1903, and was named as such as its surface was designed to resemble a miniature oil painting.

The flagstaff of Fort Cornwallis can be seen in the centre; the lighthouse is behind it. A group of Chinese with queues lean against the railing of the fort, c. 1900.

*Opposite:*
The Esplanade, c. 1920. In the centre, the new double storey Cricket Club stands between the Town Hall building (*left*) and the Municipal Offices building (*right*). A group of Jawi Peranakan men and a boy pose beneath the *angsana* tree.

The Town Hall stands on the left; the Cricket Club is in the centre, c. 1910.

The new double-storey (*centre*) Cricket Club, c. 1940.

Boutcher & Co., and rebuilt in time for the Armistice Day ceremony on 11 November 1948.[41]

While the original Cenotaph [129] had no bronze plaque at its foot (below the tip of the sword), the rebuilt Cenotaph [128] did. In the 1990s, a metal fence was built around the Cenotaph.

## The Padang Kota Lama

The Padang Kota Lama [131-136] or Padang ("field" in Malay) is adjacent to TE. It had been the venue for significant events such as the proclamation of Independence on 31 August 1957, and cultural festivities such as the Chingay Parade.

In the 1900s, the sepoy regiment used the Padang for target practice and the Manila Band played at the bandstand [131-133] from 1890 to 1954. The Padang was also known as the Cricket Field as cricket was played there.[42]

## The Penang Cricket Club

The Penang Cricket Club (CC) started on the Padang c. 1907. It was initially a single-storey building [131; 132; 137]; by 1910, it had been replaced by a two-storey building (*below left*; [124; 127; 134; 138-140]). In 1939, the CC moved to its present club house on Western Road (today known as Jalan Utama) and changed its name to the Penang Golf Club. This was timely as the CC's original building on the Padang was destroyed in 1941 when the Japanese invaded Penang. In 1947, the Penang Golf Club became known as the Penang Sports Club.

## The Ben Vermont Monument

The Ben Vermont Monument [135-136; 141-142] stood on the grounds of the Padang beside Light Street. It was built in honour of The Hon. J.M.B. Vermont, manager and part-proprietor of the Batu Kawan Estate in Province Wellesley (Seberang Perai). He was known as the "Grand Old Man" for his contribution towards the abundant sugar supply in the 1880s and 1890s.

The monument was built in the 1920s [136]. What started off as a simple brick monument with a cupola was later replaced by a much more elaborate structure of wrought iron with a fenestrated roof that housed a drinking fountain [141-142]. The monument was destroyed during World War II, never to be rebuilt again.

## The Town Hall

The Town Hall (*top left*; [143]), situated next to the Municipal Offices building and opposite Fort Cornwallis, was built between 1879 and 1883. During his visit to Penang in 1880, the Governor of the SS, Sir Frederick Weld, described the Town Hall as a "fine building".[30]

During the colonial era, the Town Hall was informally known as the European Club as non-Europeans were not allowed inside. It was primarily used as a venue for social events. Currently it is used for public speeches, art exhibitions and concerts.

The Town Hall was occupied by the Municipal Offices until the latter moved to its own building in 1906.[30,82]

## The City Hall (Municipal Offices)

Originally called the Municipal Offices, the City Hall [144-148] was formerly the seat of the City Council of George Town. The Municipal Offices building was commissioned to be built in 1903 to house the municipal offices which at that time occupied the Town Hall, and also because the Town Hall had taken on a more social function.[42] The Municipal Offices building opened in 1906 and was one of the the first buildings in Penang to be fitted with electric lights and fans.[42]

The building was renamed City Hall when George Town was granted city status in 1957. Both the Town Hall and Municipal Offices buildings have been much photographed (*top left*; [132; 134; 142-148]).

## Queen Victoria Memorial Clock Tower

The Queen Victoria Memorial Clock Tower (*below right*; [130; 149-154; 158]) was presented to George Town by Penang millionaire Cheah Chen Eok J.P. (1852–1922)[44] to commemorate the Diamond Jubilee of Queen Victoria (r. 1837–1901) in 1897. It cost $35,000 to build.

The clock tower is 60 feet tall (18 metres), with one foot (0.3 metres) for each year of the Queen's reign; and the six steps leading to the main door also denote each decade of the Queen's reign. The clock tower is located at King Edward Place (Pesara King Edward), opposite FC and the Penang Port Commission.

## The Hub of Government Administration

From the late 1890s to c. 1941, the hub of government administration in Penang stretched from Weld Quay into King Edward Place and Beach Street, and round into Downing Street. It was here that the Government Buildings and Offices were located. Called the Government Quadrangle, the U-shaped building ensemble here included the Resident Councillor's Office, the Governor's Office, the Education Department, the Treasury Office, the Audit Office, the Public Works Department, the Land Office, the General Post Office, the Penang Chamber of Commerce, the Penang Turf Club, and the Town Club.[4,9,46] Government Buildings and Offices from various views are depicted: facing the Queen Victoria Memorial Clock Tower [155-158], looking towards Weld Quay [159-162], and on Beach Street [163-166].

In late 1941, all the above-mentioned buildings were badly damaged by bombs. Only the building that housed the Telegraph Co. Ltd, which today houses the Penang State Islamic Council,[42] survived.

## The British East India Company Headquarters

The British East India Company (EIC) headquarters was Penang's first government building;[47] it was established after Francis Light took possession of Penang. The EIC headquarters c. 1900 [161] was a single-storey building that stood at the corner of Beach Street and Downing Street. The site was later occupied by the Hong Kong and Shanghai Bank (HSBC) from 1906 onwards.[48]

## The Chinese Protectorate and Downing Street

The Chinese Protectorate [162] was established in 1877 and stood on the junction of Downing Street [163-166] and Beach Street. Junks arriving from China were required to report here to check on the excesses of the Chinese coolie trade.[48] In colonial times, Downing Street was known as "The Street of the Chinese Protectorate".[49]

Downing Street was named after Downing Street in London, and stretches from Weld Quay to Beach Street. Besides the Chinese Protectorate, and other government and commercial buildings mentioned earlier, buildings and offices along Downing Street included the HSBC, the Fire Insurance Association, the Mercantile Bank of India, Messrs Adams & Allan (Advocates & Solicitors), and Adamson, Gilfillan & Co. Ltd.[22]

## General Post Office

The General Post Office (GPO) (*top right*; [167-168]) was built in 1903. It replaced two earlier post offices built in 1881 and 1892.[51] In 1941, during World War II, the GPO was destroyed; after the war, the post office operated from a building along Light Street opposite the Queen Victoria Memorial Clock Tower. Today, the GPO is housed in the Bangunan Tuanku Syed Putra on Downing Street.

## The Town Club

The Town Club [169] shared a building with the Chamber of Commerce, which stood at the corner of Weld Quay and Downing Street, facing the GPO [166]. It was formed in 1901 largely through the efforts of Robert Yeats of Boustead & Co., who was its first chairman. The

The General Post Office at the corner of Weld Quay and Downing Street. An electric tram is on the right, c. 1920.

8. The Clock Tower, Penang, S.S.

A sepia ppc of the Queen Victoria Memorial Clock Tower, published by Raphael Tuck & Sons, c. 1915.

The address side of [172]. This postcard was sent to Belgium; the sender used a "Nederlandsch-Indie" (Dutch East Indies) stamp. The first Nederlandsch-Indie stamp was issued on 1 April 1864.

The Engineers' Institute at the junction of Farquhar Street and Leith Street, c. 1900.

club was largely patronised by businessmen for "tiffin and commercial talk".[9] The Town Club was destroyed by Japanese bombing in December 1941.

## The Police Courts

The Police Courts [170-171] were located on Light Street; hence to the Hokkiens in Penang, Light Street is known as "Po-le-khau", meaning "Entrance to the Police Courts".[136] They were built in the 1820s in the Anglo-Indian Classical Style with major renovations in 1874 and 1890. The Police Courts used to house the Recorder's Court and Magistrates' Courts; these all once formed part of the Central Police Station.[42] Today the Police Courts have been transformed and enlarged into the State Assembly Buildings (Dewan Undangan Negeri).

## The Supreme Court and Penang Library

The Supreme Court [172-176] stands at the junction of Light Street, Pitt Street (Jalan Masjid Kapitan Keling) and Farquhar Street (Lebuh Farquhar). It opened in 1904, replacing its predecessor which had served since 1809, also on this same site. Recently, in 2007, the Penang Supreme Court was extensively renovated; a new three-storey wing was added to the original structure.

The Penang Library [173] used to occupy the southern portion of the Supreme Court building. Prior to this, it was housed in several places, including the Chinese Protectorate on Downing Street, before moving to the Town Hall. The library relocated to the Supreme Court building in 1905 where it remained until 1973 when it moved to the Dewan Sri Pinang.[14]

## The Logan Memorial

The Logan Memorial was erected in memory of J.R. Logan, a respected lawyer, in 1869.[9] The Gothic-style memorial stands in the grounds of the Supreme Court [174-177]. On top of its octagonal base are four life-sized females sculptures representing the four virtues of Temperance, Wisdom, Fortitude and Justice. In 2007, the memorial was moved to a new location across Light Street. Although it has since been restored, years of neglect and its relocation have caused damage to some parts of the memorial. Today, Fortitude is headless and Justice is handless.

## The Penang Free School/Hutchings School/ Penang State Museum and Art Gallery

The Penang Free School (PFS; [176; 178-180]) was founded by the Reverend R.S. Hutchings, Colonial Chaplain of Penang, on 21 October 1816. It was named "Free" as it was open to all regardless of religion or ethnicity. The PFS then stood along Farquhar Street. It was built in two phases: the first part in 1896 [178], and the second [179] in 1906.[42] By the 1920s, the school had become overcrowded. A bigger building was thus required. So, a new 12-hectare site on Green Lane (Jalan Masjid Negeri) [180] was identified, and the new school building was completed by 1925.

Hutchings School (HS) was established in January 1928. The HS, named after Rev. Hutchings, occupied the old PFS building. On 1 February 1945, the east wing of the main building was bombed by Allied forces. The school reopened on 4 October 1945[56] and, in 1963, HS moved out of the old PFS building which, in turn, housed the Penang State Museum and Art Gallery from 1965 onwards.[14]

## The Engineers' Institute

The Engineers' Institute (*below left*; [181;182]), established for the recreation and general convenience of European engineers, stood at the junction of Leith and Farquhar streets. It was a casualty of the Japanese Occupation of Penang which began in 1941. Today, Farquhar Street runs through where the institute once stood.[4]

**[113]**

**PENANG./DITCH OF FORT CORNWALLIS.**

*Cancellation:* PENANG/16 DEC/1920
*Back:* Divided
*Publisher:* Raphael Tuck & Sons, "Oilette"
    Postcard No. 8961

A watercolour ppc of Fort Cornwallis, dated c. 1910. During this time, the moat was still filled with water. A malaria outbreak in the 1920s caused the moat to be filled up. The Queen Victoria Memorial Clock Tower can be seen in the background, and the dome of the Hong Kong and Shanghai Bank building beside it.

**[114]**

**THE FORT, PENANG**

*Cancellation:* Nil; but written in 1909
     (not posted)
*Back:* Divided
*Publisher:* Not stated

Another view of Fort Cornwallis is shown in this colour ppc dated c. 1910. This view looks towards the Municipal Offices building (*right*). The moat and its bridge are shown in the foreground.

No. 53. Clock-Tower.

**[115]**
**No. 53. Clock-Tower.**

*Cancellation:* Nil
*Back:* Undivided
*Publisher:* Not stated

This ppc shows the moat and thick wall surrounding Fort Cornwallis. The Queen Victoria Memorial Clock Tower (*centre*) and Government Buildings (*left*) are clearly visible. Fort Cornwallis is the largest standing fort in Malaysia. Although originally built for military purposes, its function became more administrative as military rule was superseded by civil administration.[9] Date: c. 1900.

Penang. Fort Cornwallis and Surroundings by Night

**[116]**
**Penang. Fort Cornwallis and Surroundings by Night**

*Cancellation:* Nil
*Back:* Divided
*Publisher:* Co-operative Agency S.S./ No. 1

A similar view to **[115]**, but from a distance. Fort Cornwallis was the centre of administration in the early days of the founding of the settlement of Penang, as evidenced by the landmarks surrounding the fort: to the south of the fort were the Police Offices and Police Courts while west of the fort was the Esplanade.[9] Date: c. 1910.

**[117]**

**ESPLANDE ROAD, PENANG.**

*Cancellation:* Nil
*Back:* Divided
*Publisher:* K.M. Mahmed Esoof, Penang.
No. 3068

This colour ppc depicts Esplanade Road in c. 1920. In the foreground are carts, rickshaws and rattan baskets. The Penang Harbour Lighthouse is clearly different from an earlier one (*see cover*); the one here is on higher ground and has a domed roof instead of the original pyramid-shaped roof. The flagstaff stands next to the lighthouse.

**[118]**

**FLAG STAFF, PENANG**

*Cancellation:* Nil
*Back:* Divided
*Publisher:* M.J., Penang.

A real photographic ppc dated c. 1900. Fort Pier (Kedah Pier) is teeming with activity; the flagstaff and Penang Harbour Lighthouse (behind the flagstaff) are visible in the centre of this ppc. The lighthouse was one of the "three principal lights" to guide vessels approaching Penang Harbour, the other two being Pulau Rimau Light and Muka Head Light.[9]

Penang. Sida View Fort Cornwallis.

78

**[119]**

336. LIGHT. HUSE. PENANG.

*Cancellation:* Nil
*Back:* Divided
*Publisher:* Not stated

The Penang Harbour Lighthouse, also called Fort Point Lighthouse (*right*) and the flagstaff (*left*). The lighthouse was erected in 1882 and underwent renovations in 1914 and 1925. In 1914, the white dioptric light was of 9,000 candle power; this was doubled to 18,000 in 1925.[9,154,155] Date: c. 1940.

**[120]**

PENANG. SIDA VIEW FORT CORNWALLIS.

*Cancellation:* Nil
*Back:* Divided
*Publisher:* Co-operative Agency, S.S./No. 23.

A closer look at Fort Cornwallis, from the bridge across the moat surrounding the fort. This ppc is dated c. 1910. A soldier with rifle is guarding the entrance to the fort.

No. 137        THE ESPLANADE, SHOWING BANDSTAND, PENANG

[121]

No. 137. THE ESPLANADE, SHOWING BANDSTAND. PENANG

*Cancellation:* Nil
*Back:* Divided
*Publisher:* Not stated; printed in England

A real photographic ppc of the Esplanade, c. 1910. The iron railings, shown so prominently here, were removed by the Japanese c. 1941 during the Japanese Occupation to make armaments; they have now been replaced by concrete walls. The bandstand is on the right.

5. The Esplanade, Penang, S.S.

[122]

5. THE ESPLANADE, PENANG, S.S.

*Cancellation:* Penang/Sept/1919
*Back:* Divided
*Publisher:* Raphael Tuck & Sons, "Sepia Platemarked" Postcard 763/ Published for Lock & Co., Penang.

A "Sepia Platemarked" series of the Esplanade, printed in Britain, and dated c. 1910. The view is towards the lighthouse and flagstaff at Fort Cornwallis. The road in the foreground is now known as Jalan Tun Syed Sheh Barakbah. Before World War II, the road was a part of the Esplanade.

No. 131          THE ESPLANADE, PENANG

**[123]**
**NO. 131 THE ESPLANADE, PENANG**

*Cancellation:* Penang/1948
*Back:* Divided
*Publisher:* Not stated; printed in England

Another real photographic ppc looking towards Fort Cornwallis. In times past, the Esplanade played a part in matchmaking Chinese maidens with their future husbands during the 15th day of the Lunar New Year (Chap Goh Meh). On this day, Nyonya maidens would be paraded in trishaws and buggies to be selected by prospective suitors. At night, during the full moon, maidens cast oranges into the sea, wishing for good husbands.[82] Chap Goh Meh is also referred to as the Chinese Valentine's Day. Date: c. 1940.

City hall & Criket club Penang.

**[124]**
**CITY HALL & CRICKET CLUB PENANG.**

*Cancellation:* Nil
*Back:* Divided
*Publisher:* Not stated

The Esplanade is in the foreground. The three buildings in the background are: the Municipal Offices building (*right*), the new Cricket Club (*centre*) and the Town Hall (*left*, hidden by the tree). The Municipal bandstand, a pavilion for public entertainment and ceremonies, stands in front of the Municipal Offices building. This c. 1910 ppc has a serrated left border, and is therefore detached from a ppc booklet.

The Municipal offices.          Sea-Beach and Esplanade.

**[125]**
PENANG./THE MUNICIPAL OFFICES.
SEA-BEACH AND ESPLANADE.

*Cancellation:* Nil
*Back:* Undivided
*Publisher:* Not stated

The Esplanade and its iron railings are on the right, while on the left is the moat of Fort Cornwallis. The Municipal Offices building is clearly seen in the centre, and the bandstand in front of the building. A bullock cart and a rickshaw are in the middle of the road. Date: c. 1900.

A 6 - Municipal Office, Penang.

**[126]**
A 6 – MUNICIPAL OFFICE, PENANG.

*Cancellation:* Nil
*Back:* Divided
*Publisher:* Nikko Studio, Penang, S.S.
              Printed in Saxony.

Typical of Nikko Studio, this ppc comes in pleasing subtle colours capturing the Esplanade as it was then, looking towards the Municipal Offices building from the flagstaff in Fort Cornwallis. Date: c. 1920.

**[127]**

THE ESPLANADE/PENANG

*Cancellation:* Nil
*Back:* Divided
*Publisher:* Not stated

A real photographic ppc showing the Municipal Offices building (*centre*); the Cenotaph (*right*); and the mock-Tudor style new Cricket Club (*left*). In the foreground is the Padang Kota Lama. The Esplanade was described in 1908 as a "comprehensive name which includes a large ground on which football, cricket, lawn-tennis, and bowls are played, and also the promenade along the sea front."[9] Date: c. 1940.

**[128]**

WAR MEMORIAL AT THE ESPLANADE/PENANG

*Cancellation:* Nil
*Back:* Divided
*Publisher:* P.M.S. Mohamed Noordin, Penang

This is the rebuilt War Memorial or Cenotaph of 1948 after the original memorial, built in 1928, was destroyed by a combination of the Japanese in c. 1941 and Allied bombing in 1945. The new Cenotaph only cost $3,500.[11] Three Cuban royal palms (*Roystonea regia*) are planted around the Cenotaph. This ppc bears the "Lusterchrome" trademark on the address side. "Lusterchrome" is a trademark by American postcard manufacturers, Tichnor Brothers Inc. in Boston. This ppc is dated c. 1960.

**[129]**
UNTITLED [CENOTAPH].

*Cancellation:* Nil
*Back:* Divided
*Publisher:* Not stated

The Cenotaph c. 1940. This was the original memorial that was built in 1928. On 11 November 1928, the foundation stone of the Cenotaph was laid by Resident Councillor Meadows Frost, in the presence of the architect and designer of the Cenotaph, David McLeod Craik (of Swan & Maclaren).[40] [Collection of Dr Toh Kok Thye.]

**[130]**
PENANG. CLOCK TOWER.

*Cancellation:* Nil
*Back:* Divided
*Publisher:* Not stated

The Queen Victoria Memorial Clock Tower, c. 1905, is shown after its completion in 1902. The clock tower serves as a "permanent memorial of the late Queen Victoria's Diamond Jubilee".[9] Queen Victoria died in 1901, a year before the clock tower was completed.

**[131]**

**PENANG**

*Cancellation:* Penang/1921
*Back:* Undivided
*Publisher:* Straits Photo Co., Penang/ No. 31.

View across the Padang (Padang Kota Lama) looking towards the Town Hall, Cricket Club, the Municipal Offices building (later known as City Hall) and the bandstand. The Padang Kota Lama was named as such to distinguish it from the Padang Brown opposite the Penang Buddhist Association on Anson Road, and the Padang Polo, located opposite the Penang General Hospital on Residency Road. This real photographic ppc is dated c. 1900.

**[132]**

**PENANG, THE ESPLANADE.**

*Cancellation:* Nil
*Back:* Undivided
*Publisher:* Not stated

The single-storey old Cricket Club is on the left, while the bandstand or pavilion (to watch cricket matches or public performances) is in the foreground. The Esplanade is out of view on the right. This ppc is dated c. 1900.

Esplanade, Penang.

**[133]**

**ESPLANADE, PENANG.**

*Cancellation:* Nil
*Back:* Divided
*Publisher:* K.M. Mahmed Esoof, Penang.
No. 3065

The Esplanade looking towards Fort Cornwallis. A portion of the Padang has been transformed into a tennis court and a tennis match is shown in progress. The pavilion or bandstand is in the centre; another pavilion is in the background. A cannon, facing the sea, is in front of the bandstand. Date: c. 1910.

**[134]**

**ESPLANAD PENANG.**

*Cancellation:* Nil
*Back:* Divided
*Publisher:* Not stated

A real photographic ppc dated c. 1930. On the back of this ppc is written: "On the left the Cricket Club. Behind that the Town Hall. On the right by the bandstand the tennis courts." The Town Hall is out of view; it stood on the right of the Cricket Club. The Municipal Offices building stands imposingly on the right of the Cricket Club. The view on this ppc is from Light Street. Many people are seen strolling and resting on the Padang, enjoying the sea breeze.

Esplanad Penang.

THE ESPLANADE, PENANG.

**[135]**
**THE ESPLANADE, PENANG.**

*Cancellation:* Nil
*Back:* Divided
*Publisher:* Not stated

A real photographic ppc of the Padang and the Esplanade from Light Street. The Ben Vermont Monument is in the centre and, in the background, the bandstand. A 1908 account stated that: "At the south side of the athletic ground is a bandstand, where a Filipino band plays for an hour or so on Mondays, Wednesdays and Fridays, besides on special occasions."[9] On "band nights", the atmosphere in the Esplanade was merrier, and rickshaws and carriages thronged the area. The southern end of the Padang would be transformed into a public park where everyone, regardless of ethnicity, strolled and listened to the music.[9] Date: c. 1930.

Esplanade, Penang.

**[136]**
**ESPLANADE, PENANG.**

*Cancellation:* Nil
*Back:* Divided
*Publisher:* K.M. Mahmed Esoof, Penang.
        No. 3026

The Ben Vermont Monument stands under the shade provided by two large *angsana* trees. In the foreground is Light Street and in the background is Fort Cornwallis. This colour ppc is dated c. 1920.

**[137]**

**No. 75. Sports in Penang**

*Cancellation:* PENANG/JU 26/1907
*Back:* Divided
*Publisher:* A. Kaulfuss, Penang.

A c. 1907 colour ppc depicting a sports carnival at the Padang. The Europeans are mainly concentrated outside the old, single-storey Cricket Club, while the Asian spectators are mostly at the fringes of the Padang. A tennis game is in progress in front of the bandstand (*background*). During colonial times, the Cricket Club only admitted Europeans. The Eurasians therefore set up the Penang Recreation Club and the Chinese, the Chinese Recreation Club.[42]

**[138]**

**Cricket Club, Penang.**

*Cancellation:* Nil
*Back:* Divided
*Publisher:* Not stated

A real photographic ppc depicting the new Cricket Club. A large *angsana* tree is in the foreground. Date: c. 1940.

PENANG CRICKET CLUB.

**[139]**
**PENANG CRICKET CLUB.**

*Cancellation:* Nil
*Back:* Divided
*Publisher:* Raphael Tuck & Sons "Oilette" Postcard No. 8961/Printed in England

Another colour ppc of the "Oilette" series from Raphael Tuck & Sons. As can be seen, the picture looks like a miniature oil painting. Here, the handsome new Cricket Club building is shown. The upper storey of the new premises is mock-Tudor styled, and looks similar to the Selangor Club building in Kuala Lumpur. This ppc is dated c. 1920.

2923 CRICKET CLUB, PENANG.

**[140]**
**2923 CRICKET CLUB, PENANG.**

*Cancellation:* Nil
*Back:* Divided
*Publisher:* Not stated

A real photographic ppc of the new Penang Cricket Club in light sepia tone, c. 1930. The European community, especially cricket enthusiasts, would regularly meet here.

**[141]**

**BEN VERMONT'S MONUMENT,/PENANG**

*Cancellation:* Nil
*Back:* Divided
*Publisher:* Not stated; printed in Germany

A sepia ppc of the Ben Vermont Monument, c. 1910. Compared to the earlier structure shown in **[136]**, this was made of elaborate wrought iron. It is hexagonal in shape, and the cupola roof is elaborately fenestrated. It also housed a water fountain. The Hon. J.M.B Vermont was a very wealthy land owner. Along with his brother, he acquired the Alma Estate in Province Wellesley (Seberang Perai).[9] He was also a prominent leader of the European community in Penang. His residence in Penang was called "Marble Hall".[32]

**[142]**

**MEMORY OF BENET VERMONT,**
**C. M. G. M. L. C./ESPLANADE, PENANG**

*Cancellation:* Eastern & Oriental Hotel,
               Penang/18 FE/1911
*Back:* Divided
*Publisher:* M.J., Penang.

A group of Indian men and a boy pose for a photograph at the Ben Vermont Monument. The elaborate cast iron structure and its roof in the form of a fenestrated dome is rendered clearly in this colour ppc. This monument used to be a focal point for band performances and ceremonial events. Date: c. 1910s.

[143]
**PENANG, THE TOWN HALL.**

*Cancellation:* Nil
*Back:* Divided
*Publisher:* Raphael Tuck & Sons, "Oilette"
Postcard No. 8961./Penang
Series I./Printed in England

An "Oilette" postcard by Raphael Tuck & Sons of the Town Hall dated c. 1920. Like the Municipal Offices building, the Town Hall building was also fitted with electric lights and fans. The Town Hall was built in 1883 with an assembly hall, a ballroom and a library.[83] The Municipal Offices originally operated from the Town Hall. But as the Town Hall became more social than administrative, a new building for the Penang Municipality, the Municipal Offices building, was commissioned to be built in 1903. The Hokkiens referred to the Town Hall as "Ang Mo Kong Kuan" meaning "European Club".[82]

90

[144]
**PENANG./MUNICIPAL OFFICES.**

*Cancellation:* Nil
*Back:* Undivided
*Publisher:* Pritchard & Co., Penang.
No. 25.

This is a very early view of the Municipal Offices building soon after it opened in 1906. Built at a cost of $100,000, this building incorporated European ironworks.[82] This real photographic ppc is dated c. 1906.

Municipal Buildings, Penang

**[145]**

**MUNICIPAL BUILDINGS, PENANG**

*Cancellation:* PENANG/OC 30/1909
*Back:* Divided
*Publisher:* Co-operative Agency S.S./
No. 13

Another early view of the Municipal Offices building, dated c. 1908. This colour ppc renders clearly the richly ornate and baroque façade of the building. It was described in 1908 as "an imposing whitewashed edifice, which is one of the architectural beauties of the town".[9] A few rickshaws can be seen waiting outside the building.

Municipal Office, Penang.

**[146]**

**MUNICIPAL OFFICE, PENANG.**

*Cancellation:* Nil
*Back:* Divided
*Publisher:* Raphael Tuck & Sons Sepia
Postcard Series. No. 893./
Penang., Printed in England.

This sepia ppc depicts the Municipal Offices building standing majestically in the background; the Esplanade and the Padang are in the foreground. This is a ppc from Raphael Tuck & Sons' "Sepia Postcard" series, dated c. 1920. It is stated that the ppc was "published expressly for C.A. Ribeiro & Co. Ltd., Stationers Etc., Singapore & Penang".

**[147]**
PENANG./MUNICIPAL OFFICE.

*Cancellation:* PENANG/Not clear
*Back:* Divided
*Publisher:* Raphael Tuck & Sons "Oilette" Postcard No. 8961/Penang. Series I./Printed in England

A handsome colour ppc dated c. 1920 of the Municipal Offices Building (renamed City Hall in 1957). A lone motor car can be seen in the foreground.

**[148]**
NO. 60. PENANG./THE RESIDENCY./ESPLANADE./CHINESE RESIDENCY.

*Cancellation:* ORCHARD ROAD SINGAPORE/SE 12/1905
*Back:* Undivided
*Publisher:* A. Kaulfuss, Penang.

The Municipal Offices building (the righthand view titled "Esplanade") is flanked by an image of the Residency (home of the highest-ranking British colonial officer until Independence; *see* [336]) on its left. The Residency has since Independence been renamed "Seri Mutiara" and houses the Yang di-Pertua Negeri of Penang. The view of the Chinese Residency (*see Chapter 4*) is on the bottom left. This triview ppc was sent to New Zealand by a ppc collector in Singapore in 1905.

PENANG.

THE CLOCK TOWER.

Clock Tower, Penang

**[149]**

PENANG./THE CLOCK TOWER.

*Cancellation:* PENANG/NOV 9/1906
*Back:* Undivided
*Publisher:* Pritchard & Co., Penang. No. 36

The Queen Victoria Memorial Clock Tower soon after its completion in 1902. This may be the official opening of the clock tower as the Union Jack is hung below the onion-domed roof; a large crowd stands at the foot of the clock tower. Dated c. 1905, this ppc was written on 8 November 1906.

**[150]**

CLOCK TOWER, PENANG

*Cancellation:* Nil
*Back:* Divided
*Publisher:* Unknown

The Queen Victoria Memorial Clock Tower has four tiers: the base is octagonal; the next two tiers comprise four distinct faces with four working clocks. The top tier is rounded off with Roman columns and roofed with a domed cupola. The clock tower looks towards Beach Street. Date: c. 1910.

No. 41. Clocktower, Penang.

**[151]**
**No. 41. Clocktower, Penang.**

*Cancellation:* Nil
*Back:* Undivided
*Publisher:* Not stated

A colour ppc dated c. 1905 of the Queen Victoria Memorial Clock Tower after its completion in 1902. This view is from Light Street looking towards Fort Road (today known as Jalan Tun Syed Sheh Barakbah) and Kedah Pier (also Fort Pier). The road is deserted except for a couple of pedestrians and rickshaws.

Clock Tower, Penang

**[152]**
**Clock Tower, Penang**

*Cancellation:* 1910
*Back:* Divided
*Publisher:* M.J., Penang.

Another view of the Queen Victoria Memorial Clock Tower. The building on its right is the government goods sheds which were built in 1907 to be leased to shipping agents.[82] This view is from Light Street. This colour ppc is dated c. 1910.

**[153]**

**Clock Tower, Penang**

*Cancellation:* PENANG/11 SE/1917
*Back:* Divided
*Publisher:* M.J., Penang.

A view of the Queen Victoria Memorial Clock Tower looking towards Fort Cornwallis. Today, the clock tower leans slightly as a result of bombing during World War II. Bombs were dropped on King Edward Place, destroying the Government Buildings. This ppc is dated c. 1915.

**[154]**

**369. View of Penang**

*Cancellation:* IPOH/1930
*Back:* Divided
*Publisher:* Not stated

A real photographic ppc, c. 1930, of the View of Penang; the Queen Victoria Memorial Clock Tower and Light Street are on the right. The clock tower was completely funded by Penang tycoon, Cheah Chen Eok. Besides the clock tower, he left behind another legacy: the "Moon Gate" near the entrance of the Penang Botanic Gardens. It was a gateway to his hillside villa, named Villae. The villa was left deserted in the 1920s[12] and today its ruins can be seen about 20 minutes' walk from the Moon Gate.

No. 72, Government Offices and Clock Tower, Penang

**[155]**

**No. 72, Government Offices and Clock Tower, Penang**

*Cancellation:* PENANG/JU 18/1906
*Back:* Divided
*Publisher:* A. Kaulfuss, Penang./75460

The Government Buildings were laid out as a U-shaped ensemble. This view shows the bottom of the "U" facing the Queen Victoria Memorial Clock Tower. Fort Cornwallis is in the foreground and Penang Harbour is in the background. This aerial view was possibly taken from the lighthouse. Date: c. 1905.

1. Government Buildings, Penang, S.S.

**[156]**

**1. Government Buildings, Penang, S.S.**

*Cancellation:* PENANG/29 DE/1919
*Back:* Divided
*Publisher:* Raphael Tuck & Sons "Sepia Platemarked" Postcard 768/ Printed in Britain

This sepia ppc, dated c. 1910, features the same Government Buildings as in **[155]**, but taken from street level, in front of the Queen Victoria Memorial Clock Tower. The Government Buildings were built c. 1900. They were described as "a great block of buff-coloured Government buildings...They comprise the General Post Office, the Government Telegraph Office, and the Government Telephone Exchange; the Governor's Office, for the use of his Excellency when visiting Pinang; the Resident Councillor's Office, the Audit Office, the Public Works Department, the Land Office, the Marine Department, including the Harbour Master's Office, and the Office of the Solicitor-General."[9]

KING EDWARD'S PLACE, PENANG

No 168

**[157]**

**No 168 KING EDWARD'S PLACE, PENANG**

*Cancellation:* Nil
*Back:* Divided
*Publisher:* Not stated; printed in England

A real photographic ppc showing the Government Buildings. The street sign "King Edward Place" is visible on the lamp post in the centre. King Edward Place is a stretch of road created between 1880 and 1904 as a result of land reclamation. Date: c. 1930.

**[158]**

**UNTITLED [QUEEN VICTORIA MEMORIAL CLOCK TOWER/GOVERNMENT BUILDINGS].**

*Cancellation:* Nil
*Back:* Divided
*Publisher:* Syonan Army Inspection Team

This photograph, showing a view of the Queen Victoria Memorial Clock Tower and the Government Buildings, was taken by the Japanese Syonan Army Inspection Team. Date: c. 1942. (Singapore was renamed Syonan during the Japanese Occupation, 1942–1945.)

Penang. Harbour & Government Officee.

**[159]**

**PENANG. HARBOUR & GOVERNMENT OFFIECE.**

*Cancellation:* PENANG/JU 29/1906
*Back:* Undivided
*Publisher:* Not stated

The Government Buildings were built in stages from 1884 and completed in 1889.[9] The block of buildings stood along Weld Quay; the first block housed the Resident Councillor's Office, the Audit Office, the Public Works Department and the Marine Department and the Harbour Master's Office.[4,82] Victoria Pier is on the right in the background. This ppc is dated c. 1900.

Government Building, Penang

**[160]**

**GOVERNMENT BUILDING. PENANG**

*Cancellation:* Nil
*Back:* Divided
*Publisher:* M.J., Penang./183549

The section of the Government Buildings that housed the Post Office, Treasury and other government offices. In 1891, the Government Buildings were extended with a western wing to accommodate the Land Office. This was followed by the construction of the eastern wing for the Post Office in 1903.[4,82] On the back of this ppc is written: "Here is the continuation of the block of buildings where the Post Office, the Treasury and other Government Offices are. This block is occupied by the Gov. Veterinary Surgeon." This ppc is dated c. 1910.

**[161]**

UNTITLED [HEADQUARTERS OF THE BRITISH EAST INDIA COMPANY].

*Cancellation:* IPOH/26 DE/1918
*Back:* Undivided
*Publisher:* Straits Photo Co., Penang, No. 16.

The British East India Company headquarters, Penang's first government building, stands on the right (*centre*). It was a single-storey building with high-ceilinged verandah at the corner of Beach Street and Downing Street. On its right was the Criterion Press (signboard is visible), and opposite it was the Beach Street Police Station.[48] This sepia ppc is dated c. 1900.

Government Building, Penang.

**[162]**

GOVERNMENT BUILDING, PENANG.

*Cancellation:* Nil
*Back:* Divided
*Publisher:* S.M. Manicum, Penang/No. 88

The Chinese Protectorate (*foreground, left*) stood at the southern side of the Government Quadrangle. The image here shows the inner part of the Government Quadrangle facing Downing Street. The Chinese Protectorate, as well as the Indian Immigration Depot, were established to process the thousands of immigrants that arrived every year.[82] Date: c. 1910. [Collection of Dr Toh Kok Thye.]

Downing Street, Penang.

**[163]**
**DOWNING STREET, PENANG.**

*Cancellation:* Nil
*Back:* Divided
*Publisher:* Not stated; printed in Germany

Downing Street, looking from Weld Quay towards Beach Street. The General Post Office is in the foreground on the right; next to it is the Chinese Protectorate building. On the left foreground is the Town Club. This colour ppc dates from c. 1910.

Downing Street, Penang.

**[164]**
**DOWNING STREET, PENANG.**

*Cancellation:* Penang/1920
*Back:* Divided
*Publisher:* Not stated; printed in Germany

This c. 1910 colour ppc depicts the Government Offices housing the Education Department and the Treasury Office (*foreground*). Two rickshaws (*left*) await customers, while a Sikh policeman watches on the right.

**[165]**

UNTITLED [DOWNING STREET].

*Cancellation:* Nil
*Back:* Divided
*Publisher:* The Federal Rubber Stamp
         Co., S.S. & F.M.S.

A real ppc, c. 1920, depicting Downing Street looking towards Beach Street. The building on the left with its distinctive dome is the Hongkong and Shanghai Bank; the building on the right is the Chinese Protectorate. Although the name "Downing Street" sounds rather impressive, it was given an unflattering review in a 1908 account: "Like Weld Quay, Downing Street is by no means one of the finest streets in Pinang...Of the fifty odd public roads and streets within municipal limits there are few within the business part of the town of any special note...".[9]

**[166]**

COPYRIGHT PHOTO No. 19/DOWNING STREET, PENANG, SHOWING IN THE DISTANCE THE NEW PREMISES OF CHARTERED BANK IN COURSE OF CONSTRUCTION

*Cancellation:* Nil
*Back:* Divided
*Publisher:* Penang Photo Store, Penang/
         Printed in England

This view of Downing Street is from Weld Quay. The General Post Office is in the foreground on the right; facing it is the Town Club. This is a real photographic ppc with fine details, dated c. 1925.

COPYRIGHT PHOTO No. 19    DOWNING STREET, PENANG, SHOWING IN THE DISTANCE THE NEW PREMISES OF CHARTERED BANK IN COURSE OF CONSTRUCTION

12. Post and Telegraph Office, Penang, S.S.

[167]
**12. POST AND TELEGRAPH OFFICE, PENANG, S.S.**

*Cancellation:* Penang/1919
*Back:* Divided
*Publisher:* Raphael Tuck & Sons "Sepia Platemarked" Postcard 768/ Penang/Printed in Britain

A sepia ppc showing the General Post Office which was completed in 1903. It also functioned as a telegraph office. The Post Office wing of the Government Buildings cost $53,579 to build.[9] Until World War II, the Penang Postal and Telegraph Department was under the purview of the Postmaster of the SS based in Singapore; Penang only had an Assistant Postmaster General. In 1916, the Assistant Postmaster General was G.G. Wilson.[22] In 1906, the sale of postage stamps in Penang amounted to $87,138.85.[9] Date: c. 1910.

Post Office, Penang.

[168]
**POST OFFICE, PENANG.**

*Cancellation:* Nil
*Back:* Divided
*Publisher:* No 35 A Beach Street, Penang

A beautiful colour ppc of the General Post Office along Weld Quay, c. 1920. This grand building replaced two earlier post offices built in 1881 and 1892, but was destroyed by bombs during the Japanese invasion of Penang in 1941. Opposite the General Post Office is Victoria Pier (*right*). Penang has a long postal history; the first letter from Penang was sent in March 1806. Prior to 1948, Penang, like Malacca and Singapore, shared the use of the SS postage stamps.[52] Only in 1948 were the first postage stamps bearing the name "Penang" issued.[52]

**[169]**

**Penang./The Town Club.**

*Cancellation:* Nil
*Back:* Divided
*Publisher:* Raphael Tuck & Sons "Oilette"
Postcard No. 8962/Penang.
Series II./Printed in England.

Another ppc from the "Oilette" series, c. 1910, depicting the Penang Town Club. The Town Club was basically a social club for European businessmen. By 1908, its membership numbered 110 and included most of the influential European businessmen and "civil and municipal servants". The club consisted of a large dining room, buffet and bar, and a long verandah overlooking the road.[9] The building was destroyed by bombs in December 1941 during the Japanese invasion of Penang.

PENANG.
THE TOWN CLUB.

**[170]**

**No. 103 Police Court. Penang.**

*Cancellation:* Scarce squared circular
cancellation of "TANJONG
RAMBUTAN/1911"
*Back:* Divided
*Publisher:* Not stated; printed in Germany

The Police Courts along Light Street, facing the Esplanade. Built in the Anglo-Indian classical style in the early 19th century, they have been described as "typical of early 19th century architecture" and they "stand dignified like a row of three Greek temples".[30] The buildings were renovated in 1874 and, in 1890, an administrative block was added.[82] The street is lined on both sides by tall and luscious *angsana* trees (*Pterocarpus indicus*); some of the trees have survived changing times and are still thriving today. A horse and carriage wait outside (*left foreground*). Date: c. 1910.

No. 103 Police Court. Penang.

Police Courts, Penang.

**[171]**

**POLICE COURTS, PENANG.**

*Cancellation:* Nil
*Back:* Divided
*Publisher:* Not stated; printed in Germany

Light Street is shown lined with large and shady *angsana* trees. On the left are the Police Courts and on the right is the Padang (Kota Lama). The Police Courts used to house the Magistrates' Courts and Recorder's Court. The Recorder's Court was established in 1807; it was a solution to the "difficulty of maintaining law and order amongst a turbulent native and European population when no legally constituted courts were in existence on the island".[137] This colour ppc is dated c. 1910.

Supreme Court, Penang.

**[172]**

**SUPREME COURT, PENANG.**

*Cancellation:* 1912
*Back:* Divided
*Publisher:* Not stated; printed in Germany

The Supreme Court, c. 1910, at the junction of Light Street and Pitt Street (Jalan Masjid Kapitan Keling). It was completed in 1904 at a cost of $206,678 and designed by John Henry McCallum, the surveyor-general of the SS.[9]

Library & Museum, Penang

**[173]**
**LIBRARY & MUSEUM, PENANG**

*Cancellation:* 1910
*Back:* Divided
*Publisher:* Not stated; printed in Germany

The Penang Library was housed in the southern portion of the Supreme Court, which faces St George's Church. The caption "& Museum" is incorrect, although the library did hold many old photographs and much archival material of Penang.[14] In 1908, it was recorded that the library was "exceptionally well equipped with books".[9] Annual subscription then was $5.00.[9] This sepia ppc is dated c. 1910.

**[174]**
**UNTITLED [SUPREME COURT].**

*Cancellation:* Ipoh/9 JU/1926
*Back:* Divided
*Publisher:* The Federal Rubber Stamp Co.,/ Penang, Ipoh, Kuala Lumpur & Singapore.

A real photographic ppc of the Supreme Court, as viewed from Farquhar Street. The original edifice of the 1904 structure was described as "very handsome" with "a statue of Justice gracefully occupying the topmost niche of the portico roof."[9] The Logan Memorial is just visible on the left. Date: c. 1925.

PENANG. THE SUPREME COURT.

**[175]**

**PENANG. THE SUPREME COURT.**

*Cancellation:* Nil
*Back:* Divided
*Publisher:* Raphael Tuck & Sons "Oilette"
Postcard No. 8962/Penang.
Series II./Printed in England

The Supreme Court as viewed from Farquhar Street, c. 1920. This view shows well life in the colonial era. The Logan Memorial is on the left. The memorial was built in memory of James Richardson Logan, a well respected lawyer especially among the non-Europeans in Penang. Besides being a man of the law, Logan was also a great scholar. He founded the *Journal of the Indian Archipelago and Eastern Asia*, wrote the *Language and Ethnology of the Indian Archipelago*, and edited the *Pinang Gazette*.

Penang Free School, Penang.

**[176]**

**PENANG FREE SCHOOL, PENANG.**

*Cancellation:* Nil
*Back:* Divided
*Publisher:* Not stated; printed in Germany

The Logan Memorial can be seen in the grounds of the Supreme Court, while the Penang Free School is opposite the Supreme Court. This colour ppc is dated c. 1910.

The Convent School, Penang.

**[177]**

THE CONVENT SCHOOL, PENANG.

*Cancellation:* Nil
*Back:* Divided
*Publisher:* The Federal Rubber Stamp
Co., Kuala Lumpur, Ipoh,
Penang, & Singapore.

A sepia ppc of Convent Light Street.
The Logan Memorial can be seen in the
foreground surrounded by a fence, and
guarded by two cannons. Date: c. 1930.

PENANG.

PRITCHARD & CO., PENANG. No. 1.

THE FREE SCHOOL.

**[178]**

PENANG./THE FREE SCHOOL.

*Cancellation:* Nil
*Back:* Undivided
*Publisher:* Pritchard & Co., Penang.
No. 1.

The Penang Free School (PFS) was
founded on 21 October 1816 largely
through the tireless efforts of Rev. Robert
Sparke Hutchings. The school began as a
day school for boys on rented premises
on Love Lane in 1816; the school building
was only completed and ready for
occupation in 1821. Enrolment to the
school increased tremendously: in 1860,
there were 296 boys; by 1906, there
were 037 boys.[9] So, a permanent school
building was planned; the first phase of
the school was completed in 1896.[9] As
can be seen, its façade is similar to that of
the Municipal Offices building.
Date: c. 1900.

Free School, Penang

**[179]**

**FREE SCHOOL, PENANG**

*Cancellation:* Nil
*Back:* Divided
*Publisher:* Not stated

A colour ppc of the newly expanded PFS; the second phase of the building (west wing) was completed in 1906, ten years after the first phase (east wing) was completed in 1896.[9] The east wing was destroyed on 1 February 1945 by Allied bombing. Date: c. 1910.

335. PENANG FREE SCHOOL

**[180]**

**335. PENANG FREE SCHOOL**

*Cancellation:* Nil
*Back:* Divided
*Publisher:* Not stated

A real photographic ppc of the PFS on its new premises on Green Lane. It shifted here from its old building on Farquhar Street. The PFS started as an independent school in 1816 but by 1 January 1920, had become a government institution.[55] On the back is written: "The Penang Free School, comprising of [*sic*] about 10 acres of land, has a large playing field, for football, hockey and cricket, a gymnasium, a pavillion [*sic*], a laboratory, a big hall, some badminton and tennis courts." Date: c. 1930.

Engineers Institute, Penang.

**[181]**

ENGINEERS INSTITUTE, PENANG.

*Cancellation:* Nil
*Back:* Divided
*Publisher:* Not stated; printed in Germany

To cater to the large number of engineers among the European expatriates in Penang before World War I, the Engineers' Institute was established on 5 March 1888. Membership was at first confined to "engineers and mechanics", and they met in rooms on Beach Street. The establishment however grew in popularity and membership was extended to even include deck officers and certain longshoreman, and a larger building had to be secured. This was done by arrangements with the Kapitan China, Chung Keng Kwee, popularly known as Ah Quee.[57] Facing it was the International Hotel (its signboard is visible, at the bottom right). Date: c. 1910.

Engineers Institute, Penang

**[182]**

ENGINEERS INSTITUTE, PENANG

*Cancellation:* Nil
*Back:* Divided
*Publisher:* Co-operative Agency S.S./ No. 17

The Engineers' Institute, c. 1910. The prominent wrought iron balcony can be seen at the front. The building, which stood at the junction of Leith Street and Farquhar Street, was a handsome building with large and lofty rooms, a reading room, a billiard room and a large ballroom.[9] It was destroyed in 1941 by Japanese bombing.

SARKIES BROS., PROPRIETORS.

THE DINING ROOM, EASTERN AND ORIENTAL HOTEL, PENANG.

# The HOTELS, SCHOOLS and HOSPITALS

## THE HOTELS

### The Eastern and Oriental Hotel

The Eastern and Oriental Hotel (E & O) (*top right*; [183-204]), at No. 10, Farquhar Street, traces its origins to the Armenian Sarkies Brothers – Martin, Tigran and Arshak.

By 1915, the E & O was a 100-room hotel, the largest in Penang and, in 1923, the 40-room Victory Annexe was added to the hotel.[58] The East Wing [198] was declared open on 7 December 1929, following which, in 1930, the E & O issued a series of ppcs [198-204] to advertise itself. A combination of heavy debts and the Great Depression (1929–1932) led to the hotel's decline in 1931. In 1938, it was sold to the Runnymede Hotel.[58] After World War II (1939–1945), management of the hotel changed hands several times, and the hotel eventually closed in 1996. It reopened in 2001 after extensive renovations.[42,58]

### International Hotel

The International Hotel [205], which stood adjacent to the E & O on Farquhar Street, was opened in the late 1890s. In 1910, it was acquired by the E & O and became an annexe to the hotel [192].

### The Runnymede Hotel

The Runnymede Hotel (*below right*; [206-212]) on Northam Road (Jalan Sultan Ahmad Shah), opened in 1921. The main three-storey seafront building [208-209] was built in the 1930s.[02] It had its own post office from 1929 to 1939,[52] and letters and ppcs cancelled here are much rarer, and thus more valuable, than those with E & O postmarks.

### Chinese Residency/Hotel Norman/Bellevue Boarding House/Raffles/Raffles By-The-Sea

Built in the 1880s by tycoon Cheah Tek Soon on Northam Road at its junction with Transfer Road, Penang's first five-storey mansion later became known as the Chinese Residency [213]. From 1908 onwards, the mansion was transformed into a hotel, albeit with different names: Hotel Norman [214], Bellevue Boarding House [215], Raffles [216], and Raffles-By-The-Sea [217]. It later housed the Shih Chung School, the Pi Joo Girls' School and the Government English School [218].

### The International Bodega and Restaurant

The proprietor of the International Bodega and Restaurant [219] was the "genial" Captain W. Joyce.[9] A branch of the Hotel Norman, this bar and restaurant stood at the corner of Union Street and Beach Street.[22]

### The Australia Hotel

The Australia Hotel [220] was located at 160 Penang Road at its junction with Argyll Road. It was later occupied by the Tai Sun Hospital.[5] The building still stands today.

### The Shanghai Hotel

The Shanghai Hotel [222] was the former mansion [221] of Chung Thye Pin (1879–1935), the last Kapitan Cina of Perak (1921–1935).[57] The mansion, which stood at No. 2 Kelawai, facing the sea at North Beach (today's Gurney Drive) [221], was a picture of grandeur. In the late 1930s the mansion was converted into the Shanghai Hotel.[1] The building was demolished in 1964.

A vintage luggage label of the E & O Hotel, c. 1920.

A luggage label of the Runnymede Hotel, c. 1900. "Runnymede" was named after the field on which King John of England sealed the Magna Carta (*top*).

*Opposite*:
The dining room of the E. & O. The menu of the hotel was said to have "achieved distinction throughout the East",[61] c. 1930.

St George's Girls' School on Farquhar Street, c. 1910.

A real photographic ppc of Chung Ling High School in Kampung Bharu, Ayer Itam. Behind the school are the hills of Penang, c. 1940.

## THE SCHOOLS
### Convent Light Street

Convent Light Street (*see Chapter 3* [177]; [223-230]) was established in 1852 by the Sisters of St Maur on Church Street. It was not just a regular school, but also functioned as a boarding school [228] and an orphanage [229-230]. In 1859, the 2.8-hectare site on which the Government House stands, was acquired for the building of the school structure.[64] From Penang, the Sisters proceeded to found convents all over Malaya and Singapore.[64]

### St Xavier's Institution

St Xavier's Institution [231-234] was founded in 1852.[66] In 1858, a two-storey building was erected; a third storey was added in 1901 [231].[5] The most striking feature of this building is a large statue of St John Baptist de La Salle [233-234].[9] By 1912, its façade evoked that of a grandiose baroque European palace.[9] The original school building suffered damage as a result of Japanese bombing in 1941 and, in 1945, from Allied bombing. The present premises were built in 1954.[127]

### St George's Girls' School

St George's Girls' School (SGGS) (*top left*; [235; 236]) was formally established on 7 January 1885 and principally funded by St George's Church.[67] It moved several times before finally arriving at its present location on Macalister Road in 1954. In 1909, the British government took over the management of SGGS, renaming it "Government Girls' School" [236]; but returned it to the church in 1920.[5,67] Views of SGGS on Farquhar Street are shown at the top left and [235].

### The Anglo Chinese Boys' School and Penang Chinese School

The Anglo Chinese Boys' School (ACS; [237-238]) was the forerunner of the Methodist Boys' School. Its school building on Maxwell Road was built in 1897.[68] In 1956, the secondary school arm of the ACS moved to its new building on Ayer Itam Road, and was renamed Methodist Boys' School, while the primary school moved to Pykett Avenue, and was renamed Pykett Methodist School.[128]

The Penang Chinese School (Chung Hwa Confucian School) [238-239] was established in 1904, and was housed in the Chinese Town Hall on Pitt Street (Jalan Masjid Kapitan Keling). In 1908, the school moved to its new building on Maxwell Road, next to ACS.

### Chung Ling High School

The Chung Ling High School (CLHS) (*below left*; [240]), established in 1917, initially occupied the upper storey of the Penang Philomatic Union. By 1918, enrolment had increased, prompting the school to move to its building on Macalister Road. In 1934, CLHS shifted to its current premises at Kampong Bharu, Ayer Itam.

## THE HOSPITALS
### Penang General Hospital

The predecessor to the Penang General Hospital (PGH; [241-247]) was the Paupers' Hospital, built in 1854 by Ah Poo (Mun Ah Foo), a leader of the Ghee Hin Society. The hospital was situated at the junction of Hospital Road and Race Course Road (Residency Road).[70] In 1882, in view of the increasing need for a hospital, the British government built the PGH on land adjacent to the Paupers' Hospital. It had European and Native wards.[82]

### Pulau Jerejak

Pulau Jerejak [248], an island off the southeastern tip of Penang, was the main leper asylum for the SS. From 1948 to 1949, the British government exiled political prisoners to the island. It served as a penal colony from 1969 to 1993. Today the Jerejak Resort and Spa is the island's chief attraction.[72]

No. 40. Eastern and Oriental Hotel, Penang

19. 6. 07

*Kind regards from Yours sincerely M. Leshu.*

**[183]**

No. 40. EASTERN AND ORIENTAL
HOTEL, PENANG

*Cancellation:* PENANG/JU 21/1907
*Back:* Divided
*Publisher:* A. Kaulfuss, Penang.

A colour ppc of the Eastern & Oriental
Hotel (E & O), c. 1900. The E & O began
as the Eastern Hotel, which faced the
Esplanade, in 1884. It was founded by
the Armenian Sarkies brothers, Martin
and Tigran.[9] In 1885, the brothers opened
the nearby Oriental Hotel and ran both
hotels simultaneously.[9,44,58] As the original
Eastern Hotel could not be extended
anymore, the brothers concentrated on
the Oriental Hotel, adding new extensions
to it.[9] In 1885, they founded the E & O
Hotel at No. 10 Farquhar Street.[58]

**[184]**

EASTERN & ORIENTAL HOTEL –
PENANG – MALAYA

*Cancellation:* c. 1960 (date not clear)
*Back:* Divided
*Publisher:* Not stated; printed in England

A real photographic ppc, c. 1960,
depicting the E & O with its wide
seafront. On the back of the ppc is
written: "...The Island of Penang is
beautiful – in some ways a lot like the
Hawaiian Islands. Our hotel (in the
picture) is a fine old English structure,
with huge rooms and a very colonial
English atmosphere, though the
British have gone..." The ppc was
sent to America.

EASTERN & ORIENTAL HOTEL - PENANG - MALAYA

## THE "E. ⅋ O." HOTEL
### PENANG

*THE GATEWAY TO MALAYA AND THE FAR EAST*

Three minutes' drive from the Wharves.

Dancing :
TUESDAYS, SATURDAYS and MAIL DAYS

Orchestral Concert :
EVERY SUNDAY EVENING
On the Lawn overlooking the Sea.

902 FEET OF SEA FRONTAGE

[185]
THE "E. & O." HOTEL/PENANG

*Cancellation:* Nil
*Back:* Nil
*Publisher:* Not stated but likely to be the E & O Hotel

This is the back of [198]. Unlike other ppcs that have an address side, this was an advertisement for the hotel. Date: c. 1930.

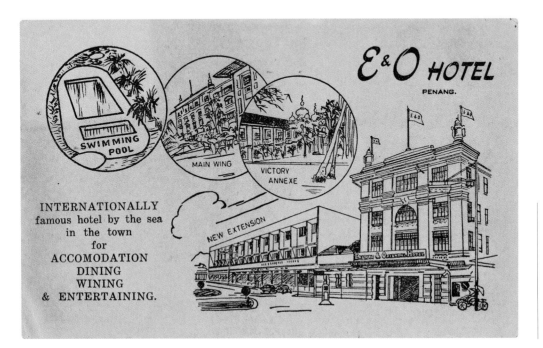

[186]
E & O HOTEL/PENANG.

*Cancellation:* Penang/1969
*Back:* Divided
*Publisher:* The Eastern & Oriental Hotel

A c. 1960 ppc of the E & O Hotel, showing drawings of the hotel's swimming pool, Main Wing, Victory Annexe, and its main frontage along Farquhar Street, including the "new extension".

Eastern and Oriental Hotel, Penang

**[187]**

**EASTERN AND ORIENTAL HOTEL, PENANG**

*Cancellation:* Nil
*Back:* Divided
*Publisher:* Not stated

An early view of the E & O, c. 1910. A horse-drawn gharry can be seen on the left, while the main entrance of the hotel is on the right. The name of the hotel is clearly visible.

**[188]**

**No. 234 E. & O. HOTEL, PENANG**

*Cancellation:* Nil
*Back:* Divided
*Publisher:* Not stated; printed in England

A view of the E & O, c. 1940; the main entrance to the hotel (constructed in 1929) had by then become a four-storey building. Remnants of the old building are visible on the left. Many rickshaws can be seen waiting for customers (*left*). The "E & O" sign is visible above the main entrance.

NO. 234                    E. & O. HOTEL. PENANG

[189]
FARQUAHARE STREET, PENANG.

*Cancellation:* Nil
*Back:* Divided
*Publisher:* S.M. Manicum, Penang, No. 35

The main entrance to the E & O is at the end of the road. The building on the left, with a domed structure, is the annexe of the hotel, occupying the site of the former International Hotel. This colour ppc is dated c. 1910.

[190]
A 31– EASTERN AND/ORIENTAL
HOTEL/PENANG

*Cancellation:* Nil; but written on 19
January 1916
*Back:* Divided
*Publisher:* Nikko Studio, Penang

A rare biview ppc of the E & O. The top view is of the main entrance, similar to [187], but showing more of the right. This part of the hotel housed a post office from 1910 to 1941 and also from 1946 to 1947.[51] The bottom view shows the seaward side of the hotel with several cannons pointing to the sea. Date: c. 1910.

Penang, Eastern and Oriental Hotel.

**[191]**

PENANG, EASTERN AND ORIENTAL HOTEL.

*Cancellation:* Not clear
*Back:* Divided
*Publisher:* Valentine & William, Penang.

A c. 1910 ppc of a row of single-storey shops facing the garden of the E & O. On the left is a hair dressing "saloon" while in the centre is Valentine & William, Manufacturing Jewellers. On the left of the jeweller's signboard is an advertisement for the *Pinang Gazette*; below it, a collection of ppcs is for sale. This ppc was published by the jewellers themselves.

No. 6        E. & O. Hotel Annexe, Penang

**[192]**

NO. 6 E. & O. HOTEL ANNEXE, PENANG

*Cancellation:* Nil
*Back:* Divided
*Publisher:* P.L.I. De Silva E. & O. Hotel/
             Printed in England/
             Photo Nikko.

The annexe of the hotel, converted from the International Hotel that stood adjacent to the E & O, was opened in 1910. Part of the E & O signboard can be seen on the left of the building. The main entrance to the E & O is in the background (*right*) behind the rickshaw and pony carriage. Date: c. 1910.

OLD WING, EASTERN AND ORIENTAL HOTEL, PENANG.

Eastern and Oriental Hotel, Penang.

**[193]**
**OLD WING, EASTERN AND ORIENTAL HOTEL, PENANG./SARKIES BROS, PROPRIETORS.**

*Cancellation:* PENANG/1919
*Back:* Divided
*Publisher:* (Photogravure) Waterlow
& Sons Limited, London,
Dunstable and Watford

This c. 1910 ppc, a photogravure by Waterlow and Sons, shows the old wing of the E & O with its seafront bungalows with long porches and full windows. A cannon can be seen pointing towards the sea (*left*). Waterlow and Sons were engravers for currency, postage stamps, stocks and bond certificates.

**[194]**
**EASTERN AND ORIENTAL HOTEL, PENANG.**

*Cancellation:* PENANG/1912
*Back:* Divided
*Publisher:* Not stated; printed in Germany

Another view of the old wing of the E & O facing the sea; its luscious lawn is planted with palms and *angsana* trees. Date: c. 1910.

Penang, Eastern and Oriental Hotel.

**[195]**

**PENANG, EASTERN AND ORIENTAL HOTEL.**

*Cancellation:* Alor Star/1919
*Back:* Divided
*Publisher:* Valentine & William, Penang

The E & O's wide seafront looking towards North Beach. The cannons are said to be from Fort Cornwallis. The North Beach is the stretch of coast on the northern side of George Town. Nowadays it is referred to as Gurney Drive and Kelawai Road. Once pronounced "the premier hotel east of Suez", the E & O boasted a 902-feet (275-metre) seafront, "the longest of any hotel in the world".[50]
Date: c. 1910.

View from the E. & O. Hotel, Penang.

**[196]**

**VIEW FROM E. & O. HOTEL, PENANG.**

*Cancellation:* Nil
*Back:* Divided
*Publisher:* The Federal Rubber Stamp Co.,
  Kuala Lumpur, Ipoh, Penang,
  & Singapore.

A real photographic ppc of the sea in front of the hotel looking northwards.
Date: c. 1930.

E & O Hotel. Penang.

[197]
E & O HOTEL. PENANG.

*Cancellation:* PENANG/24 AU/1931
*Back:* Divided
*Publisher:* Not stated

A view of the E & O's Victory Annexe, built in 1923.[58] It was a 40-room addition by Arshak Sarkies. A new Victory Annexe, unveiled in 2013, features suites with private balconies facing the sea. The large tree in the centre, a *Sterculia foetida* (also known as *Kelumpang Jari*), still flourishes today.[59] Date: c. 1930.

SARKIES BROS., PROPRIETORS.

EASTERN AND ORIENTAL HOTEL, PENANG, THE NEW WING.

[198]
EASTERN AND ORIENTAL HOTEL, PENANG, THE NEW WING./SARKIES BROS., PROPRIETORS.

*Cancellation:* Nil
*Back:* See [185]
*Publisher:* The Sarkies Bros

The picture side of [185]. This sepia ppc was issued by the hotel to advertise the opening of its new East Wing. The new wing was declared open on 7 December 1929 by Mary Sarkies, wife of Arshak.[58] The advertisement on the back of this ppc is shown in [185]. Date: c. 1930.

THE LAWN, EASTERN AND ORIENTAL HOTEL, PENANG.

**[199]**
THE LAWN, EASTERN AND ORIENTAL HOTEL, PENANG./SARKIES BROS., PROPRIETORS.

*Cancellation:* Nil
*Back:* Divided
*Publisher:* (Photogravure) Waterlow & Sons Limited, London, Dunstable and Watford.

This sepia ppc, dated c. 1930, was part of a series of ppcs to advertise the hotel. The lawn, beside the sea and next to the Victory Annexe, was used for outdoor dining.

MAIN BUILDING, EASTERN & ORIENTAL HOTEL, PENANG.

**[200]**
MAIN BUILDING, EASTERN & ORIENTAL HOTEL, PENANG./ SARKIES BROS., PROPRIETORS.

*Cancellation:* Nil
*Back:* Divided
*Publisher:* The Sarkies Bros

The main building of the E & O, c. 1930. Chairs and benches face the sea, partially shaded by large *angsana* trees. This is another sepia ppc advertising the hotel. During the E & O's heyday, it hosted famous guests such as British playwright Noel Coward; actors Douglas Fairbanks, Mary Pickford and Charlie Chaplin; and writers Herman Hesse, Rudyard Kipling and Somerset Maugham.[42,58]

SARKIES BROS., PROPRIETORS.

ENTRANCE TO THE VICTORY ANNEXE, EASTERN AND ORIENTAL HOTEL, PENANG.

SARKIES BROS., PROPRIETORS.

EASTERN AND ORIENTAL HOTEL, PENANG, THE PALM COURT.

**[201]**

ENTRANCE TO THE VICTORY ANNEXE, EASTERN AND ORIENTAL HOTEL, PENANG./
SARKIES BROS., PROPRIETORS.

*Cancellation:* Nil
*Back:* Divided
*Publisher:* (Photogravure) Waterlow & Sons Limited, London, Dunstable and Watford.

A sepia ppc, dating from c. 1930 showing the entrance to the Victory Annexe. Rattan chairs can be seen lining the entrance amidst potted palms. Although it was Martin and Tigran Sarkies who founded the E & O (Arshak only joining the firm of Sarkies Bros in 1891),[9] it was Arshak who took charge of the hotel from 1894 till his death in 1931. This ppc is part of a series of ppcs in sepia issued by the E & O for advertising purposes.

**[202]**

EASTERN AND ORIENTAL HOTEL, PENANG, THE PALM COURT./
SARKIES BROS., PROPRIETORS.

*Cancellation:* Nil
*Back:* Similar to [198]; see [185]
*Publisher:* The Sarkies Bros

The lobby ceiling of the E & O features an illuminated dome which is also a whispering gallery. The Waygood-Otis lift, looking like a standard door frame, is at the far right of the fountain. It still functions.[58] When Noel Coward stayed at the E & O in 1929, he was hosted by George Bilainkin, editor of the *Straits Echo*. Bilainkin described the E & O as: "an oasis of so-called civilization...a magnificent hotel with large and palatial suites, with telephones in every bedroom, and the rare luxury in the East, constant hot and cold running water in English baths. Rich carpets, a sea frontage of eight hundred feet, a tremendous dome, a large permanent orchestra."[60] Date: c. 1930.

THE BALL ROOM, EASTERN AND ORIENTAL HOTEL, PENANG.

**[203]**

THE BALL ROOM, EASTERN AND
ORIENTAL HOTEL, PENANG./
SARKIES BROS., PROPRIETORS.

*Cancellation:* Nil
*Back:* Divided
*Publisher:* (Photogravure) Waterlow
& Sons Limited, London,
Dunstable and Watford.

The E & O's ballroom, c. 1930. Ilsa Sharp,
in her book *The E & O Hotel: Pearl of
Penang*, captured the spirit of the E & O's
heyday: "...the scene of many glittering
social events, the E & O's ballroom
was legend in Penang – this was where
Arshak Sarkies loved to perform his
favourite party trick, waltzing around the
floor with a glass of whisky perched on
his bald head."[58]

BALLROOM, EASTERN & ORIENTAL HOTEL, PENANG.

**[204]**

BALLROOM, EASTERN & ORIENTAL HOTEL,
PENANG./SARKIES BROS., PROPRIETORS.

*Cancellation:* Nil
*Back:* Divided
*Publisher:* The Sarkies Bros

The ballroom was described in a 1930
publication in this manner: "The large
new Ball-Room, daintily adorned with
rose-coloured lights, welcomes sojourners
and visitors to its numerous and delightful
dances."[61] This sepia ppc is one of a
series of eight (*chapter opener*; [198-204].

International Hotel, Penang

*One of the hotels here. This is a most picturesque place. Every nation is*

**[205]**

INTERNATIONAL HOTEL, PENANG

*Cancellation:* EASTERN AND ORIENTAL
HOTEL/10 AP/1914
*Back:* Divided
*Publisher:* M.J., Penang.

The International Hotel, c. 1910. Opened in the late 1890s, it was acquired by the E & O Hotel in 1910 and renamed as its Annexe (*see* [192]). It was described as a hotel that "provides everything that most people can desire and affords unique facilities for getting to every part of the town in the shortest possible time."[9] The International Hotel was situated in a very convenient location; it was within five minutes' rickshaw ride of Swettenham Pier and the General Post Office.[9]

ENTRANCE
RUNNYMEDE HOTEL
PENANG

**[206]**

ENTRANCE/RUNNYMEDE HOTEL/PENANG

*Cancellation:* Nil
*Back:* Divided
*Publisher:* Not stated

A real photographic ppc showing the entrance to the Runnymede Hotel, c. 1930s. The main three-storey building in the background was built in the 1930s. The hotel was opened by two Scotsmen, W. Foster and H. Parker, in 1921. On 22 October 1924, Foster, the hotel manager, wrote to a patron: "Our New Annexe is now ready for occupation and will be opened as from 1st November 1924. On the ground floor is a commodious Billiard Room and a spacious lounge, while upstairs there are eight up-to-date bedrooms and a modern bathroom for each room..."[63] The structure stands at No. 40 Northam Road.

**[207]**
**RUNNYMEDE HOTEL PENANG**

*Cancellation:* Nil
*Back:* Divided
*Publisher:* Not stated

Another real photographic ppc of the Runnymede Hotel. The original single-storey brick building on the site was the home of Stamford Raffles and his wife Olivia, built in 1807. He was then a junior administrator in Penang. The newlyweds stayed there until 1810 when Raffles was posted to Malacca. Date: c. 1930.

**[208]**
**NO. 247 RUNNYMEDE HOTEL PENANG**

*Cancellation:* Nil
*Back:* Divided
*Publisher:* Not stated; printed in England

A real photographic ppc, c. 1930, showing the new wing of the hotel at No. 40 Northam Road. It was open from 1921 to 1940.

**[209]**
**VIEW – BALLROOM/RUNNYMEDE HOTEL/PENANG.**

*Cancellation:* Nil
*Back:* Divided
*Publisher:* Not stated

The new wing of the Runnymede Hotel, built in the early 1930s. It housed a huge ballroom on the ground floor.[62] After Stamford Raffles left Penang for Malacca in 1810, the house was put up for sale, and changed hands many times. In 1921, the building caught fire and was rebuilt by new owners, W. Foster and H. Parker, who retained the name "Runnymede".[42] This real photographic ppc dates from c. 1930.

**[210]**
**BALLROOM./RUNNYMEDE.HOTEL/PENANG.**

*Cancellation:* PENANG/28 DE/1934
*Back:* Divided
*Publisher:* Not stated

A real photographic ppc dating from c. 1930 of the Runnymede Hotel's ballroom. The dining room is in the foreground. The ballroom and dining room were in the new wing built in the 1930s.

Runnymede Hotel, Penang, (from the Sea.)

**[211]**

RUNNYMEDE HOTEL, PENANG,
(FROM THE SEA.)

*Cancellation:* Nil
*Back:* Divided
*Publisher:* Not stated

This real photographic ppc dating from
c. 1930 shows the old building (*left*)
and the new building (*right*) with tall
casuarina trees between the two. In 1940,
the Royal Navy took over the hotel, and
during the Japanese Occupation it was
used as a base by the Japanese. From
1951 to 1957, the hotel was used by the
British military, and then sold to the
Malayan Government. Renamed Wisma
Persekutuan, the hotel was used as a
government resthouse.[62] In the 1980s,
the hotel was occupied by the Malaysian
Armed Forces, who moved out in 2006.[42]

**[212]**

UNTITLED [RUNNYMEDE HOTEL].

*Cancellation:* Nil
*Back:* Divided
*Publisher:* Not stated

A real photographic ppc of the
Runnymede Hotel, c. 1930. It operated as
a hotel from 1921 to 1940, and at its peak
rivalled the E & O. In 1938 it acquired
the E & O, only to be taken over itself
in 1940.

Chinese Residence, Penang

[213]

CHINESE RESIDENCE, PENANG

*Cancellation:* PENANG/4 MR/1911
*Back:* Divided
*Publisher:* Not stated; printed in Germany

A close-up view of the magnificent Chinese Residency. To the Hokkiens in Penang, it was known as "Goh Chan Lau" (literally five-storey mansion), for it was indeed Penang's first five-storey mansion. It later became known as the Chinese Residency. The residency was built in the 1880s by tycoon Cheah Tek Soon at No. 11 Northam Road at its junction with Transfer Road. The mansion's layered architecture is a distinctive mix of British and Chinese style.[30] Notice the wide entrance to the driveway. Date: c. 1910.

356 - Hotel Norman, Penang.

[214]

356 - HOTEL NORMAN, PENANG.

*Cancellation:* PARIT BUNTAR/9 MR/1916
*Back:* Divided
*Publisher:* Federal Rubber Stamp Co., Penang, Kuala Lumpur & Ipoh

In 1908, "Goh Chan Lau" was sold to Tye Kee Yoon, the Chinese Vice-Consul of Penang.[5] It was subsequently transformed into a hotel, albeit with different names, several times: Hotel Norman; Bellevue Boarding House; Raffles; and Raffles-By-The-Sea. According to *The Singapore & Straits Directory* for 1916, the proprietors of Hotel Norman were listed as Mr and Mrs K.N. Brunel-Norman.[22] It could be that the name of the hotel was derived from the proprietors. This ppc, dated c. 1910, has a serrated left margin, indicating it was detached from a ppc booklet.

**[215]**

**BELLEVUE BOARDING HOUSE, PENANG.**

*Cancellation:* Nil
*Back:* Divided
*Publisher:* Not stated; printed in Germany

The Bellevue Boarding House, previously known as the Chinese Residency, c. 1920. Note the two rickshaws to the left of the hotel.

**[216]**

**RAFFLES, PENANG.**

*Cancellation:* Nil
*Back:* Divided
*Publisher:* No. 35.A. Beach Street, Penang/No. 44

The Bellevue Boarding House was renamed Raffles in the 1920s. This beautifully coloured ppc dates from that decade.

Raffles By-The-Sea
The Leading Hotel, Penang

**[217]**
RAFFLES BY-THE-SEA/
THE LEADING HOTEL, PENANG

*Cancellation:* Nil
*Back:* Divided
*Publisher:* M.J. Penang.

This ppc, dated c. 1920, shows the same building as **[216]**, but with a different name. On the back of the ppc, the hotel advertised itself as "Situated in the best part of Penang overlooking the Sea and Hills...The only cuisine under the direct supervision of the European Proprietor.../A Suitable Hotel for Ladies travelling alone./Terms:- Strictly Moderate." After the failure of all their hotel ventures, owner Tye Kee Yoon and tycoon Leong Fee set up the Shih Chung School on the premises of the former hotel. A girls' school, Pi Joo Girls' School, was located on the upper floor of the building.

130

**[218]**
UNTITLED [GOVERNMENT ENGLISH SCHOOL].

*Cancellation:* Nil
*Back:* Divided
*Publisher:* Not stated

A real photographic ppc, c. 1950, showing the Chinese Residency converted to the Government English School. The building was leased to the Government English School when the Shih Chung School relocated (it later re-established itself in the same premises). In the 1990s, the building was sold to the Malaysia Vegetable Oil Refinery Sdn Bhd. Today, it is vacant, neglected and in danger of collapsing.

No 118 International Bodega & Restauraut.

**[219]**

**No 118 International Bodega
& Restaurant.**

*Cancellation:* Nil
*Back:* Divided
*Publisher:* A. Kaulfuss, Penang

A branch of the Hotel Norman, this
*bodega* was described in the following
words: "The Bodega provides plain and
wholesome meals at all hours of the
day, and stocks the best brands of liquor
and cigars. Its internal appointments are
homely and cheerful, and the attendance
is all that can be desired."[9] Note the
punkahs or old-fashioned fans in
its rooms.

**[220]**

**Australia Hotel, Penang**

*Cancellation:* PENANG/15 AU/1912
*Back:* Divided
*Publisher:* M.J., Penang.

The Australia Hotel, c. 1900, along Penang
Road at its junction with Argyll Road. The
plain shophouses along Penang Road
(*left*) no longer exist but some of those
along Argyll Road (*right*) still do.

A Chinese Palacial Residence, Penang.

**[221]**

**A Chinese Palacial Residence, Penang.**

*Cancellation:* Nil
*Back:* Divided
*Publisher:* S.M. Manicum/No. 113

This palatial mansion was the Residence of Chung Thye Pin (1879–1935), the last Kapitan Cina of Perak (1921–1935).[57] It stood at No. 2, Kelawai, facing today's Gurney Drive. Following his death, the mansion was transformed into the Shanghai Hotel **[222]**. In the 1950s, it was a popular venue for weddings and other special occasions. The hotel was closed in the early 1960s. Date: c. 1900.

Shanghai Hotel, Penang

**[222]**

**Shanghai Hotel, Penang**

*Cancellation:* Nil
*Back:* Divided
*Publisher:* The Federal Rubber Stamp Co., Penang, S.S.

A real life photographic ppc of the Shanghai Hotel, c. the 1950s. At the back of this ppc was written: "This Hotel used to be the home of a local millionaire with eccentric ideas. The building has an underground floor – I believe you call it a basement in England. The openings on the left and right of the steps lead to this underground floor. It is now turned into a hotel and faces New Coast Road. Visitors like to sit on the lawn and enjoy the sea breezes." The building was demolished c. 1964. On its site, a high-end condominium was built at No. 1 Persiaran Gurney.

No. 49.  Convent Garden, Penang

**[223]**

**No. 49. CONVENT GARDEN, PENANG**

*Cancellation:* Written on 7 March 1907, and cancelled on the same day
*Back:* Divided
*Publisher:* A. Kaulfuss, Penang.

A colour ppc dating from c. 1900, of the Convent Garden. The present site of Convent Light Street, which includes Government House, was acquired in 1859. The land on which Government House stands used to belong to Francis Light, and his original home is said to have been located in the area. A 1908 account stated that "The Penang Convent, standing upon a site embracing three acres and extending from Farquhar Street to the sea, is one of the most valuable properties in the centre of the town".[9] On the site were built, in various stages, the school, chapel, and orphanage.

The Convent, Penang.

**[224]**

**THE CONVENT, PENANG.**

*Cancellation:* Nil
*Back:* Divided
*Publisher:* The Federal Rubber Stamp Co., Kuala Lumpur, Ipoh, Penang & Singapore.

A real photographic ppc of Convent Light Street, c. 1930, taken at the junction of Farquhar Street and Light Street. The grounds of the Supreme Court are in the foreground on the right. The Convent Light Street is one of the all-girls' schools under the umbrella of the Convent of the Holy Infant Jesus. It is also known as Town Convent, to differentiate it from the other convents in Penang and Butterworth.

CONVENT St MAUR PENANG — The Entrance. — L'Entrée

**[225]**

CONVENT ST MAUR PENANG — THE ENTRANCE. — L'ENTRÉE

*Cancellation:* Nil
*Back:* Divided
*Publisher:* Not stated; printed in France

A sepia ppc, c. 1920, of the entrance of the main building of the Convent, referred to here as the "Convent St Maur". The convent was established following the invitation of the Apostolic Vicar of Malaya, Bishop Jean-Baptiste Bucho in 1852. After which, a batch of Sisters of St Maur (or more commonly known as "Sisters of the Holy Infant Jesus") arrived in Penang from Singapore to start schools for the education of girls in Malaya.[64]

CONVENT St MAUR PENANG — The Chapel

**[226]**

CONVENT ST MAUR PENANG — THE CHAPEL

*Cancellation:* Nil
*Back:* Divided
*Publisher:* Not stated; printed in France

A sepia ppc showing the ornate convent chapel with its altar and striking ceiling. Convent Light Street began in 1852 as an attap hut which started with nine boarders, 30 day pupils and 16 orphans.[64] This was the earliest girls' school in Southeast Asia.[65] The convent was not just a regular school, but also functioned as a boarding school and an orphanage. Date: c. 1920.

CONVENT St MAUR PENANG — Lay Teachers. — Les Adjointes

**[227]**

**CONVENT ST MAUR PENANG — LAY TEACHERS. — LES ADJOINTES**

*Cancellation:* Nil
*Back:* Divided
*Publisher:* Not stated; printed in France

The Sisters of St Maur were assisted by many lay teachers (many of them alumni of the school). The lay teachers were of various ethnic backgrounds. In 1908, the teaching staff consisted of 17 European Choir Sisters and 14 lay Sisters.[9]
Date: c. 1920.

CONVENT St MAUR PENANG — Boarders at play
Pensionnaires aux jeux

**[228]**

**CONVENT ST MAUR PENANG — BOARDERS AT PLAY/PENSIONNAIRES AUX JEUX**

*Cancellation:* Nil
*Back:* Divided
*Publisher:* Not stated; printed in France

In the early years of Convent Light Street, boys were also admitted as boarders. The boarders were charged $25 a month for the first class, and $15 for the second class, in 1908.[9] Date: c. 1920.

CONVENT St MAUR PENANG — La Crèche

**[229]**

**CONVENT ST MAUR PENANG — LA CRÈCHE.**

*Cancellation:* Nil
*Back:* Divided
*Publisher:* Not stated; printed in France

The Convent orphanage is well known in Penang. This ppc shows the large orphanage (La Crèche) of the school in the 1920s. A 1908 account stated that the government made a special monthly grant of $100 towards the upkeep of the orphanage. The "grant-in-aid...amounts to between $2,000 and $3,000 a year".[9] The balance of the yearly expenditure amounting to about $16,000, was raised by public subscription, school fees and selling "fancy work, bouquets and other articles made by the Sisters and the orphans."[9]

CONVENT St MAUR PENANG
Babies in the Garden. — Bébés au Jardin

**[230]**

**CONVENT ST MAUR PENANG/BABIES IN THE GARDEN. — BÉBÉS AU JARDIN**

*Cancellation:* Nil
*Back:* Divided
*Publisher:* Not stated; printed in France

This real photographic sepia ppc shows the orphans raised by the Sisters in the convent. Date: c. 1920.

**[231]**
St. Xavier's Institution
(New Building), Penang

*Cancellation:* PENANG/19 MR/1919
*Back:* Divided
*Publisher:* S.M. Manicum, Penang.

A ppc of the St Xavier's Institution (SXI) building, c. 1905. The school was founded in 1852 and was originally known as St Xavier's Free School.[9] It was named after St Francis Xavier, the pioneering Roman Catholic missionary and co-founder of the Society of Jesus.[66] The school owes its founding to the Roman Catholic Order known as the Christian Brothers.[9] In 1858, a two-storey building was erected; a third-storey (*just visible*) was added in 1901.[5]

St.-Xavier's Institution. — Penang S. S.

**[232]**
St-Xavier's Institution. — Penang, S.S.

*Cancellation:* Nil
*Back:* Divided
*Publisher:* Not stated

The palatial façade of the SXI with three turrets; the central turret is fronted by a clock tower topped with a cross. This building was described in 1908 as "a distinguished pile in a classical style of architecture".[9] Date: c. 1910.

**[233]**
**ST. XAVIER'S INSTITUTION – PENANG
SOUVENIR OF DIAMOND JUBILEE**

*Cancellation*: Written but not posted
*Back*: Divided
*Publisher*: S.M. Manicum, Penang/
No. 3002

A colour ppc commemorating SXI's
Diamond Jubilee in 1912. On the arch
across its entrance (*right*) is written
"1852–1912". This ppc was written by a
former student of the school. He wrote:
"This indicates the school where I used
to attend, and was taken during the
celebrations of the Diamond Jubilee...".
The expansion of the SXI was necessary
as enrolment grew rapidly: sixfold by
1892 and, by 1907, the school achieved a
"record number of 1,150" students.[9] The
constant expansion of the school was
made possible by government aid and
the generosity of wealthy Chinese.
Date: 1912.

**[234]**
**ST. XAVIER'S INSTITUTION, PENANG**

*Cancellation*: PENANG/14 MR/1912
*Back*: Divided
*Publisher*: M.J., Penang./184022

This ppc shows the SXI, at the time it
celebrated its Diamond Jubilee in 1912.
Its crowning jewel is a large statue of
St John Baptist de la Salle, founder of the
congregation of the Brothers, on top of
the central porch. This building suffered
serious damage as a result of Japanese
bombing in 1941, and again in 1945, this
time bombed by American planes. The
present premises were built in 1954.[127]

**[235]**

**ST. GEORGE'S GIRL SCHOOL HOME, PENANG**

*Cancellation:* PENANG/3 NOV/1912
*Back:* Divided
*Publisher:* M.J., Penang./184034

A colour ppc of the St George's Girls' School (SGGS), c. 1900. The name "St George's Girls Home" is on a board above the front porch. This building, one of several premises occupied by the school before finally moving to its permanent building on Macalister Road, was on Farquhar Street. The SGGS traces its origins to informal classes provided by Mrs Biggs, wife of Rev. L.C. Biggs, Anglican Chaplain of St George's Church in Penang, on the verandah of their house, "The Manse", on Leith Street Ghaut.[67]

**[236]**

**2. GOVERNMENT GIRLS' SCHOOL, PENANG, S.S.**

*Cancellation:* Penang/1920
*Back:* Divided
*Publisher:* Raphael Tuck & Sons "Sepia Platemarked" Postcard 768; printed in Britain

A ppc of the Government Girls' School (renamed from SGGS in 1909 before reverting to the original name again in 1920) from Raphael Tuck & Son's "Sepia Platemarked" postcard series. The government took over the reins of the SGGS in 1909, renaming it Government Girls' School. This building which stood on Northam Road, was erected in 1911; the Annexe (*right*) was built in 1930.[67]
Date: c. 1920.

2. Government Girls' School, Penang, S.S.

No. 134 Anglo Chinese Boy's School.

AngloChinese School. Penang.

**[237]**

**No. 134 Anglo Chinese Boy's School.**

*Cancellation:* Nil
*Back:* Divided
*Publisher:* A. Kaulfuss, Penang./
Printed in Germany

The Anglo-Chinese Boys' School (ACS) in c. 1910. The ACS, which commenced operations in 1891, was the forerunner of the Methodist Boys' School. The ACS was pioneered by Rev. B.H. Balderstone. It opened on 28 May 1891 in a shophouse in Carnarvon Street to just one student on the first day of school![128] The numbers, however, increased steadily and, by 1893, the school had acquired five houses in Carnarvon Street.[9] That same year, Rev. Balderstone had to resign due to health issues. He was replaced by Rev. G.F. Pykett, who served until 1932.[128] This building, completed in 1897, was constructed on land along Maxwell Road, purchased in 1895 for $6,000.[08]

**[238]**

**AngloChinese School. Penang.**

*Cancellation:* Nil
*Back:* Divided
*Publisher:* Not stated

A real photographic ppc showing the ACS (*background*) and the Penang Chinese School (*foreground*) along Maxwell Road. The Penang Chinese School was established in 1904 chiefly through the efforts of famed Chinese tycoon Cheong Fatt Sze, who was also a Mandarin in the Manchu government. Today, neither the ACS (later renamed Methodist Boys' School) or the Penang Chinese School (Chung Hwa Confucian School) are on Maxwell Road: the Methodist Boys' School (secondary school) is on Ayer Itam Road, while the secondary school of the Chung Hwa Confucian School is in the residential area of Island Park. This ppc is dated c. 1920.

**[239]**

**PENANG CHINESE SCHOOL, PENANG**

*Cancellation:* Nil
*Back:* Divided
*Publisher:* M.J., Penang./183546

A c. 1920 ppc of the Penang Chinese School or Chung Hwa Confucian School along Maxwell Road, adjacent to the ACS. This school is one of the oldest formal Chinese schools in Southeast Asia, and the first to use Mandarin as its medium of instruction. It is also the only overseas Chinese school to be sanctioned by the Chinese Qing dynasty, which, through its consulate and Cheong Fatt Sze himself, presented the school with royal seals bearing the name of the school. This handsome building was designed by famed architect H.A. Neubronner, who designed numerous other landmarks in Penang including the old Hongkong and Shanghai Bank building, the new Cricket Club pavilion, the Commemorative Monument to the Armenian Church and the Kapitan Keling Mosque.[18]

Penang Chinese School, Penang

**[240]**

**64/51 CHUNG LING HIGH SCHOOL PENANG.**

*Cancellation:* Nil
*Back:* Divided
*Publisher:* Not stated; printed in England

Chung Ling High School, c. 1950. The large playing field can be seen in the foreground. The school also had hostels for boarders. It was initially a Chinese-medium school but it was converted into a National Type School in 1956. This meant that teachers were thereafter supplied by the government.[69]

64/51          CHUNG LING HIGH SCHOOL. PENANG.

General Hospital. Penang

**[241]**

**GENERAL HOSPITAL, PENANG**

*Cancellation:* Penang/1914
*Back:* Divided
*Publisher:* Not stated; No. 35. A.,
Beach Street, Penang

This colour ppc of the Penang General Hospital (PGH) dates from c. 1900. The earliest hospital in Penang to cater to the Asian poor was the Paupers' Hospital built in 1854 by Bengal-born Chinese Mun Ah Foo (Ah Poo), head of the Ghee Hin Society from 1823 to 1858.[82] The aim of the hospital was to provide healthcare for the poor, opium addicts and lepers. In 1882, the British government built the PGH on land adjacent to the Paupers' Hospital[82] with convict labour at a cost of $90,997; a Dr MacDowell was the Chief Medical Officer.[70]

142

No. 184 Penang Hospital.

**[242]**

**No. 184 PENANG HOSPITAL.**

*Cancellation:* Nil
*Back:* Divided
*Publisher:* A. Kaulfuss, Penang.

The main building in the centre is for Europeans; to the right are the Nurses' Quarters. The two *angsana* trees in the centre are still alive and are the largest in Penang.[59] Apart from the main building, there were 18 pavilion wards for local patients. Patients were charged between $1 and $3. Date: c. 1900.

**[243]**

**PENANG. GENERAL HOSPITAL.**

*Cancellation:* Penang/JU 14/1907
*Back:* Undivided
*Publisher:* Not stated

The block for Europeans is in the foreground, while on the extreme left is the "lunatic asylum". The PGH was built in 1882 on land adjacent to the Pauper's Hospital. The hospital building had European and "Native" wards, male and female wards, and a psychiatric ward.[82] In 1886, the Ghee Hin Society donated the site of the Paupers' Hospital to the Municipality which, by 1908, became known as the District Hospital.[9]
Date: c. 1900.

Penang. General Hospital

**[244]**

**COPYRIGHT PHOTO No. 8/**
**THE GENERAL HOSPITAL, PENANG**

*Cancellation:* Nil
*Back:* Divided
*Publisher:* Penang Photo Store,
49 Leigh Street, Penang/
Printed in England

A real photographic ppc, c. 1930, showing the main entrance to the PGH, and its beautiful arched gateway. This view is from Sepoy Lines Road; in the foreground is the Padang Polo (Polo Ground).

COPYRIGHT PHOTO No. 8          THE GENERAL HOSPITAL, PENANG

NEW GENERAL HOSPITAL, PENANG

No. 207

[245]

No. 207 NEW GENERAL HOSPITAL PENANG

*Cancellation:* Nil
*Back:* Undivided
*Publisher:* Not stated

A real photographic ppc showing the "A" Block, constructed in 1935. It housed the First Class wards as well as most of the Central Service facilities,[70] and the Dental Clinic. The Dental School was started in 1949.[70] The surrounding *angsana* trees are among the largest and oldest in Penang. Date: c. 1940.

144

NEW GENERAL HOSPITAL, PENANG

No. 183

[246]

No. 183 NEW GENERAL HOSPITAL, PENANG

*Cancellation:* Nil
*Back:* Divided
*Publisher:* Not stated; printed in England

A real photographic ppc of the new General Hospital, rebuilt in 1935. This ppc shows the "Class B" and "Class C" wards of the PGH; the walls of the Penang Gaol are on the right. Date: c. 1940.

**[247]**
GENERAL HOSPITAL, PENANG. NO. 8.

*Cancellation:* Nil
*Back:* Divided
*Publisher:* Not stated; printed in England

A Royal Australian Air Force helicopter landing on the Polo Ground in front of the new block of the PGH. This real photographic ppc is dated c. 1960.

General Hospital, Penang. No. 8.

**[248]**
THE LEPER CAMP

*Cancellation:* Not clear
*Back:* Divided
*Publisher:* Not stated

A real photographic ppc dating from c. 1930 of the leper colony on Pulau Jerejak (Malay for Leper Island). It was the main leper asylum for the SS in 1868, and a Quarantine Station was established here in 1875.[9] It was made a Penal Colony in 1969. In 1908, the Leper Hospital had 14 wards with a total of 138 beds. Initially, the Leper Hospital was part of the Paupers' Hospital. When the founder of the Paupers' Hospital, Mun Ah Foo, died, management of the hospital passed on to a committee headed by the Lieutenant Governor of Penang, Archibald Anson. It was during this time that the Leper Hospital was moved to Pulau Jerejak.[82]

THE LEPER CAMP

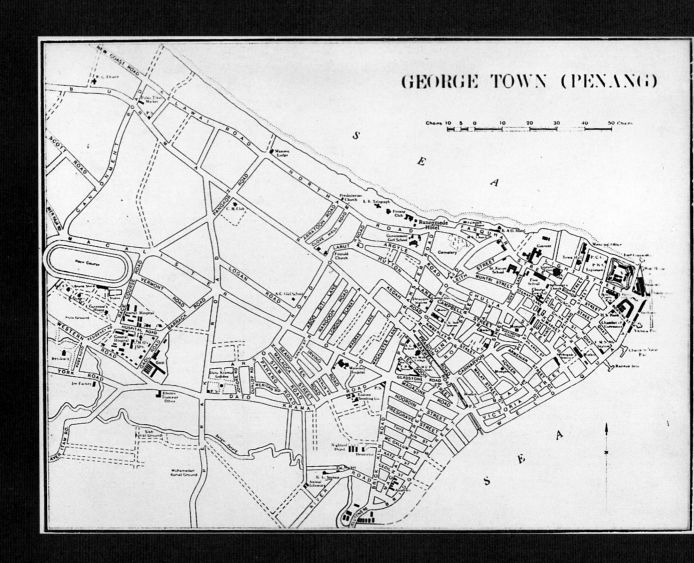

GEORGE TOWN (PENANG)

# The STREETS, ROADS and TRANSPORT

## Light Street

When Francis Light, first superintendent of Penang (1786–1794), took possession of the island, he named the first street after himself (*top right*; [274-276]). Many early civic buildings, such as Fort Cornwallis, the Supreme Court and the Padang, line Light Street (*see Chapter 3*).

## Beach Street

Beach Street [249-266] is one of the oldest roads in George Town, dating to c. 1786. It has always been a commercial street, stretching from King Edward Place [249-253] to nearly as far as Prangin Market [266]. The Hokkien Chinese refer to the beginning of the street, from King Edward Place to China Street, as "Ang Mor Thau Kay" ("European Commercial Street").[73]

The section between Acheen Street and Malay Street is known in Hokkien as "Phah Thih Kay" ("Ironmongers' Street")[73] as foundries [265] were found there. Originally, prior to land reclamation, commercial buildings lined one side of the street, while on the other was the sea and pockets of mangrove. Piers or stone steps ("ghauts") leading to the sea were placed along the coastline so that arriving ships could berth.[73]

Land reclamation in the 1880s to the early 1900s caused the street to become an inland road running parallel to Weld Quay.[73]

## Bishop Street

Religious persecution faced by the Portuguese Eurasians and their leader, Bishop Arnold Garnault, in Siam led them to flee to Penang. The first Catholic church in Penang, the Church of the Assumption, was founded on 15 August 1786 on Church Street,[74] and the Bishop's presbytery, on Bishop Street [267-269].

Before World War II, the street was a busy commercial street. The leading department store catering to Europeans, Whiteaway, Laidlaw & Co., was at the junction of Bishop Street and Beach Street [268-269].

The Commemorative Monument to the Armenian Church [270] stood at the corner of Bishop Street and King Street. It was built to mark the site of the demolished Church of St Gregory the Illuminator c. 1906. The monument itself was demolished in the 1930s.[75]

## Church Street

Church Street [271] runs adjacent to Bishop Street. It was so called as the church of the Portuguese Eurasians, the Church of the Assumption, was originally sited here.

The Hokkiens in Penang refer to Church Street as "Ghee Hin Kay" ("Ghee Hin Street"), as the secret society was based here for almost a century, until it was taken over by the Hai San Society, led by Chung Keng Kwee (1829–1901), the Kapitan Cina of Perak. Today, Church Street is famous for the Penang Peranakan Mansion, also known as "Hai Kee Chan" (Sea Remembrance Store), and the Chung Keng Kwee Temple [272]. The former was the Kapitan's residence and office, and today is a museum, while the latter is an ancestral temple.[57]

## China Street

China Street [273] is one of the oldest streets in George Town. The Hokkiens call it "Toa Kay" ("Main Street") as

Light Street is shown in this c. 1900 ppc. The civic buildings were concentrated on this street.

The address side of [270]. It was sent from Penang to Portugal; it bears the cancellation from Lisbon.

*Opposite*:
A map of George Town, c. 1930.

The address side of [278]. The stamps are from the George V Series issued from 1911 to 1915. These India Postage and Revenue stamps are each worth half an Anna. The "Anna" was a currency unit formerly used in India, equal to one-sixteenth of a rupee.

The oldest temple in Penang: the Guanyin Temple, built on Pitt Street c. 1800.

it was the original Chinatown. China Street is said to have been established by pioneer settler, Koh Lay Huan soon after Francis Light founded Penang in 1786.[57] He was later appointed the first Kapitan Cina of Penang in 1787. Land reclamation in the 19th century, around the area where China Street meets the sea, extended China Street and created a new road for warehousing and commercial offices, China Street Ghaut.

## Chetty Street/King Street/Queen Street

These streets are situated in the centre of Penang's "Little India". They were laid out soon after the founding of Penang, and run parallel to each other and to Beach Street and Pitt Street.

Indians settled in Little India from the 1800s. This is reflected in the name, Chetty Street [277], which is the southern end of Penang Street (Chetty is a title used by various South Indian mercantile castes). The influx of Chinese settlers here led to the establishment of Chinese temples, clan houses and shops.

King Street [278] is named after King George III (r. 1760–1820) and Queen Street [279], after his consort.

## Chulia Street

Chulia Street [280-282] or Lebuh Chulia was named after early Indian Muslim settlers, known as "Chulias" from the coast of Coromandel.[32] It was originally called Malabar Street in the late 18th century.[77] It is one of the oldest streets in George Town and is one of the main streets laid out during the time of Francis Light.

## The Streets of Harmony

From its founding in 1786, Penang has been a melting pot of races, religions and cultures. Acheen Street (Lebuh Acheh), Farquhar Street (Lebuh Farquhar), Cannon Square and Pitt Street (Jalan Masjid Kapitan Keling), have several mosques, temples and churches lining them.

Acheen Street was named after the Arab traders from Sumatra who lived here. The Acheen Street Mosque [283] was founded in 1808 by Syed Sheriff Tengku Syed Hussain Al-Aidid, a prominent Acehnese trader.[42] The Hokkiens call this street "Phak Chiok Kay" ("Stonemasons' Street") as many stonemasons were based here.[50]

Cannon Square (Medan Cannon) was named after the cannons used there by the British government to quell the Penang Riots in 1867. In Hokkien, it is called "Leong-San-Tong-Lai" ("Within Leong San Tong Khoo Kongsi").[50] The Khoo Kongsi (Khoo Clan House) [284] is the most famous and elaborate clan temple in Malaysia. The rebuilt temple was completed in 1906 after the earlier one was razed by fire in 1901.[79,129]

Pitt Street [285] (Jalan Masjid Kapitan Keling), named after British Prime Minister William Pitt the Younger, is one of the four major streets in the original grid of George Town. Before World War II, the section of Pitt Street between China and Chulia streets was named "Toa Ba Lai" ("Big Police Station"); the police station can be seen in [285]. Pitt Street was renamed Jalan Masjid Kapitan Keling after the main Indian Muslim mosque along it.

The head of the Indian Muslim community was Caudeer Mohudeen who became the Kapitan Keling. The Masjid Kapitan Keling [286-288] was built c. 1801. Over the years the mosque has undergone several extensions and renovations. It remains the grandest Indian Muslim mosque in Malaysia to this day.

The Arulmigu Mahamariamman Hindu Temple lies between Pitt Street and Queen Street. It was built c. 1833 and has a seven-metre tall sculptured tower (*gopuram*).[42]

Further along Pitt Street, opposite China Street, is the Guanyin Temple (*below left*; [289-290]). It was built c. 1800 by the Hokkien and Cantonese communities and is the oldest temple in Penang. The temple is dedicated to the Goddess of Mercy (Guanyin) and the patron deity of seafarers, Ma Chor Poh.[42]

Farquhar Street [291-292; 296] was named after Colonel Robert Townsend Farquhar, lieutenant governor of Penang (1804–1805). Along Farquhar Street are St George's Church and the Church of the Assumption.

St George's Church [293-295], built in 1817,[9] is the oldest Anglican church in Southeast Asia, and was built by the British East India Company using convict labour.

The Church of the Assumption [296-298] was named after the Christian Feast of the Assumption. The present church on Farquhar Street was built in 1860.[81.]

## Penang Road

Penang Road (Jalan Penang) [299-309] was the first road that extended out of George Town. Many Indians and Sumatrans settled around here in the 1800s; they are remembered in names such as Kampung Deli, Kampung Malabar, Sri Bahari Road and Kampung Ambon.

Before World War II, Penang Road was a popular commercial road with hotels, restaurants, a bazaar, a market, retail shops, cinemas, etc. The police headquarters [299], fire station and jinricksha office (*see Chapter 1,* [27]) and Australia Hotel (*see Chapter 4* [220]) no longer exist. Gone too are the electric trams that plied Penang Road [300]. The Penang Bazaar [302] was built by prominent tin mine owner Ng Boo Bee in 1905[12] and was an upmarket shopping place. The rear portion of the bazaar was known as "Picadilly Bazaar".[14] In the centre of Penang Road was the Cheong Lye Hock Cinema [303] (opposite Campbell Street); this was converted into the Cathay Cinema [304] c. 1940.[14]

Chowrasta Market [305-306], built in 1890, is a wet market along Penang Road. In its early days, the traders were predominantly South Indians.[5] Today, it is known as Bazaar Chowrasta. Argyll Road is a small side road off Penang Road (opposite Chulia Street). The Penang branch of beverage manufacturer Fraser and Neave Ltd [309] was located at No. 190, Argyll Road.

## Campbell Street

Campbell Street (Lebuh Campbell) (*top right*; [310-315]) was named after George William Robert Campbell, acting lieutenant governor of Penang (1872–1873).

The Campbell Street Market was built c. 1900, and resembles the Chowrasta Market. The front façade of the Campbell Street Market [315] has two arches while Chowrasta Market's façade has three arches [306].

## Northam Road

Northam Road [316-323] was named after the town of Northam in England[32] and renamed Jalan Sultan Ahmad Shah after the Yang di-Pertuan Agong who visited Penang in 1982.[50] During the 19th century, Northam Road was the preferred choice of residence for many Europeans, hence the Hokkien name "Ang Mor Lor" ("European Road").

When the Europeans moved out, the wealthy Chinese moved in, building ostentatious mansions here such as Soon Eng Kong's "Soonstead", Yeap Chor Ee's "Homestead", Lim Lean Teng's "Woodville", and Lim Cheng Ean's "Hardwicke".

Istana Kedah (Kedah House), belonging to the Sultan of Kedah, was built in 1935 on the location of the wooden mansion shown in [319].

The Penang Club, established in 1868, was the focal point of social life in Penang. It stands facing the seafront.[9] The club is shown c. 1910 in [320] and [321]. The present building was constructed in 1964 to accommodate the growing membership of the club.[84]

The Presbyterian Church [322-323], also known as the "Scot's Kirk" stood near the junction of Northam Road and Larut Road.[14] The church was built c. 1900 and demolished c. 1940.

## Burmah Road

Burmah Road [324-326] or Jalan Burma was named after the Kampung Ava Burmese village on Burmah Lane. The

Campbell Street, c. 1910. The street was created in the mid-19th century.[82]

149

The address side of [304]. This ppc is dated c. 1956. Hence, the Federation of Malaya (1948–1957) stamps used here.

The Golf Club on Macalister Road, c. 1910.

AUTOMOBILE DRIVES
Allowing time to see the sights and take Photographs.

The back of [350], issued by Leng Brothers Motor Garage, c. 1930, and printed locally, by G.H. Kiat & Co. Ltd. This ppc advertised tour services offered by Leng Brothers, using their motor cars.

Dhammikarama Burmese Temple [328] and roads such as Salween Road, Moulmein Close, Rangoon Road, and Mandalay Road, are lasting reminders of the Burmese presence in Penang.[50,85] Locals refer to Burmah Road as "Jalan Kreta Ayer" (in Malay) and "Chia Chooi Lar" (in Hokkien). Both mean "Water Cart Road", in reference to the ox carts [325] transporting water, or men carrying water on their shoulders [326].[85]

The Siamese community have lived in Penang since the 19th century. Their temple, Wat Chaiyamangkalaram [329], is shown here.

The Chinese Recreation Club was formed in 1892 "for the encouragement of all kinds of sports and recreation among the Chinese".[9] In 1901, the club purchased the "Eastbourne" mansion [327] which stood at the corner of Burmah Road and Pangkor Road. In the 1920s, a new structure was built to replace the dilapidated "Eastbourne". The new club house was completed in 1931.

## Macalister Road

Macalister Road [330] was named after Colonel Norman Macalister, a confidante of Captain Francis Light and later governor of Penang from 1807 to 1810.

Prior to World War II, Macalister Road was best known as the location of the Penang Turf Club (PTC) [331-334]. The PTC was founded in 1864, although another source states it as 1867.[9] It received generous assistance from the colonial government including a free grant of land for the racecourse. In 1900, new and substantial stands were erected.[9] The PTC experienced its golden years from 1912 to 1928; the race course on Macalister Road was the most modern in Malaya at that time. It shifted to new and grander premises at Bukit Gantong in 1939.

The Golf Club (*top left*; [335]) occupied a section of the PTC grounds on Macalister Road. In 1939, it shifted to Batu Gantong with the PTC. Today, it is known as the PTC Golf Section.

Race Course Road [336] was so named as it led to the PTC on Macalister Road. It was renamed Residency Road after Independence in 1957.

## Peel Avenue and Piccadilly Circus

Peel Avenue [337] was named after William Peel, resident councillor of Penang (1925–1926). Piccadilly Circus [338] was located at the junction of Peel Avenue, Codrington Avenue, Macalister Road and Residency Road.

## Transport

From the 1800s to 1945, the main transport on Penang roads was the rickshaw or jinricksha [339-341]. These were licensed by the rickshaw office on Penang Road (*see Chapter 1*, [27]). The rickshaw office was also referred to as the "Hackney Carriage Department".

Other human-powered transport was the hand cart [342] and "chair coolies" (*see Chapter 6*, [378-380]).

The bullock supplemented man as a means of transport for carrying goods and men [343-344]; horse-drawn carriages (*see Chapter 3*, [175], [182]; *Chapter 4*, [187]) were also used in Penang from its founding.

Trams were a major feature on the roads of pre-World War II Penang. The use of steam trams (*see Chapter 2*, [94]) in Penang began in the 1880s, while in 1898 horse-drawn trams (*see Chapter 3*, [170]) plied the areas from Magazine Road to Weld Quay.[87]

Electric trams [345-346] began regular service in 1906. Trolley buses were first introduced in 1925 and serviced the Magazine Road to Jetty route. For economic reasons, trams were replaced by trolley buses. The change to trolley buses was completed in 1937. Trolley buses were in time replaced by motor buses [347].[87]

Following the tin and rubber boom of the early 1900s, cars became a common sight in Penang [348-349]. Motor garages (*below left*; [350]) flourished with the boom in motor cars.

PENANG. *Lightstreet*

**[249]**

PENANG. LIGHTSTREET

*Cancellation:* Nil
*Back:* Divided
*Publisher:* C.H. 456 Copyright

This is the beginning of Beach Street as viewed from King Edward Place, with Light Street on the right foreground. The building with the red roof on the left was the Chinese Protectorate. Beach Street was so named as it was laid out to follow the curve of the beach. This colour ppc dates from c. 1900.

BEACH STREET, Penang.

**[250]**

BEACH STREET, PENANG.

*Cancellation:* Nil
*Back:* Divided
*Publisher:* Not stated

A real photographic ppc of the same area as **[249]** but 40 years later. The buildings have changed and the street is now used by motor cars. The four-storey British Palladian-style building on the right is the Standard Chartered Bank, built in 1930. Opposite it is the old Hongkong and Shanghai Bank (HSBC) building, with its prominent domed turret. Date: c. 1940.

Hongkong and Shanghai Banking Corporation, Penang.

**[251]**

**HONGKONG AND SHANGHAI BANKING CORPORATION, PENANG.**

*Cancellation:* PENANG/6 JY/1912
*Back:* Divided
*Publisher:* Not stated; printed in Germany

The old HSBC building in Penang was built between 1905 and 1906. Designed by prominent architect Henry Alfred Neubronner, its magnificent domed turret characterises the building. The bank was situated at the corner of Downing Street and Beach Street. This view is from Downing Street. Date: c. 1910.

Hong & S'hai Bank Buildings, Penang

**[252]**

**HONG & S'HAI BANK BUILDINGS, PENANG**

*Cancellation:* PENANG/1913
*Back:* Divided
*Publisher:* Co-operative Agency S.S./ No. 16

Another view of the beginning of Beach Street from King Edward Place. The lefthand side is dominated by the HSBC building and, beyond that, is the Netherlands Trading Society (Nederlandsche Handel Maatschappij). A branch of the Dutch bank was established in Penang in 1889. This Neo-Classical style building was also designed by Neubronner's firm, Wilson & Neubronner, and completed in 1905.[9] The bank was later renamed ABN-AMRO. The building today houses the Royal Bank of Scotland. Date: c. 1910.

[253]
No. 128 Hongkong & Shanghai Banking Corporation./ Netherlands Trading Society & Chartered Bank of India, Australia & China.

*Cancellation:* PENANG/19 MY/1912
*Back:* Divided
*Publisher:* A. Kaulfuss, Penang.

This ppc shows the HSBC (*centre*) and the Netherlands Trading Society building (*right*). Date: c. 1910.

[254]
A 20 – Beach Street, Penang.

*Cancellation:* Nil
*Back:* Divided
*Publisher:* Nikko Studio, Penang, S.S./Printed in Saxony.

The street joining Beach Street in the centre of the picture is Market Street; at the corner of Beach Street and Market Street is the Kee Guan Co. (No. 63 Beach Street). Date: c. 1910.

Logan Building, Penang.

**[255]**

LOGAN BUILDING, PENANG.

*Cancellation:* Penang/1913
*Back:* Divided
*Publisher:* S.M. Manicum, Penang/No. 1

This colour ppc shows the building along Beach Street between Union Street (*foreground*) and Bishop Street. This building was named after the much respected Penang advocate and solicitor James Richardson Logan. As shown in this ppc, it was originally a three-storey building when it was built in the late 19th century.[82] By the 1930s, the building had to be renovated as it was dilapidated and became hazardous. Date: c. 1910.

Beach Street, Penang.

**[256]**

BEACH STREET, PENANG.

*Cancellation:* Nil
*Back:* Divided
*Publisher:* Not stated; printed in Germany

The HSBC is on the left, and beyond that the Netherlands Trading Society. On the right is the Logan's Building. The thoroughfare is pretty busy with people and rickshaws. This colour ppc is dated c. 1910.

**[257]**

**PENANG. BEACH STREET.**

*Cancellation:* SINGAPORE/1904
*Back:* Undivided
*Publisher:* Not stated

A ppc of Beach Street dating from c. 1900. Pritchard & Co. Ltd, a shop selling a variety of merchandise ("universal providers"), stood at the corner of Union Street and Beach Street. Opposite it were the earlier premises of the Standard Chartered Bank. Pritchard & Co. was established in 1880, and also produced ppcs of Penang. This ppc was written on 1 October 1904 on board the S.S. *Palawan*.

**[258]**

**PENANG,/BEACH STREET.**

*Cancellation:* Nil
*Back:* Undivided
*Publisher:* Not stated

A real photographic ppc of a busy Beach Street, c. 1900. Pritchard & Co. Ltd is on the right. Its advertisement in 1917 read: "Complete House Furnishers/ Tailors/Provisions, Wine Merchants, etc."[12] The founder of the business, G.H. Pritchard, initially set up a tailoring and outfitting store, gradually diversifying to include general, provision, hardware and outfitting departments.[9] Date: c. 1900.

Beach Street, Penang.

[259]
BEACH STREET, PENANG.

*Cancellation:* Nil
*Back:* Divided
*Publisher:* K.M. Mahmed Esoof, Penang. No. 3035

Beach Street is festooned with flags and decorations. On the right is Robinson Piano Co. Ltd, and the next shop on the right is the Georgetown Dispensary. This colour ppc dates from c. 1900.

Beach Street, Penang.

[260]
BEACH STREET, PENANG.

*Cancellation:* Penang/1917
*Back:* Divided
*Publisher:* S.M. Manicum, Penang./No. 3

The signboard of the Georgetown Dispensary Ltd can be seen outside the building in the middle. It was established in 1889, and moved into this building at 37A Beach Street in 1895. The dispensary imported all kinds of drugs and chemicals from the United Kingdom, United States, and Europe. It also specialised in optical appliances and photographic materials.[9] In 1908, the dispensary employed "a qualified English chemist and a staff of trained assistants."[9] Date: c. 1910.

**[261]**

**BOMBAY SHOP, PENANG.**

*Cancellation:* Nil
*Back:* Divided
*Publisher:* S.M. Manicum, Penang/ No. 8

A colour ppc, c. 1910, of the shop of Bombay merchants Tollaram Dholiamall & Co. Located at No. 8 Beach Street, this store sold Indian, Chinese and Japanese products including jewellery and sundry goods. Tollaram Dholiamall moved into these premises when its previous tenant, the upmarket department store Whiteaway, Laidlaw and Co., moved out in 1914 to larger premises on Bishop Street.

**[262]**

**BEACH STREET, PENANG**

*Cancellation:* Nil
*Back:* Divided
*Publisher:* Not stated

In the foreground on the right above the gentleman in white can be seen the road sign "Che Em Lane". This is a branch of Beach Street located between China Street and Market Street, and named after Chinese merchant, Chee Eam (Chu Yan). Francis Light, in his account of brick buildings in Penang in 1793, identified Chee Eam as the largest Chinese property owner on the island, possessing three shophouses worth 2,700 Spanish dollars.[82] The Tamils call Che Em Lane "Koli Kadai Sandhu", in reference to poulterers who operated near the wet market at Market Street Ghaut. Date: c. 1910.

Beach Street, Penang.

**[263]**

**BEACH STREET, PENANG.**

*Cancellation:* Nil
*Back:* Divided
*Publisher:* Not stated

A real photographic ppc of Beach Street in c. 1930. By this time, Beach Street was in stark contrast to its early years; the street is crowded with cars, rickshaws, bicycles, and pedestrians. The Che Eam Lane signboard is visible on the right.

Beach St. Penang

**[264]**

**BEACH ST PENANG**

*Cancellation:* Nil
*Back:* Divided
*Publisher:* Not stated

A real photographic ppc dating from c. 1930. Grosvenor Motors (*right*) is visible at the junction of Church Street Ghaut. On the left, at the far end, is Kongsoon House, built in 1914, and originally the premises of Goh Teik Chee & Co., wholesale store and ship chandlers, suppliers of mining, engineering and industrial machinery.[42,82] Goh Teik Chee was the leader of the Anti-Opium Movement in Penang. He was awarded the Order of the British Empire for helping to relieve the food shortage during World War I (1914–1918), the first Penang Chinese to receive such an honour.[82]

Penang. Beach Street.

**[265]**

**PENANG, BEACH STREET.**

*Cancellation:* PENANG/JA 28/1902
*Back:* Undivided
*Publisher:* A. Kaulfuss, Penang, No. 15

A very early ppc, c. 1900, of Beach Street. On the right the signboard of "Penang Foundry/Company/Engineers", can be seen; on the left, the "Penang Sales Room" signboard is visible. This section of Beach Street, from Acheen Street to Malay Street, is called "Phah Thih Kay", literally meaning "Striking Iron Street" ("Ironmongers' Street"), in Hokkien.[136]

372 - Prangin Market, Penang.

**[266]**

**372 – PRANGIN MARKET, PENANG.**

*Cancellation:* Written but not posted.
*Back:* Divided
*Publisher:* Federal Rubber Stamp Co.,
 Penang, Kuala Lumpur & Ipoh.

This ppc is of Prangin Market, c. 1910. The market used to be beside Prangin Canal, which in the 19th century marked the limits of George Town. Hence, the Hokkien name "Sia Boey", meaning end of the town or village. The market was near the southern end of Beach Street where it intersects with Lebuh Noordin to become Lebuh C.Y. Choy.

**[267]**

**No. 208 PENANG, BISHOPSTREET.**

*Cancellation:* 1909
*Back:* Divided
*Publisher:* A. Kaulfuss, Penang./
Printed in Germany

A beautiful colour ppc of Bishop Street, c. 1905. The street is crowded with pedestrians, hand carts and rickshaws. On the right can be seen the signboard of "The Dispensary", while on the left are "The Retreat Bar/Tiffin Room" and "Choon Hin/Shoemaker". Bishop Street came to be with the arrival of Bishop Arnold Garnault and his persecuted congregation from Siam. They had fled Siam for Kuala Kedah, and at Francis Light's invitation, settled in Penang.

**[268]**

**BISHOP STREET, PENANG**

*Cancellation:* Nil
*Back:* Divided
*Publisher:* Not stated; printed in Germany

Bishop Street, c. 1910. "Whiteaway, Laidlaw Co. Limited/Home Furnishings" is on the left. It was referred to as "The Whiteley of the East"[9] after London's first department store. According to a 1908 account, the original store opened in March 1903 with only £500 worth of goods in small premises on Beach Street.[9] Just a year later, it relocated to this much larger building on Bishop Street. Its clientele consisted mostly of Europeans, "better-class Chinese and Malays".[9]

Junction of Bishop Street, Penang

The Commemorative Monument to the Armenian Church, Penang

[269]

JUNCTION OF BISHOP STREET, PENANG

*Cancellation:* Nil
*Back:* Divided
*Publisher:* M.J. Penang./184028

The junction of Bishop Street and Beach Street was marked by Whiteaway, Laidlaw & Co. and the Eastern Extension Telegraph Co. on the left and The Dispensary (Chemists/Opticians) on the right. Date: c. 1910.

[270]

THE COMMEMORATIVE MONUMENT TO THE ARMENIAN CHURCH, PENANG

*Cancellation:* Penang/Date unclear
*Back:* Divided
*Publisher:* M.J., Penang./184069

The Commemorative Monument to the Armenian Church built in c. 1906 to mark the site of the demolished Church of St Gregory the Illuminator on Bishop Street. The construction of the church in 1824 is largely attributed to Armenian merchant and philanthropist, Catchatour Galastaun. Date: c. 1910.

Church Street, Penang.

**[271]**

**CHURCH STREET, PENANG.**

*Cancellation:* Penang/1917
*Back:* Divided
*Publisher:* S.M. Manicum, Penang/No. 36

A lovely colour ppc of Church Street, c. 1910. The three shophouses in the centre (18, 20, 22) belonged to Goh Teik Chee & Sons. They owned two other shophouses (34 and 38) further down the street.[22] The tenant above shop number 22 is the "Hongkong Yuen On Fire & Marine Insr. Co. Ltd", as stated on the signboard. Church Street was so called after a makeshift church, the predecessor of the Church of the Assumption, was sited there. To the Chinese however, it is known as "Ghee Hin Kay", in reference to the Ghee Hin secret society building, which was also the family residence of Captain Ah Quee.[136]

**Penang.** Captn Ah Kevie House, Church Street.

**[272]**

**PENANG. CAPTN AH KEVIE HOUSE, CHURCH STREET.**

*Cancellation:* Nil
*Back:* Divided
*Publisher:* Not stated

The address shown on this ppc is No. 29 Church Street. The bullock cart stands in front of the private temple of Chung Keng Kwee (1829–1901), the Kapitan Cina of Perak. Two streets in Penang were named after him: Keng Kwee Street and Ah Quee Street, both built by him and presented to the Municipality.[57] The temple is dedicated to the Kapitan himself. It is a unique private house of worship, containing a life-sized bronze statue of the Kapitan.[57] This sepia ppc is dated c. 1910.

[273]

PENANG, NO. 16.—A STREET SCENE
IN CHINA TOWN

*Cancellation:* PENANG/1902
*Back:* Undivided
*Publisher:* British Empire Series/
"Sanbride"

The original Chinatown was in China
Street. Although it was shorter than Beach
Street and Chulia Street, it contained
more shops.[157] It is strategically located
in the heart of George Town: between
Chulia and Market streets to the south;
Church and Bishop streets to the north;
and intersected by Beach Street to the
east and Pitt Street on the west.[157] Francis
Light had actually designated China Street
to be the centre of the commercial area;
that is why there were more brick than
attap houses there.[157] This ppc shows
some of the many shops on China Street.
The three-storey building in the centre
was the "Yin Oi Tong Medical Hall",[42]
originally established at Pitt Street in 1796,
and was one of the oldest medical halls in
Southeast Asia.[82] Date: c. 1890.

Penang, No. 16.—A Street Scene in China Town

[274]

LIGHT STREET, PENANG

*Cancellation:* Nil
*Back:* Divided
*Publisher:* Not stated

An early view of Light Street, c. 1900.
The Padang is on the right. Tall *angsana*
trees line the street; some of them are
still alive today. When Francis Light arrived in
Penang, he did not prepare a blueprint
for the town. Instead, he decided that
the commercial areas of the town would
be between Light Street, Beach Street,
Malabar (later Chulia) Street and Pitt
Street. All these streets were named
by him.[157]

Light Street, Penang

LIGHT STREET, PENANG, NAMED AFTER CAPTAIN LIGHT,
THE FOUNDER OF PENANG

COPYRIGHT PHOTO
No. 12

[275]
COPYRIGHT PHOTO No. 12/LIGHT STREET, PENANG, NAMED AFTER CAPTAIN LIGHT,/THE FOUNDER OF PENANG

*Cancellation:* Nil
*Back:* Divided
*Publisher:* Penang Photo Store,
49 Leight Street, Penang/
Printed in England

Light Street, c. 1920. On the right, behind the *angsana* trees are the Town Hall, Cricket Club and the Municipal Offices building (City Hall).

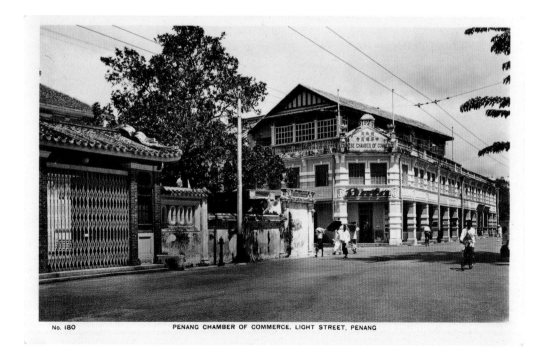

No. 180                PENANG CHAMBER OF COMMERCE, LIGHT STREET, PENANG

[276]
No. 180 PENANG CHAMBER OF COMMERCE, LIGHT STREET, PENANG

*Cancellation:* Nil
*Back:* Divided
*Publisher:* Not stated; printed in England

A real photographic ppc of Light Street facing the Padang. The Penang Chinese Chamber of Commerce dominates this photograph. The organisation was established in June 1903,[9] the building here was built in 1928 (the date is visible on the gable). The Bata shoe shop occupied the ground floor. Date: c. 1930.

**[277]**

CHETTY STREET, PENANG.

*Cancellation:* SINGAPORE/1914
*Back:* Divided
*Publisher:* S.M. Manicum, Penang/No. 25

A colour ppc of Chetty Street, c. 1910. The part of Penang Street which is between Market Street and Chulia Street is known as Chetty Street. Here was where the Chettiars settled and went on to acquire a lot of property due to forfeited mortgages.[82] Many of the wealthy Chettiars became moneylenders and businessmen. They worked and lived in this row of shophouses. Many of the wealthier Chettiar families returned to India after Malaya achieved independence in 1957.

**[278]**

KING STREET, PENANG.

*Cancellation:* PENANG/1915
*Back:* Divided
*Publisher:* S.M. Manicum, Penang/No. 24

King Street, c. 1910, with a view towards the Esplanade. The Ben Vermont Monument is in the distance, left of centre, and the bandstand or pavilion is in the centre. At the corner of King Street and Light Street is the mansion of Foo Tye Sin (*right*), an influential Chinese community leader. King Street, along with Penang Street, runs parallel to Beach Street to the east and Pitt Street (Jalan Masjid Kapitan Keling) to the west.[137] The shops on King Street, some of which are visible on the left, were diverse: they were European-, Chinese-, Indian-, and Malay-owned, and were mostly built of brick. Fires had broken out several times in King Street and Penang Street – in 1789, 1812, 1814. As a result, by 1818, there were no attap-roofed shops on King Street, while there was only one shop roofed with attap on Penang Street.[137]

Queen Street, Penang.

[279]
QUEEN STREET, PENANG.

*Cancellation:* PENANG/1918
*Back:* Divided
*Publisher:* S.M. Manicum, Penang/No. 4

Queen Street, c. 1910. Queen Street was named after the consort of King George III of England, Queen Charlotte. The three-storey building on the right belonged to the government and used to house the Penang Opium and Spirit Farm Office. From 1971 to 1997, *The Star* newspaper's Penang office and printing presses occupied the premises.

Chulia Street, Penang.

[280]
CHULIA STREET, PENANG.

*Cancellation:* Nil
*Back:* Divided
*Publisher:* S.M. Manicum, Penang/No. 10

Chulia Street, c. 1910, at its junction with Pitt Street. The Pitt Street market is on the far right; the gables of the Penang Teochew Association are visible (*centre right*). The tower of the Central Fire Station is just visible in the distance. Chulia Street was the scond busiest street in Penang, and more than 18 percent of George Town's shops were located there. It was so named as most of the people who owned shops and other property there were Chulia merchants who originated from the Coromandel Coast and Bengal.[137]

Chulia Street, Penang

**[281]**

CHULIA STREET, PENANG

*Cancellation:* Nil
*Back:* Divided
*Publisher:* Not stated; printed in Germany

Chulia Street, at its junction with Love Lane (*right*); the road sign is just visible. On the left is the signboard advertising "Theem Poh Wah/Photographer/C. Tackson/Dentist". This view is towards Penang Road. In the early 1800s, the area surrounding Chulia Street was a Malay settlement.[137] This ppc is dated c. 1910.

Chulia Street, Penang.

**[282]**

CHULIA STREET, PENANG.

*Cancellation:* 3 AP/1914
*Back:* Divided
*Publisher:* S.M. Manicum, Penang/No. 9

An electric tram (introduced in 1906) shares the street with rickshaws. A row of three-storey Chinese shophouses dominates the street. Today, Chulia Street is well known as the street of backpackers (budget travellers), with an abundance of budget hotels, restaurants, pubs and shops catering to their needs. This colour ppc is dated c. 1910.

Penang. Malay Mosque, Acheen street.

**[283]**

**PENANG. MALAY MOSQUE, ACHEEN STREET.**

*Cancellation:* Nil
*Back:* Divided
*Publisher:* Not stated

A c. 1920 ppc of the Acheen Street Mosque. A large crowd gathers around the mosque, and the British Union Jack is flown prominently in the centre; suggesting the visit of a colonial officer. The mosque was built in 1808 by Syed Sheriff Tengku Syed Hussain Al-Aidid, a prominent Acehnese trader, as well as a member of the Acehnese royal family. He was the richest Malay in Penang at that time. The architecture of the mosque combines Mughal influence, oriental influence and Neo-Classical features. Prior to the late 1960s, the mosque complex also functioned as a hub for religious pilgrims who travelled by ship to Jeddah.

3. Seh Khoo Kongsi (Khoo Family House), Penang, S.S.

**[284]**

**3. SEH KHOO KONGSI (KHOO FAMILY HOUSE), PENANG, S.S.**

*Cancellation:* Nil
*Back:* Divided
*Publisher:* Raphael Tuck & Sons "Sepia Platemarked"/Postcard 768/ Printed in Britain

A sepia ppc showing the most famous and elaborate Chinese clan temple in Penang. It was originally a simple clanhouse of the Khoos, built in 1851 at Cannon Square, and named Leong San Tong. But by 1894, it had shown signs of deterioration, and the Board of Trustees rebuilt a newer and more magnificent clanhouse in 1894. This was however razed by fire on Chinese New Year's eve in 1901. In 1902, a new clanhouse was built, and took four years to complete. This ppc is dated c. 1920.

Pitt Street, Penang

**[285]**

**PITT STREET, PENANG**

*Cancellation:* Nil
*Back:* Divided
*Publisher:* M.J., Penang./184210

A real photographic ppc of Pitt Street, c. 1910. The view in this ppc shows the market in the centre, and behind it the police station. Pitt Street was renamed Jalan Masjid Kapitan Keling after Independence in 1957.[82]

Penang, No. 20— Mohammedan Mosque. A Malay Festival

British Empire Series

**[286]**

**PENANG, NO. 20—MOHAMMEDAN MOSQUE. A MALAY FESTIVAL**

*Cancellation:* Nil
*Back:* Undivided
*Publisher:* British Empire Series/ "Sanbride"

An early ppc of the Kapitan Keling Mosque along Pitt Street. The mosque was named after the "Kapitan Keling" who was "head of the Indians" (here meaning Indian Muslims). This mosque was originally built by the Kapitan, Caudeer Mohudeen, c. 1801, on a 7.3-hectare lot provided by the British government. Caudeer Mohudeen imported labour and materials from India.[82] This ppc is dated c. 1900.

*Malay Mosque, Chulia Street, Penang.*

**[287]**

**Malay Mosque, Chulia Street, Penang.**

*Cancellation:* Dated 24 September 1919, but not posted
*Back:* Divided
*Publisher:* K.M. Mahmed Esoof, Penang. - No. 3015

The Kapitan Keling Mosque, c. 1910. The mosque also has an entrance at Chulia Street. The message on the ppc reads: "This will impress upon you that the Malays have also their own church commonly known as "Mosque". Their building is of a queer architecture...before entering, however, they have to wash their hands and feet in a tank which is just outside the Mosque as a sign of purity."

*Worship Hall of Mohammedan. Penang.*

**[288]**

**Worship Hall of Mohammedan./Penang.**

*Cancellation:* Nil
*Back:* Divided
*Publisher:* Not stated

A real photographic ppc of the Masjid Kapitan Keling, c. 1930. Although the mosque was built c. 1801, it was extended and underwent renovations, including re-roofing and the construction of the wall around the compound.[82] Renovation work can be seen in progress here.

PENANG.

PRITCHARD & CO., PENANG. No. 8.

CHINESE TEMPLE.

**[289]**

**PENANG./CHINESE TEMPLE.**

*Cancellation:* Nil
*Back:* Undivided
*Publisher:* Pritchard & Co., Penang./
No. 8.

An early ppc of the Guanyin (Goddess of Mercy) Temple along Pitt Street opposite China Street. It is the oldest Chinese temple in Penang and was built c. 1800. This was the first temple built by the early settlers from China.[82] To the Chinese, China Street was linked to this temple; the Cantonese refer to China Street as "Kum Yam Miu Chek Kay", meaning "The street going straight from the Temple of the Goddess of Mercy".[136] Date: c. 1900.

**[290]**

**No. 124 CHINESE TEMPLE, PITT STREET, PENANG**

*Cancellation:* Nil
*Back:* Divided
*Publisher:* Not stated; printed in England

A real photographic ppc of the Guanyin Temple, c. 1930. Several rickshaws are in the foreground; while in the background is the Chinese Town Hall. The Guanyin Temple was originally named "Kong Hock Keong", meaning "Canton-Hokkien Temple"; and hosted the council and tribunal for the Chinese community in the early days of Penang. The Chinese Town Hall was established in the 1880s to take over the economic and social functions of the Kong Hock Keong; thus the temple now only serves its religious functions.[82]

No. 124

CHINESE TEMPLE, PITT STREET, PENANG

No. 88. Farquhar Str. Penang

**[291]**
**No. 88. Farquhar Str. Penang**

*Cancellation:* Nil
*Back:* Divided
*Publisher:* A. Kaulfuss, Penang./
Printed in Germany

A view of No. 88 Farquhar Street, near Northam Road. A variety of trees including coconut and *angsana* line the street. Farquhar Street, along with Love Lane, Penang Road and Battery Lane, were new roads built to accommodate the further expansion of George Town due to an increase in population, in the early 19th century.[157] Date: c. 1900.

Farquhar Street, Penang.

**[292]**
**Farquhar Street, Penang.**

*Cancellation:* Nil
*Back:* Divided
*Publisher:* No. 35. A. Beach Street,
Penang/No. 51

A view of Farquhar Street from Pitt Street, c. 1910. On the left, hidden by trees, is St George's Church, and next to it is the Penang Free School.

Penang No 10.   St. George's Church.   Built 1817.

**[293]**

**PENANG NO 10. ST. GEORGE'S CHURCH. BUILT 1817.**

*Cancellation:* PENANG/NO 15/1905
*Back:* Undivided
*Publisher:* British Empire Series. "Sanbride"

A real photographic ppc of St George's Church, standing at No. 10 Farquhar Street. Completed in 1817, the church was an initiative of the Penang Colonial Chaplain, the Rev. Robert Hutchings, and consecrated by the Bishop of Calcutta, the Right Rev. T.F. Middleton on 11 May 1819.[80] The most prominent feature is the Greek temple-like portico of Doric columns at the front of the building.
Date: c. 1900.

ST. GEORGE'S CHURCH.

**[294]**

**PENANG./ST. GEORGE'S CHURCH.**

*Cancellation:* PENANG/1918
*Back:* Undivided
*Publisher:* Pritchard & Co., Penang./ No. 38.

The Francis Light Memorial stands in front of the church. It was erected in 1886 on the centenary of the founding of Penang, and built in the form of a circular Greek temple. On one side of the wall of the rotunda is a white marble plaque inscribed "In memory of Francis Light Esquire who first established this island as an English Settlement, and was many years Governor; born in the county of Suffolk in England and died October 21st 1794. In his capacity as Governor, the settlers and natives were greatly attached to him, and by his death had to deplore the loss of one who watched over their interests and cares as a father."
Date: c. 1900.

173

St. Georges Church (Interior).

**[295]**
**ST. GEORGES, CHURCH (INTERIOR).**

*Cancellation:* SINGAPORE/1913
*Back:* Divided
*Publisher:* Not stated; printed in Germany

The interior of the St George's Church, c. 1910. The "two rows of Tuscan columns form a central nave and side aisles."[30] In 1907, the church was re-roofed. The following year, electric lights and fans were installed for the comfort of the congregation of between 200 and 300 that the church could accommodate.[9] Several carved memorial tablets are located on the walls of the church.[9]

174

Farquhar Street, Penang

**[296]**
**FARQUHAR STREET, PENANG**

*Cancellation:* Nil
*Back:* Divided
*Publisher:* Not stated; printed in Germany

The Church of the Assumption on Farquhar Street, c. 1910. Farquhar Street is deserted except for a few rickshaws. Established on 15 August 1786, the church was originally located on Bishop Street; it moved to its present location on Farquhar Street in 1860. This Catholic church is built with a floorplan of a cross, and has two bell towers. Its pipe organ was installed in 1916.

[297]

SOUVENIR/OF/THE CONSECRATION/OF/THE BISHOP OF MALACCA/15TH APRIL 1934.

*Cancellation:* Nil
*Back:* Divided
*Publisher:* Not stated

The Church of the Assumption is shown in this ppc commemorating the consecration of the Bishop of Malacca, the Right Rev. Adrian Devals, D.D., on 15 April 1934. The *Straits Times* reported that the three-hour consecration ceremony was attended by Catholic priests from all parts of Malaya and the Church of the Assumption "was filled by two thousand members of the public". A portrait of the bishop is on the left.

[298]

ROMAN CATHOLIC CHURCH, PENANG.

*Cancellation:* Nil
*Back:* Divided
*Publisher:* Norddeutscher Lloyd, Bremen/
Ocean Comfort Company
m.b.H., Bremen/H 34 - 3

A real photographic ppc showing the Church of the Assumption in a run-down and neglected state following its disuse during the Japanese Occupation of Penang (1941–1945). In 1955, the church was elevated to a cathedral. However, in 2003, its status as cathedral was moved to the more recently built Cathedral of the Holy Spirit. Date: c. 1945.

**[299]**

POLICE STATION, PENANG RD, PENANG.

*Cancellation:* PENANG/27 NO/1920
*Back:* Divided
*Publisher:* Not stated

An early ppc of the police station (*centre*) on Penang Road, c. 1900. This police station was at the junction of Penang Road and Leith Street. It is no longer in existence. The shop on the far right states that it is a laundry.

**[300]**

UNTITLED [PENANG ROAD].

*Cancellation:* Nil
*Back:* Divided
*Publisher:* Norddeutscher Lloyd, Bremen/
            Ocean Comfort Company
            m.b.H., Bremen/H 34 - 3

This colour ppc depicts Penang Road at its junction with Chulia Street. The Australia Hotel is just visible in the foreground on the righthand edge of the ppc. In the early 19th century, Penang Road was largely populated by Indian Muslim shops; most of these gave way to Chinese businesses at the turn of the 20th century.[82] Date: c. 1900.

Penang Road, Penang

**[301]**

**PENANG ROAD, PENANG**

*Cancellation:* Nil
*Back:* Divided
*Publisher:* M.J., Penang.

A real photographic ppc of Penang Road, c. 1910. Tram tracks are visible on the road. Penang Road was the first road that extended out of George Town.[82]

Penang Bazaar, Penang.

**[302]**

**PANANG BAZAAR. PANANG.**

*Cancellation:* Nil
*Back:* Divided
*Publisher:* Not stated

A real photographic ppc of the Penang Bazaar that was built by Ng Boo Bee, a rich tin miner in Taiping in 1905. The signboards in front of the roof advertise many goods including the "Umbrella" soap brand (fourth billboard from left). The bazaar sold affordable apparel, earning it the name "Jual Murah" or "Cheap Sale". The bazaar was rebuilt in 1937 as a two-storey concrete structure to replace the original building that was destroyed in a fire. Today, it is an ideal place to shop for affordable Muslim clothes and textiles. Date: c. 1930.

COPYRIGHT PHOTO
No. 24

ONE OF THE MAIN THOROUGHFARES,
SHOWING THE CINEMA HALL ON THE LEFT, PENANG

[303]
COPYRIGHT PHOTO NO. 24/ONE OF THE
MAIN THOROUGHFARES,/SHOWING THE CINEMA
HALL ON THE LEFT, PENANG

*Cancellation:* Nil
*Back:* Divided
*Publisher:* Penang Photo Store,
49 Leith Street, Penang/
Printed in England

A large cinema can be seen on the left.
The cinema is screening the movie
*Square Crooks* which was produced
in 1928. The three-storey building
further down the road is the Tong Aik
Department Store. Date: 1928.

PENANG ROAD. PENANG

[304]
PENANG ROAD. PENANG

*Cancellation:* Not clear
*Back:* Divided
*Publisher:* Not stated

The police headquarters (*centre*), built
c. 1940, and the Cathay Cinema. The
movie *Anastasia* is showing in Cathay
Cinema; it was produced in 1956, thus
dating this ppc. Date: 1956.

Chowrasta Market, Penang

**[305]**

CHOWRASTA MARKET, PENANG

*Cancellation:* Nil
*Back:* Divided
*Publisher:* Not stated; printed in Germany

A ppc of the Chowrasta Market, c. 1900. It is a wet market along Penang Road adjacent to the Penang Bazaar. In its early days, stallholders were predominantly Tamil Muslims. The part of Penang Road near Chowrasta Market was called "Ku Kha Khu", meaning "old jail", alluding to the prison, formerly opposite the market.[136]

**[306]**

PENANG, NATIVE MARKET.

*Cancellation:* Nil
*Back:* Divided
*Publisher:* Raphael Tuck & Sons "Oilette"
Postcard No. 8962./Penang.
Series II./Printed in England

An "Oilette" postcard by Raphael Tuck & Sons of the Chowrasta Market, dubbed the "Native" Market. As can be seen in the ppc, many of the traders and shoppers are Indians. The traders sold their produce and wares inside and outside the market building. Date: c. 1920.

PENANG. NATIVE MARKET.

**[307]**

PENANG ROAD.

*Cancellation:* Nil
*Back:* Divided
*Publisher:* Not stated

Penang Road, c. 1940. This real photographic ppc looks northeast along Penang Road from the junction with Prangin Road (which leads to the right) to Leith Street. The Boston Bar occupied the top floor of the large building on the right. Behind the row of shophouses on the left are the police headquarters. An electric trolley bus is in the centre of the road. This section of Penang Road was a mixed commercial area.

No. 244  WINDSOR BUILDINGS. JUNCTION. PENANG. MAXWELL AND BURMAH ROADS

**[308]**

No. 244 WINDSOR BUILDINGS. JUNCTION. PENANG. MAXWELL AND BURMAH ROADS

*Cancellation:* Nil
*Back:* Divided
*Publisher:* Not stated; printed in England

This real photographic ppc depicts Windsor Buildings at the junction of Penang Road, Maxwell Road and Burmah Road, c. 1940. On the top of the building was a popular restaurant, "Theang Nan Low", advertised in three large Chinese characters. The shops on the ground floor included newsagents, and textile and photographic equipment sellers. This section of Penang Road was a mixed commercial area.

[309]

**WITH CHRISTMAS GREETINGS FROM FRASER & NEAVE LIMITED.**

*Cancellation:* Penang/1909
*Back:* Divided
*Publisher:* Not stated

A rare sepia ppc cum Christmas card issued by Fraser & Neave Limited
(F & N), c. 1905. It depicts F & N factories in Ipoh, Kuala Lumpur, Bangkok,
Singapore and Penang. In Penang, F & N was at No. 190 Argyll Road. Its
"Red Lion Lemonade" was well known in Penang prior to World War II.

[310]

**A 49 – CAMPBELL STREET/PENANG.**

*Cancellation:* Nil
*Back:* Divided
*Publisher:* Nikko Studio, Penang, S.S./Printed in Saxony.

A cake peddlar walks towards three oncoming rickshaws on Campbell Road,
c. 1910. Campbell Road was named after Sir George William Robert
Campbell, who served as inspector general of Penang (1866–1891) and later
as acting lieutenant governor of Penang (1872–1873).

Campbell Street, Penang.

**[311]**
**CAMPBELL STREET, PENANG**

*Cancellation:* Nil
*Back:* Divided
*Publisher:* No. 35. A. Beach Street, Penang

A traffic jam of rickshaws! The vegetable sellers on the left identify the location as near to the Campbell Street Market. Campbell Street was known as "Sin Kay" ("New Street") as it was a new street created between Pitt Street and Penang Road in the mid-19th century. However, it could also mean "fresh prostitutes" brought in from China. The Malays call it "Jalan Nona Baru" meaning "Street of New Maidens".[82] Date: c. 1910.

Campbell Street, Penang.

**[312]**
**CAMPBELL STREET, PENANG.**

*Cancellation:* PENANG/10 AU/1912
*Back:* Divided
*Publisher:* Not stated; printed in Germany

An aerial view of Campbell Street looking towards Buckingham Street (the start of Campbell Street). The clock tower of the FMSR Station building is visible in the distance. This colour ppc is dated c. 1910.

6. Campbell Street, Penang, S.S.

**[313]**

**6. Campbell Street, Penang, S.S.**

*Cancellation:* Penang/1921
*Back:* Divided
*Publisher:* Raphael Tuck & Sons "Sepia Platemarked" Postcard 768/ Printed in Britain

A sepia ppc, c. 1910, showing a peddlar, pedestrians and rickshaws on Campbell Street. Another name for this street was "Jalan Makau", in reference to the Cantonese people who arrived in Penang from Macau which was the main port of emigration for people from the Kwangtung province in China.[82]

CAMPBELL ST. PENANG

**[314]**

**CAMPBELL St./PENANG**

*Cancellation:* Nil
*Back:* Divided
*Publisher:* Not stated

This real photographic ppc shows shophouses on both sides of Campbell Street, advertising "International Hair Dressing Salon" and "A.S. Varisai –/ General Merchants", among other things. Campbell Street was a popular shopping area for jewellery, apparel, watches and shoes. In 1999, the Penang Road end of Campbell Street was pedestrianised.[83] This ppc dates from c. 1930.

**[315]**
**CAMPBELL STREET/PENANG**

*Cancellation:* Nil
*Back:* Divided
*Publisher:* Not stated

This real photographic ppc, c. 1930, shows the Campbell Street Market on the left. The market was built c. 1900. Architecturally, the difference between this structure and Chowrasta Market is that the former has two arches while the latter has three arches. This view is from Buckingham Street looking towards Penang Road.

No. 38. Natham-Road, Penang.

**[316]**
**No. 38. NATHAM-ROAD, PENANG.**

*Cancellation:* PENANG/AU 22/1906
*Back:* Undivided
*Publisher:* Not stated

An early ppc of Northam Road (misspelt Natham Road). On the left are large bungalows of the type favoured by Europeans at the time. The road's Hokkien name "Ang Mor Lor", literally means "Red Hair Road" or "Road Where Europeans Live".[136] Northam Road was the first residential suburb. Here the upper echelon of Penang society made their homes, including Stamford Raffles's "Runnymede" and Major General Archibald Anson's "Peninsula Cottage".[82]
Date: c. 1900.

NORTHAM ROAD, PENANG

**[317]**
NORTHAM ROAD, PENANG

*Cancellation:* Nil
*Back:* Divided
*Publisher:* S.M. Manicum, Penang/No. 18

Northam Road, c. 1910. The large *angsana* tree in the foreground was planted in the late 1800s. Behind it are splendid bungalows with ornate fences and gates. Northam Road was described as "one of the prettiest roads in George Town...It is the beginning of villadom – fine, large residences enclosed in spacious grounds (locally called 'compounds'), with tropical foliage on every side. The road itself is well kept, and is beautifully shaded with overhanging trees."⁹

No. 9 – Penang.
Northam Road

**[318]**
NO. 9 – PENANG./NORTHAM ROAD

*Cancellation:* Nil
*Back:* Divided
*Publisher:* T.C.B., Penang

No wonder Northam Road was described as the prettiest road in George Town; the road is lined on both sides by huge *angsana* trees, many of which still survive today. When the Europeans vacated the area for other residential areas, wealthy locals moved in, as evidenced by this description in 1908: "The first building of note is the pagoda-like residence of a wealthy Chinaman, which is four-storeys in height..."⁹ An electric arc streetlight can be seen in the foreground. Date: c. 1910.

Rajah Rest House, Penang.

**[319]**
RAJAH REST HOUSE, PENANG.

*Cancellation:* 1913
*Back:* Divided
*Publisher:* S.M. Manicum, Penang/No. 16

This wooden mansion was in 1935 replaced with the present Istana Kedah or Kedah House along Northam Road. Kedah House is the residence of the Sultan of Kedah in Penang. Date: c. 1910.

Penang Club, Penang

**[320]**
PENANG CLUB, PENANG

*Cancellation:* PENANG/24 JU/1910
*Back:* Divided
*Publisher:* Not stated; printed in Germany

The Penang Club, c. 1910, situated beside the sea, along Northam Road. The club was established in 1868 with Walter Scott, a member of the Legislative Council, as its president and F.C. Bishop as honorary secretary. The club is described as "pleasantly situated on the sea-front...".[9] It was equipped with a billiard room, card rooms, a "breezy verandah facing the sea", and a "modern American" bowling alley attached to the club.[9] "Cinderella dances" were held by members every month, and balls organised twice a year during the race weeks.[9]

**[321]**

**No. 14 – Penang./Town Club, Northam Road**

*Cancellation:* Penang/1910
*Back:* Divided
*Publisher:* T.C.B. Penang

A colour ppc of the Penang Club, c. 1910. The club was a building "of pink hue" with a "well-groomed, spacious lawn and fine approaches from the roadway".[9] When the club was founded in 1868, it was the most exclusive in Penang.[82] The present clubhouse was built in 1964.[84]

**[322]**

**Penang**

*Cancellation:* Tientsin (China)/1906
*Back:* Undivided
*Publisher:* C.H. 462 Copyright

The Presbyterian Church, also known as the "Scot's Kirk" (as the Presbyterian Church originated in Scotland). It was a beautiful, whitewashed building set amidst coconut palms and *angsana* trees. It was built c. 1900 and demolished in c. 1940.

No. 119 Scotch Church.

**[323]**
**No. 119. Scotch Church.**

*Cancellation:* Penang/13 MR/1911
*Back:* Divided
*Publisher:* A. Kaulfuss, Penang.

The "Scotch Church" was also known as St Andrew's Kirk or the Presbyterian Church of Scotland. It was in the vicinity of the junction of Northam Road and Larut Road. This ppc dates from c. 1910.

Penang. Burmah Road. Chinese Quarter

**[324]**
**Penang, Burmah Road Chinese Quarter**

*Cancellation:* Nil
*Back:* Undivided
*Publisher:* Not stated

An early view of Burmah Road, c. 1900. A group of Chinese labourers are on the left and, beyond them, a shoplot with two Chinese characters "gong yan" (meaning opium den). On the right Europeans pass on open horse-drawn carriages with Sikh attendants. Date: c. 1900.

No. 12 - Penang.
Burmah Road.

**[325]**
**No. 12 – Penang./Burmah Road**

*Cancellation:* Nil
*Back:* Divided
*Publisher:* T.C.B. Penang

Burmah Road, c. 1910. Burmah Road was
called "Jalan Kreta Ayer" (in Malay) and
"Chia Chooi Lor" (in Hokkien); both mean
"Water Cart Road". This was because prior
to the construction of the Municipal Water
Service, water sellers would come to a
well here to obtain water and transport it
in bullock carts for sale in the town.[136]

Penang. Burmah Road.

**[326]**
**Penang. Burmah Road.**

*Cancellation:* Nil
*Back:* Divided
*Publisher:* Co-operative Agency S.S./
No. 63.

Burmah Road in c. 1910. The man in the
foreground is peddling bottled drinks.
The road is lined with *angsana* trees.
Burmah Road was also described as a
"pretty avenue".[9]

373 - Chinese Recreation Club, Penang.

**[327]**

**373 – CHINESE RECREATION CLUB, PENANG.**

*Cancellation:* 1916
*Back:* Divided
*Publisher:* Federal Rubber Stamp Co.,
Penang, Kuala Lumpur
& Ipoh.

The "Eastbourne" bungalow was acquired as the premises of the Chinese Recreation Club (CRC) in 1901. The members of the CRC, who considered themselves the "Queen's Chinese", named the club grounds "Victoria Green" as a show of loyalty to Queen Victoria. In the 1920s, a new structure was built to replace the dilapidated "Eastbourne". It was a Victorian-style edifice. During the Japanese Occupation, the club house was used as a broadcasting station.[42] The serrated left border of this ppc indicates that it was detached from a ppc booklet.

Penang, No. 14—Burmese Buddhist Temple and Pagoda

**[328]**

**PENANG, No. 14—BURMESE BUDDHIST TEMPLE AND PAGODA**

*Cancellation:* PENANG/DE 7/1906
*Back:* Undivided
*Publisher:* British Empire Series/
"Sanbride"

A ppc of the Dhammikarama Burmese Temple, c. 1900. Widely believed to be founded in 1803, this temple is the oldest Theravada Buddhist temple in Penang.[139] Theravada Buddhism is the oldest surviving branch of Buddhism, and is mostly practised in Sri Lanka, Myanmar, Thailand, Laos and Cambodia. The oldest part of the temple is the stupa, consecrated in 1805. The temple stands opposite the Siamese Temple. Today, the temple is significantly larger than its original structure.

No. 31. Penang. Siamese Temple.

**[329]**

**No. 31. Penang. Siamese Temple.**

*Cancellation:* Nil
*Back:* Undivided
*Publisher:* Not stated

A ppc of the Siamese Wat Chaiyamangkalaram, c. 1900. It stands on a two-hectare site donated by Queen Victoria to the Thai and Burmese communities of Penang in 1845.[139] Today, the temple has been enlarged several times and houses a 33-metre statue of the reclining Buddha.

No. 10 - Penang.
Maclister Road

**[330]**

**No. 10 – Penang./Maclister Road**

*Cancellation:* PENANG/16 JY/1910
*Back:* Divided
*Publisher:* T.C.B. Penang

Macalister Road runs from Magazine Junction to Western Road (Jalan Utama). It is called "Tiong Lo" ("Middle Road"), meaning the middle road of the six roads meeting at Magazine Junction.[136] From the late 1800s to the present, it has been lined with *angsana* trees; each year in April, yellow flowers from these trees fall and carpet the road, creating a beautiful sight. Date: c. 1910.

Races, Penang

[331]
RACES, PENANG

*Cancellation:* Nil
*Back:* Divided
*Publisher:* Not stated

The racecourse and grandstand of the Penang Turf Club at Macalister Road, built in 1900. Date: c. 1910.

No. 1 - Penang    Grand Stand & Race Course

[332]
No. 1 – PENANG/GRAND STAND & RACE COURSE

*Cancellation:* PENANG/12 NO/1910
*Back:* Divided
*Publisher:* T.C.B. Penang

The grandstand and race grounds are packed with spectators on race day. The first president of the Penang Turf Club (PTC) was David Brown, a "well-known sportsman".[9] The PTC received generous assistance from the colonial government including a free grant of land for the racecourse. In 1869, gymkhanas began with prize money of "not more than $600 a year" rising to $5,950 by 1898.[9] As horse racing was encouraged during the Japanese Occupation, the PTC survived the war relatively unscathed.[86] Date: c. 1910.

Race course Road, Penang.

[333]
RACE COURSE ROAD, PENANG.

*Cancellation:* Nil
*Back:* Divided
*Publisher:* S.M. Manicum, Penang/No. 22

A view of the racecourse from the junction of Ayer Rajah Road (its signboard is above the stone gate post; centre of the right foreground), c. 1910.

[334]
RACECOURCE PENANG

*Cancellation:* Nil
*Back:* Divided
*Publisher:* Not stated

A sepia real photographic ppc of the racecourse, c. 1930. It shows the race course on the right from the junction of Ayer Rajah Road and Macalister Road. The sides of Macalister Road are lined with tall *angsana* trees. Although both locals and British enjoyed horse racing, locals were underrepresented and confined to the native stands. In 1927, prominent businessman Quah Beng Kee led the local cause for representation on the PTC Committee.

RACECOURCE PENANG

**[335]**

**No. 114 Golf Club. Penang.**

*Cancellation:* Nil
*Back:* Divided
*Publisher:* A. Kaulfuss, Penang.

A colour ppc of the Golf Club on the grounds of the PTC along Macalister Road. It relocated to Batu Gantang when the PTC moved there in 1939, and is today known as the PTC Golf Section. It started with nine holes and, in 1966, was expanded to 18 holes, of which seven were constructed within the racetrack. Date: c. 1910.

**[336]**

**Race Course/Road,/Penang.**

*Cancellation:* Nil
*Back:* Divided
*Publisher:* K.M. Mahmed Esoof, Penang.
          - No. 3056

This ppc shows the PTC on the left and, on the right, peddlars setting up their business (it could have been a race day). A 1900 publication records that the road was known in Chinese as "Toa Chai Hui", meaning "Big Vegetable Garden Road", a reference to many vegetable plantations there.[136] After Malaya achieved independence in 1957, the road was renamed Residency Road. Notably, a Residency Road already existed before 1957; the residence of the resident councillor of Penang was situated on it![9] Date: c. 1910.

A ROAD OF PALMS, PENANG

No. 178

**[337]**

**No. 178 A Road of Palms, Penang**

*Cancellation:* Nil
*Back:* Divided
*Publisher:* Not stated; printed in England

A row of royal palms (*Roystonea regia*), lends the road an air of grandeur. Peel Avenue (Lebuhraya Peel) has been lined with royal palms since they were planted in 1935.[82] Peel Avenue is named after William Peel, resident councillor of Penang (1925–1926). This sepia ppc dates from c. 1940.

PICCADILLY CIRCUS
PENANG

**[338]**

**Piccadilly Circus/Penang**

*Cancellation:* Nil
*Back:* Divided
*Publisher:* Not stated

The Piccadilly Circus was located where Peel Avenue, Macalister Road, Codrington Avenue and Residency Road converged. Adjacent to the circus was perhaps the most famous tree in Penang, the Baobab (*Adansonia digitata*) (not visible here), planted by Captain T.C.S. Speedy in 1871. The tree still lives, and is considered young, as the Baobab can live up to 2,000 years.[59] This ppc is dated c. 1930.

No. 20. A Rickshaw, Penang.

[339]
No. 20. A Rickshaw, Penang.

*Cancellation:* Nil
*Back:* Divided
*Publisher:* A. Kaulfuss, Penang

A c. 1910 ppc depicting a rickshaw puller and customers. The man on the right is a Jawi Peranakan. In 1908, there were about 5,000 public rickshaws in Penang.[9]

Malay Boys in Rickshaw, Penang.

[340]
Malay Boys in Rickshaw, Penang.

*Cancellation:* PENANG/1911
*Back:* Divided
*Publisher:* No. 35. A. Beach Street, Penang/No. 77

A posed photograph of Jawi Peranakan or Indian Muslim boys in and around a rickshaw. The message at the back of the ppc reads: "I have been riding all the afternoon in one of those little carts. It is very hot here." Date: c. 1910.

**[341]**
**Penang/Jin Rickshaw Department**

*Cancellation:* Nil
*Back:* Divided
*Publisher:* Not stated

Rows of rickshaws wait to be licensed by the Hackney Carriage Department (they had to be registered three times a year).[9] On the left are bullock carts also waiting to be registered. It was stated in a 1908 account that "for some reason or other there are no rubber-tyred rickshas plying for public hire, and the number of public gharries (58) is inadequate to meet the demand in wet weather."[9] Date: c. 1910.

Penang
Jin Rickshaw Department.

**[342]**
**Maxwell Road, Penang**

*Cancellation:* Nil
*Back:* Divided
*Publisher:* Not stated, printed in Germany

Two human-powered modes of transportation are showed in this ppc: the rickshaw on the right and, on its left, a man-pulled hand cart. Tram tracks are visible in the foreground. Date: c. 1910.

Maxwell Road, Penang

A Rice Load, Penang

Bullock Carts, Penang.

**[343]**

**A Rice Load, Penang**

*Cancellation:* Nil
*Back:* Divided
*Publisher:* Co-operative Agency S.S./
No. 4

Sacks of rice being carried on a bullock cart. While rickshaws were mostly associated with the Chinese in Penang, bullocks carts were linked with Indians. Bullock carts were also issued licences by the Hackney Carriage Department: "The Department charged with this duty issues licences also for horses and ponies, private carriages, private rickshas, motor-cars, bullock-carts, hand-carts, and public gharries."[9] This colour ppc is dated c. 1920.

**[344]**

**Bullock Carts, Penang.**

*Cancellation:* PENANG/1918
*Back:* Divided
*Publisher:* Not stated

The bullock cart was a sturdy mode of transport: two examples here are shown, transporting goods (*left*) and people (*right*). Date: c. 1910.

Tram Car, Penang

**[345]**
**TRAM CAR, PENANG**

*Cancellation:* Nil
*Back:* Divided
*Publisher:* M.J., Penang./184056

This c. 1910 colour ppc shows an electric tramcar at a tram stop at the Penang Road junction. The fire station tower at Penang Road is visible on the right. Electric trams began regular service on 1 January 1906. That year, they carried 1,457,357 passengers. The trams were operated by the George Town Municipal Council.[87]

No. 135 Penang Electric Trams.

**[346]**
**NO. 135 PENANG ELECTRIC TRAMS.**

*Cancellation:* PENANG/FE 19/1910
*Back:* Divided
*Publisher:* A. Kaulfuss, Penang.

Two trams are seen at the Magazine Road junction (an intersection of six roads, or "Simpang Enam" in Malay – Magazine Road, Gladstone Road, Penang Road, Macalister Road, Dato Kramat Road and Brick-kiln Road).[136] Date: 1910.

[347]

**SUPREME COURT/PENANG**

*Cancellation:* Penang/1924
*Back:* Divided
*Publisher:* Not stated

Penang's first municipal motorbus was introduced in 1921.[87] This motorbus displaying the sign "Special Direct to Races", is driving along Light Street towards Weld Quay. The Supreme Court is in the background.

The Monkys In Botanical Garden. Penang.

[348]

**THE MONKYS IN BOTANICAL GARDEN. PENANG.**

*Cancellation:* Nil
*Back:* Divided
*Publisher:* Not stated

A real photographic ppc showing Europeans and their attendants watching the monkeys at the Penang Botanic Gardens (*see Chapter 6*). In Malaya, the first motor car was imported by the philanthropist Loke Yew, in 1899. The rubber and tin boom helped spur the use of cars here in the early 1900s. This ppc is dated c. 1930.

**[349]**

Eɴᴛʀᴀɴᴄᴇ. P.H.R.

*Cancellation:* Nil
*Back:* Divided
*Publisher:* Not stated

Many cars can be seen parked outside the Penang Hill Railway (PHR). A 1908 account described the driving experience in Malaya as follows: "Malaya is a delectable land to the automobilist, for the roads are excellent, there is no speed limit, and there are no import duties on cars...It has now become the fashion for wealthy Chinese to own at least one car, with the result that the largest and most expensive cars on the road belong, as a rule, to Chinamen."[9] This ppc is dated c. 1930.

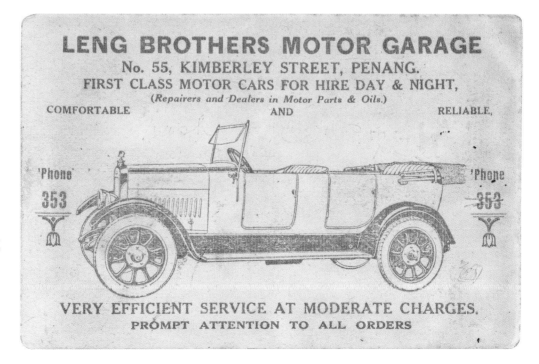

LENG BROTHERS MOTOR GARAGE
No. 55, KIMBERLEY STREET, PENANG.
FIRST CLASS MOTOR CARS FOR HIRE DAY & NIGHT,
(Repairers and Dealers in Motor Parts & Oils.)
COMFORTABLE        AND        RELIABLE,
'Phone 353        'Phone 353
VERY EFFICIENT SERVICE AT MODERATE CHARGES.
PROMPT ATTENTION TO ALL ORDERS

**[350]**

Lᴇɴɢ Bʀᴏᴛʜᴇʀs Mᴏᴛᴏʀ Gᴀʀᴀɢᴇ

*Cancellation:* Nil
*Back:* Advertising charges for the hire of "Automobile Drives"
*Publisher:* G.H. Kiat & Co. Ltd, Penang.

An early motor garage advertisement ppc, c. 1930. Leng Brothers Motor Garage, was located at Kimberley Street in Penang, and provided "first class motor cars" for hire. One of the pioneers to set up a motor garage and import cars to Penang was Cheah Leong Keah J.P. (1875–1941), an entrepreneur and property owner.[88] His company, Chin Seng & Co, was the first importer of motor cars in Penang.

Ayer Itam Temple,
Penang

# BEYOND GEORGE TOWN

## Penang Botanic Gardens

The Penang Botanic Gardens (PBG) are a public park on Waterfall Road (known today as Jalan Air Terjun) located about eight kilometres from George Town. They are also known as the Waterfall Gardens because of the cascading waterfall at the back of the gardens.

### History

Earlier botanic gardens had been established in Penang prior to the present gardens.[89,90] The establishment of Penang as a British East India Company (EIC) settlement in 1786 was an opportunity for the British to challenge the Dutch spice trade and maritime supremacy in the region.

The EIC recruited Irish botanist Christopher Smith in 1794 to explore and establish a spice garden in Penang. Although the exact location of the garden in unclear, he is recorded to have created a smaller garden of 10.5 hectares in Ayer Itam, and a larger one of 158 hectares at Sungei Keluang.[130] Smith collected and planted nutmeg, clove, pepper, canary nuts and sugar palms,[130] but died unexpectedly in 1805. The Lieutenant Governor of Penang, Colonel Robert Townsend Farquhar then sold the Spice Gardens and all their contents for $9,656.[130]

The second botanic gardens, nicknamed the "Kitchen Gardens" were established in 1822 by Governor William Edward Phillips (1819–1824). These gardens were also sited in Ayer Itam. In 1834, the Kitchen Gardens were sold by Governor Kenneth Murchison (1833–1836), who alleged that the gardens were not producing enough vegetables to supply the Residency kitchens.

The present PBG are the third botanic gardens, sited in the Waterfall River Valley.[130] In 1884, Nathaniel Cantley, superintendent of the Singapore Botanic Gardens, established the present PBG and appointed Charles Curtis as the assistant superintendent of gardens and forests of Penang district.[130] Curtis was largely responsible for the forest reserves, including those of the Waterfall Gardens, as well as the design and development of the gardens.

### The Penang Botanic Gardens, 1900-1940

The entrance to the PBG are shown in [351] to [354]. All three ppcs depict a large rain tree (*Pukul lima* or *Samanea saman*). This rain tree was planted in 1887 to commemorate the golden jubilee of Queen Victoria; it is still standing.[59]

Two of the earliest ppcs of the PBG (c. 1900) are shown in [355] and [356]. A large number of trees, palms, shrubs and flowers [357-362] were collected and planted in the PBG. They still maintain their plant houses such as the Orchidarium, Cactus House, Bromeliad and Begonia House [359-361]. The roads around the gardens are shaded by tall and flowering trees [362-364]; and a small stream meanders through the gardens [365-366].

Numerous monkeys used to inhabit and roam freely around the gardens. The most common monkeys were the rhesus monkey, long-tailed macaque and dusty leaf monkey [367-368].

The waterfall [369-370; 372] was once a popular tourist spot in Penang. Early visitors to Penang, such as Ibrahim Munshi (son of writer Abdullah Munshi), made the compulsory visit to the "Waterfall Garden".[82] The Waterfall Reservoir (*below right*; [371; 373-374]) was completed in 1894 by British engineer James MacRitchie who also built the MacRitchie Reservoir in Singapore.[89]

In 1910, there was a proposal to turn the Waterfall River Valley into a reservoir. This plan was, however, abandoned in 1912 and only a small reservoir was built at

A real photographic ppc cum Christmas card in sepia with colour tinting of Guillemard Reservoir at Batu Ferringhi, c. 1948.

An early ppc of the Waterfall Reservoir, c. 1900.

*Opposite*:
The Kek Lok Si temple complex, c. 1910. Its upper tier is shown; in the foreground is the pavilion.

A real photographic ppc of Bel Retiro, c. 1948.

A cigarette card showing the Moon Gate near the Waterfall Gardens, c. 1920. A footpath leads from the gate to Penang Hill.

the foot of the waterfall. By the 1920s, the management of the gardens was placed under the Gardens Department.[90] After World War II, the PBG were gradually restored to their original splendour and Cheang Kok Choy was appointed the first Malayan curator of the gardens in 1956. He retired in 1976.[90]

## Penang Hill

Penang Hill (PH) consists of a group of hills including Flagstaff Hill, Fern Hill, Haliburton's Hill, Strawberry Hill, Western Hill, and Tiger Hill.[91,92] It is located in Air Itam, which is six kilometres from George Town. It is the oldest hill station in Malaysia, and traces its founding to Francis Light who plotted a horse track up the hill in 1788.

The Malay name for PH is "Bukit Bendera" ("Flagstaff Hill") in reference to the flagstaff outside "Bel Retiro", which was the official residence of the governor (*top left*; [375-377]).

Bel Retiro was built for the governor of Penang c. 1789; the building shown in [375] was built much later. The cannon [376] weighs 2.75 tonnes and was cast in the 18th century.

### The Road Up the Hill

Before the funicular railway was completed in 1924, the only way up the hill was by foot, horseback, or dooly (sedan chair). The journey began at the entrance of the Botanic Gardens [378-379] or at the Moon Gate (a short distance from the entrance to the PBG; *below left*).

The road from the PBG to the top of the hill is about six kilometres, and the journey by foot takes about two hours. The wealthy often preferred to travel up the hill by dooly [378-380].

### The Funicular Railway

The Penang Hill Funicular Railway (PHFR) was officially opened on 1 January 1924. An earlier attempt to build

one in 1906 failed and the two carriages of the Penang Hills Railway Co. Ltd were abandoned [383]. The PHFR of 1924 was designed by Arnold R. Johnson, an engineer with the FMS Railways, and based on a Swiss design. It was inaugurated on 21 October 1923 by Sir Laurence Guillemard, governor of the SS. The trains carried 35,201 passengers and made 4,021 trips that year.[87]

The PHFR ([384-388]; *see Chapter 5*, [349]) was built in two sections with an interchange at the Middle Station. The 2,007-metre journey took about 30 minutes, and the train would stop at intermediate stations upon request.[91]

The PHFR was closed for renovation and upgrading in March 2010. The upgraded funicular train service reopened the following year. Today, the trip up the hill takes just five minutes in new air-conditioned coaches that can accommodate 100 passengers each! The trains travel from the station at the foot of the hill to the station at the top directly and with no stops in between.

## Life at the Summit

A bird's eye view of George Town [389-390] depicts stunning day and evening views.

In 1890, Scotsman Captain J. Kerr built a bungalow on a commanding hill shoulder; this was taken over by the Sarkies Brothers in 1895 who renamed it the Crag Hotel [392-396]. In 1925, the hotel was completely rebuilt, comprising a village of bungalows grouped around a central building. During its heyday, the Crag Hotel was *the* place to stay on the hill.[42]

The Crag Hotel ceased operations during the Japanese Occupation. After the war, it remained closed till 1955 when it was occupied by the Uplands School. When the school vacated it in 1977, the former hotel was left neglected. In 2011, it was announced that the Crag Hotel would be refurbished and reopened.

There is a police station [397] and a post office [398] at the summit of PH; the post office was opened in 1894.[51] Near the police station and post office are a garden and tea kiosk *(top right)* sited on Strawberry Hill.

Between 1920 and 1940, many of the rich and famous built holiday villas and bungalows on PH, such as "The Great Wall" *(below right)*, built by tycoon and Municipal Commissioner, Khoo Sian Ewe.

## Kek Lok Si Temple at Air Itam

Air Itam or Ayer Itam [399-401] ("Black Water" in Malay) incorporates a wide area that includes Farlim, Thean Teik Estate, Hill Railway Road and Rifle Range.[98]

Ayer Itam's most recognisable landmark is the Kek Lok Si temple (KLS) [402-412]. Also known as the Temple of Supreme Bliss, it is the largest Buddhist temple in Malaysia. The founder of the KLS was Abbot Beow Lean (1844–1907)[23] from the Kushan Abbey in Fujian, China,[99] who was invited to be the chief monk of the Guanyin Temple on Pitt Street in 1887. In 1891, he and other representatives of the Kushan Abbey began to collect funds for the construction of the KLS. The original temple was built over a period of 15 years on a 12.1-hectare site donated by a Yeoh Siew Beow in 1893.[23]

The KLS received the sanction of the Chinese Emperor, Guangxu (r. 1875–1908), who bestowed to the KLS a royal tablet and 70,000 volumes of the Imperial Edition of the Buddhist Sutras.[98]

The KLS [403-406], sited at the foot of the Penang hills, consists of many prayer halls, pavilions, carved pillars, tortoise and fish ponds, and flower gardens linked by winding and ascending pathways. In 2002, a 30.2-metre bronze statue of the Goddess of Mercy, Guanyin was built.

The crowning glory of the KLS is its majestic pagoda [407-412]. It is named the Pagoda of Rama VI as the foundation-laying ceremony of the pagoda was performed by Siamese King Chulalongkorn (King Rama VI) when he visited Penang in 1915.[100,139]

## Snake Temple

The Snake Temple [413-414] or Temple of the Azure Clouds ("Ban Kah Lan" in Hokkien) is a small temple in Sungai Keluang. On the altar of this temple are a variety of pit vipers; perhaps the only such temple in the world!

The temple was built in 1850, and dedicated to a Song dynasty Buddhist monk, Chor Soo Kong. He was also a healer and was known to give shelter to snakes.[102]

The land on which this temple is sited was donated by the planter David Brown, who was Penang's largest landowner at that time, when he was healed of a mysterious illness.

## Province Wellesley

Province Wellesley (PW), also known as Prai or Prye, is today officially called Seberang Perai. It is a strip of land on the Malay Peninsula opposite Penang Island.

Province Wellesley was named after Richard Wellesley, the Marquess of Wellesley, governor of Madras and governor-general of India (1795–1805).[103] Its principal town is Butterworth, named after William John Butterworth, governor of the SS (1843–1855).[104]

The residents of Penang commonly refer to PW as the "mainland". Penang Island and the mainland are linked by the 13.5-kilometre Penang Bridge. In 1903, the railway at PW was connected to Kuala Lumpur and Seremban. The railway station at PW and train, c. 1910, are shown in [415] to [417].

The Prye River, c. 1910 is shown in [418]; the Prye Harbour and the Butterworth Pier are shown in [419] and [420] respectively. The Prai Dock is shown in [421], while the Butterworth Smelters, built in 1902 by the Straits Trading Co. Ltd, is shown in [422].[105]

The main road in Butterworth, Jalan Bagan Luar, is shown in [423]; while the interior of a church in Machang Bubok is depicted in [424]. The beach at Butterworth and a coconut factory are shown in [425] and [426].

Strawberry Hill, c. 1930. A children's playground is visible on the right; adjacent to it is a tea kiosk. The tea kiosk is now the David Brown's Restaurant.

A beautifully tinted real photographic ppc of Khoo Sian Ewe's villa "The Great Wall", c. 1940.

205

No. 117    Entrance to Bot. Gardens.

[351]
117 ENTRANCE TO BOT. GARDENS

*Cancellation:*  Nil
*Back:*  Divided
*Publisher:*  A. Kaulfuss, Penang.

The large tree in the centre is the rain tree (*Samanea saman*) planted in 1887 to commemorate the Golden Jubilee of Queen Victoria in June 1887.[59] This colour ppc is dated c. 1910.

Entrance to Botanical Gardens, Penang.

[352]
ENTRANCE TO BOTANICAL GARDENS, PENANG.

*Cancellation:*  Nil
*Back:*  Divided
*Publisher:*  K.M. Mahmed Esoof, Penang.
           No. 3043

A colour ppc, c. 1910 depicting the entrance to the PBG; the large rain tree is on the right.

[353]

**BOTANICAL GARDEN. PENANG**

*Cancellation:* Nil
*Back:* Divided
*Publisher:* Not stated

A real photographic ppc of the PBG; the large rain tree dominates the ppc. This tree was about 43 years old in this ppc, and still stands till today (about 115 years old). Charles Curtis, assistant superintendent of forests in the SS, planted 20 rain trees along the sides of the entrance road to the Gardens on Jubilee Day (Golden Jubilee of Queen Victoria) in 1887. Date: c. 1930.

Botanical Garden Penang

[354]

**ENTRANCE TO THE BOTANICAL GARDEN, PENANG.**

*Cancellation:* Nil
*Back:* Divided
*Publisher:* No. 35. A. Beach Street, Penang

The entrance to the PBG, c. 1910; luscious bamboo and shrubs line the road.

Entrance to the Botanical Garden, Penang.

Penang. Cacteen group.

[355]

PENANG, CACTEEN GROUP.

*Cancellation:* PENANG/23 DE/1901
*Back:* Undivided
*Publisher:* A. Kaulfuss, Penang. No. 17

This ppc, c. 1900, shows a group of cacti belonging to the *Cactaceae* family from the Americas on a rocky terrain. The PBG have a Cactus House, as part of their plant houses and open collections.

Penang. In the gardens.

[356]

PENANG. IN THE GARDENS.

*Cancellation:* PENANG/MR 23/1903
*Back:* Undivided
*Publisher:* Not stated

The PBG in c. 1900. These botanic gardens, the third to be established in Penang, were founded in 1884 with Charles Curtis appointed assistant superintendent of forests, SS. He immediately set out to develop a plant nursery and undertook a visionary programme to create a "pleasurable recreational and botanical gardens in the Valley (Waterfall River Valley)".[138]

No. 37. Traveller-Palm. Penang.

**[357]**

No. 37. TRAVELLER-PALM. PENANG.

*Cancellation:* PENANG/DE 15/1906
*Back:* Divided
*Publisher:* A. Kaulfuss, Penang/
Printed in Germany

The traveller's palm (*Ravenala madagascariensis*) is not, in fact, a palm but a member of the banana family; it originates from Madagascar. Several specimens are planted in the PBG. Assistant Superintendent Charles Curtis erected a new palm cultivation shed in the nursery, measuring 36.6 by 6 metres, of "hardwood scantling 5'6" [1.7 metres] in diameter" and "green-painted Bertam chicks to the roof".[138] Date: c. 1905.

**[358]**

BOTANICAL GARDENS, PENANG.

*Cancellation:* Alor Setar/1922
*Back:* Divided
*Publisher:* The Continental Stamp
Company Singapore
No. 100 2

A colour ppc dated c. 1920 depicting tall and slender *pinang* or betel palms (*Areca catechu*), the palm that lent its name to the island of Penang.

BOTANICAL GARDEN, PENANG

**[359]**

**BOTANICAL GARDEN, PENANG**

*Cancellation:* Not clear
*Back:* Divided
*Publisher:* S.M. Manicum, Penang/No. 5

The plant houses in the PBG, c. 1920. The PBG have several plant houses; this is a large one and it could be the Bromeliad and Begonia House. It is set amidst lush greenery at the foot of a hill. Charles Curtis erected the first plant shed in the PBG in 1887. The "show-house structure" was filled with ferns growing from a centre-piece rock-work feature.[138] Curtis was a keen plant collector, and under his supervision and management, the PBG became a major centre of plant and seed propagation and distribution; from this began the herbarium collection. By 1890, this collection comprised over 3,000 specimens.[138]

No. 122 Orchid House, Bot. Gardens.

**[360]**

**No. 122 ORCHID HOUSE, BOT. GARDENS.**

*Cancellation:* Nil
*Back:* Divided
*Publisher:* A. Kaulfuss, Penang./
          Printed in Germany

The PBG's Orchidarium with many beautiful blooming orchids. A shed for orchid cultivation, measuring 14 by 6 metres, was built in 1887. In 1889, Charles Curtis supervised the construction of a new orchid cultivation plant house, measuring 30 by 5.4 metres, and roofed with Bertam chicks.[138] Date: c. 1910.

**[361]**

**A 50 – PALM HOUSE/TRAVELLER PALM/ ORCHID HOUSE/PENANG.**

*Cancellation:* Nil
*Back:* Divided
*Publisher:* Nikko Studio, Penang, S.S./
Printed in Saxony

This ppc shows plants and plant houses at the PBG: the Palm House; traveller's palm and Orchid House. Typical of ppcs produced by Nikko Studio, this ppc has beautiful and subtle colours. The vignettes show decorative palm leaves and lanterns. Date: c. 1910.

**[362]**

**A 35 – BOTANICAL GARDEN/PENANG**

*Cancellation:* Penang/Date not clear
*Back:* Divided
*Publisher:* Nikko Studio, Penang, S.S./
Printed in Saxony.

A biview colour ppc, c. 1910, showing the bridge across a stream near the entrance (*right*) and the undulating valley between the Upper Circular Road (*left*). The bridge was a "substantial granite arch that is in keeping with the surroundings and will last for ever".[138] This is a scarce ppc produced by Nikko Studio.

Entrance to the Botanical Gardens, Penang.

**[363]**
**ENTRANCE TO THE BOTANICAL GARDENS, PENANG.**

*Cancellation:* Nil
*Back:* Divided
*Publisher:* Not stated; printed in Germany

The entrance to the Botanic Gardens is shown in this c. 1910 colour ppc. The Circular Road crosses the stream, and on both sides of the road are trees and shrubs. A house is visible on top of the hill; this is likely to be the house of the curator of the PBG. In 1887, Charles Curtis arranged for the hill site to be cleared for an access track and levelled the site for his quarters. The house, built in late 1887, was surrounded by an extensive designed and planted garden. Both office and house, with furniture included, cost $4,171.75. Curtis occupied the bungalow on 1 February 1888.[138]

No. 3 - Penang.
Entrance to the Botanical Garden

**[364]**
**No. 3 - PENANG./ENTRANCE TO THE BOTANICAL GARDEN**

*Cancellation:* PENANG/1911
*Back:* Divided
*Publisher:* T.C.B., Penang

The tall flowering tree in the foreground is an *angsana* tree and next to it in the foreground are *Pandanus* (*mengkuang*) plants. This ppc of the Botanic Garden's entrance is dated c. 1910.

No. 21.  Botanical Gardens, Penang

**[365]**
**No. 21. Botanical Gardens, Penang.**

*Cancellation:*  Nil
*Back:*  Divided
*Publisher:*  A. Kaulfuss, Penang./
                Printed in Germany

A small waterfall breaks the gentle stream running through the valley of the Botanic Gardens. This ppc is dated c. 1910.

BOTANICAL GARDENS
PENANG

**[366]**
**Botanical Gardens/Penang**

*Cancellation:*  Nil
*Back:*  Divided
*Publisher:*  Not stated

A real photographic ppc, c. 1930, showing the waterfall, stream and bridge. Between 1886 and 1887, three small footbridges were built over the Waterfall River. One of the footbridges was rebuilt in 1889 at a cost of only $97.31.[138]

[367]

MONKEYS/BOTANICAL GARDENS/PENANG

*Cancellation:* Nil
*Back:* Divided
*Publisher:* Not stated

This c. 1930 real photographic ppc shows a European woman feeding monkeys in the PBG. The PBG were nicknamed the Monkey Garden because of their large monkey population.

No. 213          MONKEYS BOTANICAL GARDENS, PENANG

[368]

No. 213 MONKEYS BOTANICAL GARDENS, PENANG

*Cancellation:* PENANG/1938
*Back:* Divided
*Publisher:* Not stated; printed in England

Visitors are shown admiring the monkeys in the PBG, c. 1930. This ppc was sent to America; on the back, the message reads: "The monkeys made funny noises and chattered a lot..."

Penang  Waterfall.

A 1 - Waterfall in Botanical Garden, Penang.

[369]

PENANG WATERFALL.

*Cancellation:* Singapore/AP 22/1903
*Back:* Undivided
*Publisher:* Not stated

The waterfall at the back of the PBG, c. 1900. At the foot of the waterfall is an Indian shrine (*left*). Most of the workers in the PBG then were Indians. They were housed in a small attap building at the Chetty Temple Nursery adjacent to the Nattukkotai Chettiar Temple on Waterfall Road.[138]

[370]

A 1 – WATERFALL IN BOTANICAL GARDEN, PENANG.

*Cancellation:* Penang/25 OC/1913
*Back:* Divided
*Publisher:* Nikko Studio, Penang, S.S./Printed in Saxony.

Another depiction of the waterfall at the back of the PBG. This ppc is dated c. 1910, and uses beautiful, subtle colours. The stamp on this ppc was cancelled in the Eastern and Oriental Hotel on 25 October 1913.

The Waterfall, Penang

**[371]**
UNTITLED [WATERFALL GARDENS RESERVOIR]

*Cancellation*: PENANG/1962
*Back*: Divided
*Publisher*: P.M.S.M.N., Penang/
           Printed in U.S.A.

A panoramic view of the Waterfall
Gardens Reservoir, c. 1960. Completed in
1894, the reservoir was reconstructed in
1950 and is still in use today. This ppc is
about twice the width of a normal ppc,
measuring 21 by 9 centimetres.

**[372]**
THE WATERFALL, PENANG

*Cancellation*: Nil
*Back*: Divided
*Publisher*: Not stated

In the early 19th century, the waterfall
was an important source of water for
ships calling at Penang Harbour.[89]
For visitors calling at Penang for just a
few hours, the Waterfall Gardens formed
the island's "principal attraction".[9]
Date: c. 1910.

**[373]**

Nr. 41. Reservoir, Penang.

*Cancellation:* Nil
*Back:* Divided
*Publisher:* (Sold by) S.K. Md. Yusoff
& Co.

A real photographic ppc of the Waterfall Reservoir, c. 1910. When a proposal to build this reservoir was made in 1889, Charles Curtis opposed it, stating that the reservoir would affect the appearance of the botanic gardens.[158] Although the idea of a major reservoir was abandoned, a smaller one went ahead. Following construction of the reservoir, a water main to George Town was built, and about 182 metres of new carriage road built to reposition the Upper Circular Road. In its early days, the reservoir was open to visitors. Today, it is a restricted area, and not open to the public.

Nr. 41. Reservoir, Penang.

**[374]**

No. 110 Reservoir of Penang
Water Supply.

*Cancellation:* Singapore/1911
*Back:* Divided
*Publisher:* A. Kaulfuss, Penang./
Printed in Germany

The Waterfall Reservoir, shown here c. 1910, was built to supply George Town with water.[9] Today only 10 to 15 percent of Penang's water supply comes from this reservoir; most of the island's water now comes from Sungai Muda on the border of Province Wellesley and Kedah.[89]

No. 110 Reservoir of Penang Water Supply.

THE FLAGSTAFF GOVERNMENT HILL.

PRITCHARD & CO., PENANG. No. 30.

PENANG

**[375]**

**PENANG/THE FLAGSTAFF GOVERNMENT HILL.**

*Cancellation:* PENANG/AU 6/1907
*Back:* Undivided
*Publisher:* Pritchard & Co., Penang.
No. 30.

A c. 1900 colour ppc of "Bel Retiro", the governor's residence on Penang Hill. This two-storey stone mansion replaced an earlier wooden residence built in c. 1789. While Bel Retiro was a holiday seat for the governor in colonial days, it is today a retreat for the Yang di-Pertua Negeri of Penang and visiting dignitaries. Since Malaya's Independence in 1957, Bel Retiro has hosted important figures such as Malaysia's first Prime Minister, Tunku Abdul Rahman, the first Yang di-Pertuan Agong, Tuanku Abdul Rahman and, in 1972, Britain's Queen Elizabeth.

Penang. Government Hill.

**[376]**

**PENANG. GOVERNMENT HILL.**

*Cancellation:* Penang/FE 14/1908
*Back:* Undivided
*Publisher:* Not stated

A real photographic ppc showing the governor's house or Bel Retiro in the background, and the flagstaff (*centre*) outside. The bronze cannon on the lefthand side of the foreground weighs 2.75 tonnes, and was a powerful symbol of British supremacy in colonial days. Date: c. 1900.

[377]
FLAG STAFF–GOVT. HILL, PENANG

*Cancellation:* Nil
*Back:* Divided
*Publisher:* Co-operative Agency, S.S./No. 22

A close-up view of the flagstaff on Government Hill, outside Bel Retiro, the official residence of the governor. The hill on which the flagstaff is sited is also called "Flagstaff Hill" or "Bukit Bendera", and is 747 metres above sea level.[91] This colour ppc is dated c. 1910.

[378]
No. 29. ROAD TO THE HILLS, PENANG

*Cancellation:* Nil
*Back:* Divided
*Publisher:* A. Kaulfuss, Penang.

A c. 1910 biview colour ppc showing the start of the journey up Penang Hill from the Botanic Gardens (*above*); workers bearing a dooly (sedan chair) get ready to carry some European children. The lower view shows a European being similarly carried while a lady is making the journey on foot.

Penang

Weg zu den Hôtels.    Personenbeförderung.

935. Chair Coolies going up Penang Hill

**[379]**
PENANG/WEG ZU DEN HÔTELS.
PERSONENBEFÖRDERUNG.

*Cancellation:* SINGAPORE/AP 22/1903
*Back:* Undivided
*Publisher:* Not stated

The German caption means "Towards the
Hotels/Passenger". Four Tamil workers
bear a European man on a dooly (sedan
or rattan chair suspended from bamboo
poles) outside the botanic gardens, as
they get ready to ascend the hill. Besides
the dooly, several rickshaws are parked
outside the botanic gardens; a horse (*left*)
waits in the background. The trip by
dooly was described in 1908 as follows:
"The journey is usually made in chairs
suspended from bamboo poles, borne on
the shoulders of Tamil coolies".[9] Today,
there is a jeep track up the hill, allowing
jeeps and motorcycles to go up the hill.[91]
This sepia ppc is dated c. 1900.

**[380]**
935. CHAIR COOLIES GOING UP PENANG HILL.

*Cancellation:* Nil
*Back:* Divided
*Publisher:* Houghton Butcher (Eastern)
Ltd., Robinson Road,
Singapore

A clearer view of the "chair coolies" and
their passenger. These dooly bearers did
not just transport people, but also things,
noted a young English bride, Joanna
Smith, who spent her honeymoon on
the Penang Hill in 1866. Smith and her
husband, a Dr King, rode up the hill on
ponies. The journey from the Botanic
Gardens to Fern Hill took an hour.
Dr King even had a piano transported
up the hill for his young bride![93] This
real photographic ppc was published
by Houghton Butcher (Eastern) Ltd for
the Malayan Government, and sold at
the Malayan Pavilion during the British
Empire Exhibition, at Wembley, Britain,
in 1924.

**[381]**
**GOV. HILL/PENANG/17B**

*Cancellation:* Unclear
*Back:* Divided
*Publisher:* H. Bodom, Penang.

A real photographic ppc, c. 1900, showing a European man with hat and a walking cane, resting on a rock. The message on the back of the ppc reads: "...This was one of our walks on the Hill. We had to be carried in chairs by coolies up there. It was so cool..."

**[382]**
**P.H.C.L. MORNING RAMBLERS AT HALFWAY HOUSE (GOVERNMENT HILL) 22.2.14. T.J.BENG/NO. 1.**

*Cancellation:* Nil
*Back:* Divided
*Publisher:* Photograph taken by T.J. Beng

A unique real photographic ppc taken by a T.J. Beng in 1914. The locals pose by the signboard "To Moniot Road". Ramblers are those who hike or walk for pleasure or health. Moniot Road is one of a series of roads on Penang Hill. It is named after Jules Moniot, surveyor-general of the SS from 1855 to 1862.

Penang Hills Railway, Penang, Straits Settlements.

PENANC HILLS RAILWAY Cº Lᵀᴰ No 2

TANG HILLS RAILWAY Cº Lᵀᴰ Nº I

222

**[383]**
**PENANG HILLS RAILWAY, PENANG,
STRAITS SETTLEMENTS.**

*Cancellation:* Nil
*Back:* Divided
*Publisher:* 170 Federal Rubber Stamp Co.,
Kuala Lumpur.

An early attempt to operate the funicular
railway on Penang Hill in 1906 failed;
two of the carriages of the Penang Hills
Railway Co. Ltd (Nos. 1 and 2 shown
here) were abandoned and ended up as
chicken coops! Construction on a new
and revamped line began in 1920 and
was opened to passenger traffic on 21
October 1923.[87]

Penang Hill Railway

**[384]**
**PENANG HILL RAILWAY**

*Cancellation:* Nil
*Back:* Divided
*Publisher:* Not stated

A real photographic ppc of the funicular
railway carriages ascending the viaduct
near the station at the foot of the hill.
Note the Ayer Itam Reservoir in the
background (*right*). Date: c. 1930.

**[385]**

COPYRIGHT PHOTO No. 5/PENANG HILL RAILWAY. FROM FOOT OF THE HILL

*Cancellation:* Nil
*Back:* Divided
*Publisher:* Not stated

A sepia real photographic ppc showing the Lower Station and behind it, trains ascending to the Middle Station. Another view of the Lower Station is shown in Chapter 5 [349]. The Penang Hill Railway was built in two sections, with an interchange at the Middle Station. Passengers had to board a train at the Lower Station, change trains at the Middle Station, and get off at the Upper Station. Today, there is no more Middle Station, and passengers are provided the luxury of travelling in air-conditioned coaches that can accommodate 100 passengers each. Date: c. 1930.

PENANG HILL RAILWAY, FROM FOOT OF THE HILL

**[386]**

COPYRIGHT PHOTO No. 3/TOP STATION, PENANG HILL RAILWAY

*Cancellation:* Nil
*Back:* Divided
*Publisher:* Penang Photo Store, Penang/ Printed in England

This sepia real photographic ppc, c. 1930, shows the topmost station, the Upper Station. A stationery carriage is visible behind the station (*centre*). The funicular railway system provides easy access to Penang Hill and is a boost to tourism. An advertisement in 1938 read: "Penang Hill Railway. Pleasurable Journey. Perfect Safety. Hill Holiday. Healthful Recreations. Harmonious Surrounds"; and "Railway rates are low. Record of Efficiency High. Reliable in all Respects."[93]

TOP STATION, PENANG HILL RAILWAY

[387]
PENANG HILL/RAILWAY

*Cancellation:* Nil
*Back:* Divided
*Publisher:* Not stated

The steep climb from the Lower to the Middle Station, c. 1930. The "passing place" is in the middle. In order to allow the coaches to pass one another, the wheels on only one side of the coaches were grooved to enable each car to be guided to follow the correct track at the passing loop.[87]

[388]
PENANG HILL

*Cancellation:* Ipoh/date not clear
*Back:* Divided
*Publisher:* Not stated

This ppc, c. 1930, shows the crossing where the upgoing train bypasses the descending train in the distance. The granite steps on the left enabled workmen to do repairs. It is common to sight monkeys and other fauna, besides plants such as pitcher plants (*Nepenthes ampullaria*), near the track.

[389]

**No. 156 Bird's Eye View
of George Town, Penang**

*Cancellation:* Nil
*Back:* Divided
*Publisher:* Not stated; printed in England

A bird's eye view of George Town from Penang Hill, about 883 metres above sea level. A panoramic view of George Town is visible on a cloudless day. Kedah Peak is in the background across the South Channel of the Straits of Malacca.
Date: c. 1940.

[390]

**No. 98 Sunrise in Penang.**

*Cancellation:* PENANG/OC 6/1910
*Back:* Divided
*Publisher:* A. Kaulfuss, Penang./
Printed in Germany

The Kedah Peak can be seen clearly in the background. Even today, the allure of Penang Hill is its view, the cool climate, flora and fauna, the walking trails, charming colonial buildings, and its easy accessibility from George Town.
Date: c. 1910.

**[391]**
**GOVERNMENT HILL, PENANG**

*Cancellation:* Nil
*Back:* Divided
*Publisher:* Not stated

Government Hill, rises to about 747 metres above sea level. The summit of the hill is occupied by "Bel Retiro", the governor's residence. It is surrounded by thick forest vegetation. Date: c. 1910.

**[392]**
**NO. 113 THE CRAG HOTEL.**

*Cancellation:* Nil
*Back:* Divided
*Publisher:* A. Kaulfuss, Penang./
Printed in Germany

The Crag Hotel, built in 1890 and originally the home of a Captain Kerr, was acquired by the Sarkies Brothers in 1895 and transformed into the Crag Hotel. In 1908, it consisted of detached bungalows for families and a bachelor's establishment.[9] Date: c. 1910.

No. 22.  Crag Hotel Hill, Penang

**[393]**
**No. 22. Crag Hotel Hill, Penang**

*Cancellation:*  Nil
*Back:*  Divided
*Publisher:*  A. Kaulfuss, Penang./
                    Printed in Germany

This ppc dated c. 1910 shows the tranquil
environment of the Penang hilltop:
two European men are seated on long
benches amid the cool atmosphere of
Penang Hill. In the background (*right*)
is the hotel. In 1925, Crag Hotel was
rebuilt and expanded into a village of
bungalows.[42] An advertisement in 1936
read: "The Crag Hotel. Situated 2,000 feet
above the sea level on Penang Hill – The
Crag is an ideal spot for recuperation,
holiday making or for only a day's stay
or just a meal. The food is frequently
referred to as being as good as any served
in Malaya."[97]

No. 50.  Crag Hotel,
Bybungalows and Walks

**[394]**
**No. 50. Crag Hotel,/Bybungalows
and Walks**

*Cancellation:*  Penang/JA 10/1910
*Back:*  Divided
*Publisher:*  A. Kaulfuss, Penang

This colour ppc, dated c. 1910, shows
the shady pathway leading to the hotel.
The message at the back reads: "The
3 bungalows are Victoria, Alexandra &
Diamond Jubilee…"

[395]

3111 ENTRANCE OF CRAG HOTEL, PENANG HILL.

*Cancellation:* Nil
*Back:* Divided
*Publisher:* Not stated

The entrance to the Crag Hotel. Doolies to transport visitors are visible in the foreground. Each doolie was borne by four Tamil porters. They were paid 46¢ per person for each trip from the foot of the hill to the hotel. Date: c. 1930.

228

[396]

No. 149 CRAG HOTEL, PENANG HILL, PENANG

*Cancellation:* Nil
*Back:* Divided
*Publisher:* Not stated; printed in England

A real photographic ppc of the main building, c. 1930. It enjoyed its best years from 1895 to 1941. From 1955 to 1977, it was occupied by the Uplands School. While it lies in a state of neglect today, it was announced in 2011 that the former hotel would be revived.

**[397]**

**No. 154 PENANG HILL, PENANG**

*Cancellation:* Singapore/14 FE/1934
*Back:* Divided
*Publisher:* Not stated; printed in England

A real photographic ppc of the two-storey police station; its sign is visible above its entrance. Adjacent to it is a children's playground. Date: c. 1930.

**[398]**

**COPYRIGHT PHOTO No. 7/POST OFFICE, PENANG HILL**

*Cancellation:* Penang/1932
*Back:* Divided
*Publisher:* Penang Photo Store,
            49 Leith Street, Penang/
            Printed in England

A real photographic ppc of the post office on Penang Hill, c. 1930. The post office here was first established in 1894;[51] a ppc posted in 1894 was cancelled with the cancellation "Government Hill". After 1896, "Penang Hill" was used, replacing the words "Government Hill".[51] According to a 1908 account, there was a post office and telephone station on the hill, near Government House, and another at Crag Hotel.[9]

AYER ETAM.

**[399]**
**PENANG/AYER ETAM.**

*Cancellation:* Penang/NO 4/1904
*Back:* Undivided
*Publisher:* Pritchard & Co., Penang, No. 4.

An early ppc depicting the village in Ayer Itam as a farming one. A small house is in the foreground with a couple of houses in the centre. Behind are coconut palms and the Penang hills. The crops in the foreground look like tobacco plants. It is believed that the soil in the Ayer Itam valley, yielded by the Sungai Ayer Itam (Black Water River), is some of the richest in Penang. This area has always been an agricultural area. The first major crop in Penang, pepper, was cultivated in the Ayer Itam area by Koh Lay Huan, Penang's first Kapitan Cina.[82]
Date: c. 1900.

No. 262                MAIN STREET, AYER ITAM VILLAGE, PENANG

**[400]**
**No. 262 MAIN STREET, AYER ITAM VILLAGE, PENANG**

*Cancellation:* PENANG/14 MR/38
*Back:* Divided
*Publisher:* Not stated; printed in England

The Ayer Itam village and its background, the Penang hills. The row of shops include the "Ghee Hee Druggist" (*right*), barber shops and foodshops. This real photographic ppc is dated c. 1930.

**[401]**
**NO. 120 AYER ETAM VALLEY.**

*Cancellation:* Nil
*Back:* Divided
*Publisher:* A. Kaulfuss, Penang./
Printed in Germany

The vast expanse of the Ayer Itam valley is framed in the background by the Penang hills. The Kek Lok Si Temple is not visible in this ppc. Date: c. 1910.

**[402]**
**NO. 47, CHINESE TEMPLE AYER ITAM, PENANG**

*Cancellation:* Penang/AP 13/1905
*Back:* Divided
*Publisher:* A. Kaulfuss, Penang

This colour ppc, c. 1910, shows the Kek Lok Si Temple (KLS) complex on the hilly slopes overlooking Ayer Itam. Abbot Beow Lean chose this site to build the KLS because the summit of the hill appeared to resemble a giant white crane with wings outstretched to the sky. The hill was thus called "Crane Hill" (the crane symbolises longevity in traditional Chinese belief). To the left of Crane Hill is a summit resembling a "Blue Dragon", a symbol of vigilance, and to its right, the summit of a white elephant, sacred to Buddhism.[139] The three summits also reminded Abbot Beow Lean of his native Fuzhou in China.[139]

**[403]**

PENANG./AYER ITAM TEMPLE.

*Cancellation:* Penang/1920
*Back:* Divided
*Publisher:* Raphael Tuck & Sons "Oilette"
Postcard No. 8962./Series II/
Printed in England

The KLS complex comprises tiers of temples and prayer halls at the foot of the Penang hills. This ppc shows the elaborate covered footpath linking the bottom tier (*right*) to the middle tier. This "Oilette" ppc dates from c. 1910.

GENERAL VIEW OF SECOND SECTION, AYER ITAM TEMPLE, PENANG

**[404]**

GENERAL VIEW OF SECOND SECTION, AYER ITAM TEMPLE, PENANG.

*Cancellation:* Nil
*Back:* Divided
*Publisher:* Photo by C.S. Foo/
Printed in England

A real photographic ppc in sepia depicting a general view of the second section of the KLS. The second section (*right*) is separated from the bottom section by the flower garden (*left*). The printed bilingual message on the back of this ppc requests for donations to the temple fund. The founder of the KLS, Beow Lean, was formally installed as the abbot of the KLS in 1905, but died two years later. He was succeeded by Poon Teong, his faithful and trusted aide, in 1907.[99] The KLS is a branch of the Kushan Abbey in Fujian, China, the abbey from which Beow Lean originated.[99]
Date: c. 1930.

**[405]**
**A 33 – Chinese Temple (Buddist)/**
**Ayer Itam/Penang**

*Cancellation:* Nil
*Back:* Divided
*Publisher:* Nikko Studio, Penang, S.S./
      Printed in Saxony.

A Nikko studio ppc with two overlapping views, and a dragon and flowery decorative vignette. The top view is that of the upper tier of the KLS, while the lower view is that of the middle tier of the temple. The KLS was described in 1908 as follows: "The building itself is in the peculiar Chinese style of architecture. It stands on the hill-side, and rises tier above tier, so that a fine kaleidoscopic view of the surrounding landscape can be obtained from the top."[9] Date: c. 1910.

**[406]**
**A 45 – Chinese Temple/Ayer Itam,/Penang**

*Cancellation:* Nil
*Back:* Divided
*Publisher:* Nikko Studio, Penang, S.S./
      Printed in Saxony.

This Nikko Studio ppc shows a statue of the Julai Sakyamuni Buddha at the top view. The view below shows a statue of the Julai Melet Buddha, and the images of Yew Thean Gods on the left. A flowery vignette is placed between the two panels. Date: c. 1910.

**[407]**

**CHNIESE. TEMPLE. AYRETAE. PENANG. 181.**

*Cancellation:* Ipoh/11 SE/1928
*Back:* Divided
*Publisher:* Not stated

The pagoda in the midst of construction, c. 1920. At the time this photograph was taken, only the base and part of the middle section of the pagoda had been built.

**[408]**

47. CHINESE TEMPLE. AYER ITAM. PENANG

*Cancellation:* Nil
*Back:* Divided
*Publisher:* Not stated

A real photographic ppc, c. 1920, of the pagoda during its construction. Construction of the KLS pagoda began in 1915 and was only completed in 1930. Building works were interrupted by a scarcity of building materials during World War I (1914–1918).[139]

**[409]**
UNTITLED [AYER ITAM TEMPLE].

*Cancellation:* KUALA LUMPUR/
12 JY/1928
*Back:* Divided
*Publisher:* Unknown

A real photographic ppc, c. 1920, of
the pagoda during its construction. The
pagoda cost around $200,000.[139]

**[410]**
**548.** CHINESE.TEMPLE.AYER.ITAM. PENANG

*Cancellation:* Nil
*Back:* Divided
*Publisher:* Unknown

Another real photographic ppc depicting
the pagoda of the KL5, c. 1923. The
pagoda is notably taller than in earlier
views. Named the Pagoda of King Rama
VI, it is more popularly known as the
Pagoda of 10,000 Buddhas ("Ban Po Thar"
in Hokkien).

[411]
**183 Chinese.Tmeple/Ayer.Itam.Penang**

*Cancellation:* PENANG/29 NOV/1929
*Back:* Divided
*Publisher:* Not stated

This ppc shows the pagoda just a year away from its completion in 1930. Scaffolding works can be seen in the middle section of the pagoda. This real photographic ppc is dated c. 1929.

[412]
**No. 179A New Pagoda, Ayer Itam Temple, Penang**

*Cancellation:* Nil
*Back:* Divided
*Publisher:* Not stated; printed in England

The crowning glory of the KLS, the completed pagoda, c. 1940. At 30 metres tall, the seven-tiered pagoda incorporates a variety of architectural styles: Chinese at its octagonal base, Thai in between and capped with a Burmese crown.[82,101]

**[413]**

UNTITLED [SNAKE TEMPLE].

*Cancellation:* Nil
*Back:* Divided
*Publisher:* The Federal Rubber Stamp
Co., Penang, Ipoh, Kuala
Lumpur & Singapore.

A real photographic ppc, c. 1930, of the Temple of the Azure Clouds ("Ban Kah Lan" in Hokkien), popularly known as the Snake Temple in Sungai Keluang, near what is now the Bayan Lepas airport. The temple was built in 1850 and dedicated to the monk, Chor Soo Kong.[102] Worship of this monk is especially prominent amongst overseas Hokkien communities.

**[414]**

SNAKE TEMPLE/PENANG.

*Cancellation:* Nil
*Back:* Divided
*Publisher:* Not stated

This biview ppc shows the altar of the temple deity, "Chor Soo Kong" at the top panel of this ppc. Pit vipers coil on the twigs and branches which are placed in large vases on the altar in the foreground. The bottom panel shows a general view of the temple. The Snake Temple is crowded with devotees on the birthday of Chor Soo Kong, which is on the sixth day of the first lunar month. Date: c. 1930.

Railway Station, P. W.

**[415]**

**RAILWAY STATION, P.W.**

*Cancellation:* Nil
*Back:* Divided
*Publisher:* Not stated

A ppc depicting the railway station at Butterworth in Province Wellesley, c. 1910. A group of European men and women pose for a group photograph beside the train. The railway line from Butterworth in Province Wellesley to Seremban in Negeri Sembilan was completed in 1903.

Railway Prye.

**[416]**

**RAILWAY PRYE.**

*Cancellation:* Nil
*Back:* Divided
*Publisher:* S.M. Manicum, Penang/No. 32

This colour ppc shows the railway in Province Wellesley (also known as Prai or Prye); the train ran south from Butterworth in Province Wellesley to Kuala Lumpur. The introduction of the railway line through Province Wellesley in 1903 had a remarkable effect on the economy of the town: its municipal revenue rose from $568,695 in 1903 to $819,531 in 1905.[9] Date: c. 1910.

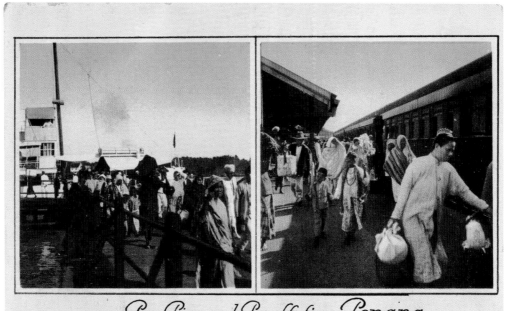

A 46 – *Pry Pier and Pry Station, Penang.*

**[417]**
**A 46 – PRY PIER AND PRY STATION, PENANG.**

*Cancellation:* Nil
*Back:* Divided
*Publisher:* Nikko Studio, Penang,
S.S./Printed in Saxony.

A colour biview ppc by Nikko Studio, c. 1910. It depicts (*left*) passengers disembarking from the Penang Island ferry at the pier in Butterworth and then walking to board the awaiting train (*right*). It is interesting to note that the racial diversity of Penang was apparent even then: a Peranakan lady wearing a pink *baju panjang* and a tiara of jasmine flowers carries a heavy bag in the foreground, and a Jawi Peranakan family is behind her. Malay women with sarongs draped over their shoulders walk behind.

**[418]**
**PRYE RIVER, PENANG.**

*Cancellation:* Nil
*Back:* Divided
*Publisher:* S.M. Manicum, Penang/
No. 100

This colour ppc depicts the harbour at the Prye River in c. 1910. The harbour is busy with ships. In 1908, an important subsidiary port to Swettenham Pier on Penang Island was constructed at the mouth of the Prye River opposite George Town. Among the facilities available there were a dry dock, foundries and workshops to enable repairs to shipping. Extensive wharves were in the course of construction.[9]

Prye Harbour, Penang.

[419]
PRYE HARBOUR, PENANG.

*Cancellation:* Nil
*Back:* Divided
*Publisher:* S.M. Manicum, Penang/
No. 103

The coal-burning steamer S.S. *Perak* docked at the Prye Harbour. It transported passengers and goods between Penang Island and Province Wellesley. Much later, during World War II, the S.S. *Perak* was converted for use as a hospital carrier and saw service in the Mediterranean. Date: c. 1910.

A 25 - Butterworth Pier, Opposite Side, Penang.

[420]
A 25 - BUTTERWORTH PIER,
OPPOSITE SIDE, PENANG.

*Cancellation:* Nil
*Back:* Divided
*Publisher:* Nikko Studio, Penang, S.S./
Printed in Saxony.

A Nikko Studio ppc, c. 1910, with subtle hues, showing the Butterworth Pier in the foreground and the town in the background. An Indian Sri Mahamariamman temple (*right*) dominates the background.

Prai Dock

**[421]**

PRAI DOCK

*Cancellation:* Nil
*Back:* Divided
*Publisher:* Not stated; printed in Germany

The Prai Dock enabled tin ore from the rest of Malaya and Thailand to be brought for smelting at Butterworth. Date: c. 1910.

Eastern Smelting Company, Butterworth.

**[422]**

EASTERN SMELTING COMPANY, BUTTERWORTH.

*Cancellation:* PENANG/1927
*Back:* Divided
*Publisher:* K.M. Mahmed Esoof, Penang. No. 3027

This colour ppc is miscaptioned "Eastern Smelting Company". This was actually the European-owned Straits Trading Co. Ltd (Butterworth Smelters),⁵ c. 1910. The narrow-gauge railway track in the foreground was used to transport tin ore from the nearby dock. The competitor to this company was the Chinese-owned Eastern Smelting Co. Ltd.

Butterworth, Main Road, Penang.

**[423]**

**BUTTERWORTH, MAIN ROAD, PENANG.**

*Cancellation:* Nil
*Back:* Divided
*Publisher:* K.M. Mahmed Esoof, Penang.
– No. 3034

The main road in Butterworth, Jalan Bagan Luar, is depicted in this ppc. Visible in the distance is the Sri Mahamariamman Hindu temple. Prior to World War II, Butterworth and the other towns of Province Wellesley were known for their gambling dens, even earning the nickname "Monte Carlo of Penang Island"![106] During Chinese New Year, gambling was done with abandon for three days and nights, and every shop was turned into a gambling house. Trouble was present wherever rival syndicates operated at the same place, often leading to fights. Eventually the gambling rackets in Province Wellesley were rooted out by the authorities. Date: c. 1907.

1. - Intérieur de l'Eglise Chinoise du Sacré Cœur
MACHANG-BUBOH. - Mission de Malacca

**[424]**

**I. INTÉRIEUR DE L'EGLISE CHINOISE DU SACRÉ CŒUR/MACHANG-BUBOH. – MISSION DE MALACCA**

*Cancellation:* Nil
*Back:* Divided
*Publisher:* Not stated

The French caption to this ppc refers to the interior of the Chinese Church of the Sacred Heart at Machang Bubok, Mission of Malacca. This is a scarce ppc, dated c. 1910.

**[425]**

**BUTTERWORTH PENANG**

*Cancellation:* Nil
*Back:* Divided
*Publisher:* Not stated

This real photographic ppc of Butterworth c. 1910 captures life as it was then. Three Europeans, clad in colonial attire, observe the beach as local fishermen go about their business.

**[426]**

**1114. DESICCATED COCOANUT FACTORY, P.W.**

*Cancellation:* Nil
*Back:* Divided
*Publisher:* Houghton Butcher (Eastern) Ltd, Singapore

A coconut factory in Province Wellesley, c. 1924. This ppc was published by Houghton Butcher (Eastern) Ltd for the Malayan government and reproduced for the Malayan Pavilion in the British Empire Exhibition in 1924.

A 27 - Malay Dancing Girls, Penang.

# The PEOPLE

## The Population

The first census of Penang was taken in December 1788, two years after Francis Light took possession of the island.[107] It recorded a total of 1,335 people, concentrated around George Town. Among the inhabitants were people from Madagascar, Malabar, Madras, Bengal, Batavia and Macau.[107] In 2010, the population of Penang was 1.56 million: 670,400 (43%) were Chinese, 642,286 (41%) Malays and other natives, 153,472 (10%) Indians, and 95,225 (6%) other races.[124]

## The British/Europeans

### Government

Sir John Anderson [427] was the governor of the SS from 1904 to 1911.

### Royal Visits

Prince Arthur, Duke of Connaught, and the third son of Queen Victoria, visited Penang in 1906 [428–430].

In 1922, the Prince of Wales (the future King Edward VIII) visited the island. He was driven from Victoria Pier through a gaily-decorated George Town [431], and then to Government House. He lunched at the Penang Club and later visited the Cricket Club [432].[109]

### Royal Celebrations

King George V and Queen Mary were crowned on 22 June 1911; their coronation was grandly celebrated in all the British colonies, including Penang [433–440]. The Silver Jubilee of King George V and Queen Mary, on 6 May 1935, was also celebrated on a grand scale in Penang [441–444]. Celebrations to commemorate the coronation of King George VI and Queen Elizabeth [445] on 12 May 1937 were rather subdued as war loomed in Europe.

Empire Day (known today as Commonwealth Day) used to be celebrated in May [446].

## The Chinese

The Chinese, numbering 534 in the 1788 census, were the largest ethnic group on the island. Most of the Chinese migrants came from the Malay Peninsula, and had lived in Kedah and Kuantan; only a few came from China.[107]

### The Peranakan

The word *peranakan* is Malay for "local born". Starting in the 15th century, some Chinese associated with and adopted local customs, particularly those of the Malays. These Chinese became known as *peranakan* Chinese. *Peranakan* Chinese women are known as *nyonyas*, while the men are *babas*.

Penang *nyonyas* in *baju panjang* and adorned with jewellery from head to foot are shown in [449] to [452] (*below right*). Children dressed for the Chinese New Year in Manchu clothing are shown in [453]. The extravagance of the *peranakan* wedding is shown in [455].

The Chinese sitting room of local-born tycoon, Cheah Chen Eok's Beeham House [454] was filled with large Chinese porcelain vases, European epergnes (table centrepieces) and Italian marble statues.[114]

### The King's Chinese

*Peranakan* Chinese men preferred to be called "Straits Chinese" to distinguish themselves from the new arrivals to Penang from China. The term "King's Chinese" was coined in 1906 by lawyer G.E. Raine. Some of the King's Chinese in Penang signed up with the Straits Settlements Volunteer Force (SSVF) [456]. They trained at the SSVF camp and practised shooting at the Rifle Range [457].

The address side of [441]. The sender uses a stamp commemorating the Silver Jubilee of King George V (*right*).

A biview ppc depicting *peranakan* Chinese women, known as *nyonyas*. They wear their customary *baju panjang* and elaborate jewellery, c. 1910.

*Opposite*:

The melting pot of Penang. This ppc depicts a Malay dancer, surrounded by Jawi Peranakans of Indian descent, and some Chinese, c. 1910.

The "Al Huda Arabic School Borea Party", c. 1930. The *boria* performers are dressed as Arabs. In the centre is a model of a camel.

The silver chariot that bears the statue of Lord Muruga in Thaipusam processions in Penang, c. 1910.

### Opium Addiction

The sale and consumption of opium were legal and encouraged by the colonial government as opium provided it with its major source of revenue.[117] Opium addicts in Penang c. 1900 are shown in [458] and [459].

In Penang, the campaign against the sale and consumption of opium was spearheaded by Dr Wu Lien-Teh (1879–1960). He founded the Anti-Opium Association and Rehabilitation Centre [460], but was forced to leave Penang partly because of his anti-opium campaign. He gained international acclaim for his work on the treatment and prevention of the pneumonic plague in China.[118] The British totally prohibited the use of opium only in 1945.

### The Chingay Procession

Chingay processions are held in honour of Chinese deities or on important occasions. In 1911, a Chingay procession [437-440] was held to celebrate the coronation of King George V and Queen Mary. In 1924, a Chingay procession was held in honour of the God of Prosperity, Tua Pek Kong [461-462]. The 1928 Chingay procession [463-470] was the grandest to be held and a special souvenir book was published for the occasion.[119] It was held in honour of the Goddess of Mercy, Guanyin, over four days: 28 and 30 October, and 1 and 2 November.

### The Malays

When Francis Light landed in Penang in 1786, there were already permanent Malay communities in Penang engaged in fishing and rice-planting.

The establishment of Penang as a trading post attracted migrant Muslim traders from the Middle East, Indian subcontinent, and the Malay Archipelago. Some of them married Malay women, creating the elite *Jawi Peranakan* (Straits Malays) or *Jawi Pekan* group.[111]

Pre-war Penang Malays are depicted in [471] to [474]; a Malay wedding is shown in [475].

The Penang *Boria* (*top left*; [476]) traditionally referred to Malay or Indian Muslim minstrels who performed at Muslim homes during the Muslim month of Muharram, singing topical songs.[112] A popular venue for *boria* used to be Padang Brown (today Padang Dato Keramat), and later, Padang Tambun. The last *boria* competition was held at Padang Tambun in 1972.[111]

The idyllic lifestyle of the rural Malays in inland and seaside kampongs is shown in [477] to [480]. Rice farming [480] was done exclusively by the Malays.

### The Indians and Other Races

Indians were early settlers of Penang; South Indian Muslims, known as Chulias, were among the earliest Indians to arrive.

The rubber boom of the 1890s to 1920 led to the arrival of large numbers of Tamil migrants to work on rubber plantations [490] and to build the railways and roads [489] used to transport tin and rubber. They also worked in the harbour and maritime industry. Money lenders, known as "chettiars", grew particularly rich.

Indian workers and bullock carts are shown in [481]. The Chettiar Temple along Waterfall Road is shown from [482] to [484]. The Hindu festival of Thaipusam (*below left*; [485-487]) is celebrated annually at the end of January or beginning of February.

An Indian Revolving Cradle [488], shown during an Indian festival such as Thaipusam, worked like a modern Ferris wheel, except that it was revolved by hand.

Penang was also home to other minority races including the Japanese [491] and Burmese [492] communities. Another prominent minority were the Armenians, who played a far greater role in the economic, social and civic life of Penang than their limited numbers would suggest. Today, the E & O Hotel and Armenian Street are a lasting reminder of the Armenian presence in Penang.[121]

[427]
SIR JOHN ANDERSON, K.C.M.G./GOVERNOR OF THE STRAITS SETTLEMENTS AND
HIGH COMMISSIONER OF THE FEDERATED MALAY STATES.

*Cancellation:* Nil
*Back:* Divided
*Publisher:* Koh & Co., Singapore.

A rare portrait on ppc. Sir John Anderson was appointed governor of the
SS, succeeding Sir Frank Swettenham, on 1 February 1904. He officially
commenced service on 15 April 1904.[9] Date: 1910.

[428]
LIGHT STREET ARCH, PENANG.

*Cancellation:* Nil
*Back:* Divided
*Publisher:* S.M. Manicum, Penang/No. 111

The Chinese words on the arch (below the roof) mean "Welcoming the
arrival of the Duke." The caption on this ppc is incorrect as the arch was
erected on Farquhar Street, not Light Street. The Duke of Connaught was the
third son of Queen Victoria. Date: 1906.

[429]

PENANG. WAITING THE ARRIVAL OF HIS ROYAL
HIGHNESS PRINCE ARTHUR OF CONNAUGHT.

*Cancellation:* Nil
*Back:* Divided
*Publisher:* Not stated

A large retinue of carriages,
horses, policemen, etc. wait outside
the Government Buildings and the
Queen Victoria Memorial Clock
Tower. A welcome arch (marked
with an "X") stands across the
entrance of Light Street.
Date: 1906.

[430]

PENANG. EN FÉTE. (THE ROYAL VISIT)

*Cancellation:* Nil
*Back:* Divided
*Publisher:* Co-operative Agency S.S./
No. 59.

Crowds line Light Street beside the
Padang as Prince Arthur, the Duke of
Connaught is driven past in an open
horse carriage. Fort Cornwallis can be
seen in the background. During their
visit to Penang, the Duke and Duchess of
Connaught and their daughter, Princess
Patricia were driven by tycoon Chung
Thye Pin in his car.[9] Date: 1906.

**[431]**

UNTITLED [THE CHINESE CLUB WELCOME OUR GLORIOUS PRINCE].

*Cancellation:* Penang/13 JY/1922
*Back:* Divided
*Publisher:* Not stated

The Prince of Wales (the future King Edward VIII who later abdicated and became the Duke of Windsor) visited Penang on 23 May 1922. According to a *Straits Times* report the following day, he drove "by way of Downing Street round the Esplanade, via Leith Street, Penang Road, Macalister Road, Western Road and Residency Road to Government House". The roads were decorated with arches welcoming the prince. This arch, situated between Light Street and Farquhar Street, was presented by the Chinese Club.

**[432]**

UNTITLED [VISIT OF THE PRINCE OF WALES].

*Cancellation:* Nil
*Back:* Divided
*Publisher:* H. Bodom, Photo. Penang

This real photographic ppc shows the Cricket Club at the Esplanade gaily decorated and packed mostly with Europeans in formal dress. This could be on the occasion of the visit of the Prince of Wales in 1922. The Prince of Wales was reported to have played tennis in Government House and lunched informally at the Penang Club. The *Straits Times* reported that at the Cricket Club, the Prince was treated to a "comic match between football teams, the players being tied up in sacks."

The Hindu Priest prays that our graceous King George V, may live long and have a properous reign, Penang

GOD SAVE THE KING

[433]

THE HINDU PRIEST PRAYS THAT OUR GRACIOUS KING GEORGE V, MAY LIVE LONG AND HAVE A PROSPEROUS REIGN, PENANG

*Cancellation:* Nil
*Back:* Divided
*Publisher:* M.J., Penang.

The interestingly posed photograph on this ppc commemorates the coronation of King George V and Queen Mary on 22 June 1911. The priest is in a meditative pose, while a woman and two children pray.

[434]

LIGHT STREET CORONATION ARCH, PENANG

*Cancellation:* Nil
*Back:* Divided
*Publisher:* S.M. Manicum, Penang.

The caption for this ppc is on the reverse of the ppc. The decorative arch features Mughal elements such as minarets and domed-shaped archways. The coronation of King George V was celebrated in a grand manner in Penang, with street arches, boat races and Chingay processions. Date: 1911.

**[435]**

**CORONATION BOAT RACES, PENANG**

*Cancellation:* Nil
*Back:* Divided
*Publisher:* S.M. Manicum, Penang.

Another ppc with its caption on the reverse of the postcard. This ppc, dated c. 1911, depicts the boat races held in celebration of the coronation of King George V in June 1911. There is a flotilla of small boats and an eager crowd watching the boat races.

**[436]**

**THE CHINESE MUSICIAL PROCESSION, PENANG**

*Cancellation:* Nil
*Back:* Divided
*Publisher:* S.M. Manicum, Penang.

A Chinese musical procession to commemorate the coronation of King George V on 22 June 1911. The musical party also carried banners and lanterns. The king's coronation was a grand celebration observed by all British colonies. Even the Sultan of Kedah, Sultan Abdul Hamid Halim Shah (r. 1882-1943) attended the "Coronation of the King-Emperor George V and Queen-Empress Mary" at Westminster Abbey, in London.

[437]
**A 26 – CHINESE FESTIVAL PROCESSION, PENANG.**

*Cancellation:* Nil
*Back:* Divided
*Publisher:* Nikko Studio, Penang, S.S./Printed in Saxony.

A Chingay procession to mark the coronation of King George V. Two maidens are seated on a float decorated with flowers; the umbrellas are for shielding them from the sun. Date: 1911.

[438]
**CHINESE CHINKAY, PENANG.**

*Cancellation:* Nil
*Back:* Divided
*Publisher:* K.M. Mahmed Esoof, Penang./No. 3040

The back of this 1911 ppc reads: "Ladies are strapped to their seats and are placed on raised wooden frame...This car is brilliantly decorated and at night beautifully illuminated..." Two maidens are seated on a cart decorated with flowers. The cart may have been pulled by bullock, horse or human.

Chinese Chingey Ppocession, Penang.     Published by Nikko-Studio.

**[439]**

CHINESE CHINGEY PPOCESSION, PENANG.

*Cancellation:* Nil
*Back:* Divided
*Publisher:* Nikko-Studio.

A similar ppc by S.M. Manicum is captioned "Coronation Naga". The dragon is mounted on carts with wheels and drawn by horses (a horse's tail is visible on the margin). "Chingay" means "true art", "decorated miniature stage" or "float" in Chinese.[110] This ppc is dated 1911.

**[440]**

A 32 – CHINESE FESTIVAL/
PROCESSION/PENANG

*Cancellation:* Nil
*Back:* Divided
*Publisher:* Nikko Studio, Penang, S.S./
Printed in Saxony.

A biview colour ppc of the Chingay procession in 1911. The upper panel shows a dragon dance, while the lower panel shows a dragon drawn by a horse (similar to [439]). Jean DeBernardi, in her book, *Rites of Belonging in a Malaysian Chinese Community* (2004), states that Chingay processions traditionally served as occasions to pray for luck for the Chinese community and to repel disasters and epidemics, but that they acquired new meanings in colonial Penang: they were used to celebrate colonial or national events. For example there were Chingay processions to celebrate the coronation of King George V in June 1911, which cost $120,000.

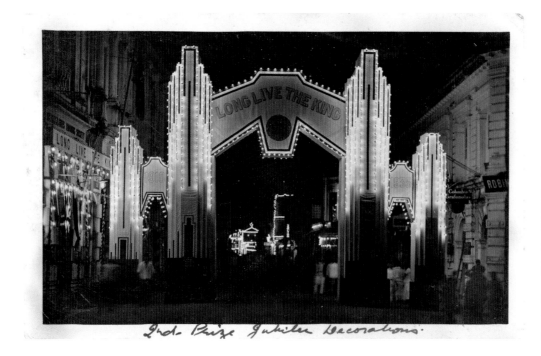

*2nd Prize Jubilee Decorations.*

**[441]**
2ND. PRIZE JUBILEE DECORATIONS.

*Cancellation:* Penang/1935
*Back:* Divided
*Publisher:* Not stated

This real photographic ppc dated 1935, shows a lighted arch across Beach Street (Robinson Store is visible on the right). The arch was built to commemorate the Silver Jubilee of King George V and Queen Mary on 6 May 1935. Across the arch is written: "Long Live the King". This arch won second prize in the Silver Jubilee decoration contest.

**[442]**
UNTITLED [DECORATIVE ARCH].

*Cancellation:* Nil
*Back:* Divided
*Publisher:* Not stated

A real photographic ppc of the Penang Buddhist Association along Anson Road decorated and illuminated for the occasion of the Silver Jubilee of King George V and Queen Mary on 6 May 1935. The Silver Jubilee was celebrated on a grand scale throughout Penang, with street arches, decorated and illuminated buildings, dragon dances and grand processions. Date: 1935.

**[443]**

UNTITLED [SILVER JUBILEE CELEBRATIONS].

*Cancellation:* Ipoh/22 JU/1935
*Back:* Divided
*Publisher:* Not stated

This 1935 real photographic ppc shows a dragon dance to celebrate the Silver Jubilee of King George V and Queen Mary in 1935. The message on the back of this ppc reads: "...This is the dragon in the Chinese Jubilee procession and thought you would like to see it..."

**[444]**

UNTITLED [SILVER JUBILEE CELEBRATIONS].

*Cancellation:* Nil
*Back:* Divided
*Publisher:* Not stated

A privately produced photographic ppc of a float during the Silver Jubilee procession on 6 May 1935. The words on the side of the float read: "Li Tek Seah/Silver Jubilee". The float is European in appearance and is in the form of a swan, with children in it. Date: 1935.

**[445]**

**UNTITLED [CORONATION OF KING GEORGE VI].**

*Cancellation:* Nil
*Back:* Divided
*Publisher:* Not stated

The Town Hall at the Esplanade is illuminated for the coronation of King George VI and Queen Elizabeth on 12 May 1937. In the centre are the words "God Save Our King" flanked by the initials "G" (for "George", *left*) and "R" (for "Regis", *right*). Date: 1937.

**[446]**

**No. 8 – PENANG./EMPIRE DAY CELEBRATION, SEPOY LINE**

*Cancellation:* PENANG/12 MY/1912
*Back:* Divided
*Publisher:* T.C.B. Penang

A parade held to celebrate Empire Day, c. 1910. The parade was held at the Polo Ground at Sepoy Lines where the barracks of the Malay States Guides (the Sikh Regiment) were also located.[9] Prior to World War II, it was an annual event held on the last school day of May.

[447]
HELVETIA-MESSE IN PENANG. [SWISS FAIR IN PENANG]

*Cancellation:* Unclear
*Back:* Undivided
*Publisher:* Not stated

The handwritten heading to this privately printed ppc "Helvetia Messe in Penang" is a coalition of languages. "Helvetia" is the Latin name of Switzerland, and "Messe" is German for "Fair". This ppc is dated c. 1900.

[448]
NO. 89. EUROPEAN BUNGALOW

*Cancellation:* Nil
*Back:* Divided
*Publisher:* A. Kaulfuss, Penang.

This beautiful colour ppc depicts an early European bungalow of timber construction. The building is on elevated wooden pillars. In the foreground are tapioca plants and there are palm trees to the right. Date: c. 1900.

[449]
UNTITLED [NYONYAS].

*Cancellation:* Nil
*Back:* Divided
*Publisher:* Tan Chin Kim, proprietor of Federal Rubber Stamp Co. (FRS)

Two Penang *nyonyas*, relatives of Tan Chin Kim, founder of the FRS, are shown in this c. 1910 ppc. They are dressed in their traditional *baju panjang* and batik sarong, adorned with tiaras and jewellery, and wearing anklets and beaded slippers. [Collection of Tan Ah Yeang, daughter of Tan Chin Kim.]

[450]
A 47 – CHINESE LADIES/(STRAITS BORN)/PENANG.

*Cancellation:* Penang/1920
*Back:* Divided
*Publisher:* Nikko Studio, Penang, S.S./Printed in Saxony.

A biview ppc of Straits-born Chinese ladies in their traditional attire. The portrait on the right also shows a glass epergne on the tea table. While the *nyonyas* adopted Malay-style dress and cuisine, they retained their traditional Chinese beliefs and lifestyle. Date: c. 1910.

[451]
UNTITLED [PENANG NYONYA].

*Cancellation:* Nil
*Back:* Divided
*Publisher:* Not stated

A c. 1920 beautiful studio portrait of a *nyonya* in pink *baju panjang* and adorned with jewellery from head to toe. This woman must have been very well-off; she has a ring on almost every finger!

[452]
UNTITLED [PENANG NYONYA].

*Cancellation:* Nil
*Back:* Divided
*Publisher:* Not stated

A formal portrait of a *nyonya* showing her jewellery in detail: her collar is held by two jewelled buttons; her *baju panjang* is fastened by a set of brooches. She is also wearing three "star" brooches and a long necklace. Portraits such as this were often given to a matchmaker. Date: c. 1930.

[453]
PENANG/CHINESE CHILDREN/IN
NEW YEAR'S/DRESS.

*Cancellation:* PENANG/JU 3/1909
*Back:* Divided
*Publisher:* Not stated

Chinese children dressed in Qing dynasty
costumes during Chinese New Year. The
two girls in front are dressed like brides
while the three boys are dressed in the
attire of Qing dynasty officials, complete
with hats. Behind them to the left is an
elaborate altar. Date: c. 1905.

[454]
UNTITLED [CHINESE SITTING ROOM].

*Cancellation:* Nil
*Back:* Divided
*Publisher:* Not stated

A real photographic ppc, c. 1920, of the
Chinese sitting room in Beeham House,
one of the palatial homes of Cheah
Chen Eok (1852–1922). It was filled
with Chinese and European antiques.
A large Chinese porcelain vase is in the
foreground (*left*) and an Italian marble
statue is on the righthand side.
An epergne – much-loved by the
*peranakans* – is seen on the table
beneath the ceiling light.

CONVENT St MAUR PENANG
Une élève de St-Maur-Penang près de son lit nuptial

[455]

CONVENT ST MAUR PENANG/UNE ÉLÈVE DE ST-MAUR-PENANG PRÈS
DE SON LIT NUPTIAL

*Cancellation:* Nil

*Back:* Divided

*Publisher:* Not stated; printed in France

An orphan raised at the Penang Convent is pictured on the occasion of her wedding to a rich *peranakan* bridegroom, c. 1910. She sits bedecked with jewellery, in front of an elaborate wedding bed with embroidered drapery.

[456]

UNTITLED [STRAITS SETTLEMENTS VOLUNTEER FORCE].

*Cancellation:* Nil

*Back:* Divided

*Publisher:* Kee Chun Studio/Penang (*bottom left*)

A real photographic ppc, c. 1940, of a Straits Chinese officer in the Straits Settlements Volunteer Force (SSVF). Known as the "King's" or "Queen's Chinese", these Anglophiles were inclined to work in the colonial service or other European commercial services.[1,2]

No. 121 Volunteers Camp & Rifle Range.

**[457]**

**No. 121. VOLUNTEERS CAMP & RIFLE RANGE.**

*Cancellation:* Not clear (c. 1920)
*Back:* Divided
*Publisher:* A. Kaulfuss, Penang.

The training camp of the Straits Settlements Volunteer Force (SSVF) at Rifle Range, near Ayer Itam, c. 1910. Although the SSVF was already formed in 1888,[116] British subjects of non-European descent including the Straits Chinese were only allowed to participate in military training in c. 1896.[115] Some of the Penang members of the SSVF saw action against the Japanese during the Japanese invasion in 1941.[116]

Opium Smokers.

**[458]**

**OPIUM SMOKERS.**

*Cancellation:* Nil
*Back:* Divided
*Publisher:* The Federal Rubber Stamp Co., Kuala Lumpur, Ipoh, Penang & Singapore.

This ppc, from c. 1920, shows a man lying down smoking opium while another man prepares the opium for him. The early history, progress and development of Penang, Malaya and Singapore is entwined with the opium trade.[117] Its sale and consumption were legal until 1945 and was, indeed, encouraged by the colonial government as it provided the government with its major source of revenue. Many of the opium revenue "farms" were run by Chinese themselves, who grew wealthy at the expense of the poor.[117]

**[459]**

PENANG NO. 6. CHINESE OPIUM SMOKERS.

*Cancellation:* Written on 23 December
              1907 but not posted
*Back:* Undivided
*Publisher:* British Empire Series./
            "Sanbride"

An early real photographic ppc, c. 1900,
showing three opium smokers. Notice the
opium smoking utensils and two tea cups
(the smokers needed to sip tea as their
mouths were parched by the hot
opium smoke).

Penang No. 6. Chinese Opium Smokers.

**[460]**

UNTITLED [PENANG ANTI-OPIUM SMOKING
AND REHABILITATION CENTRE].

*Cancellation:* Nil
*Back:* Divided
*Publisher:* Not stated

A rare ppc of the Penang Anti-Opium
Smoking and Rehabilitation Centre in
Muntri Street in 1906.[118] Dr Wu Lien-Teh
is seated in the centre. The banner in
front has the words "The Penang Anti-
Opium (Association)" surmounting a cross
with the words "Penang Rehabilitation
Centre". Although Dr Wu was forced to
leave Penang as a result of his anti-
opium campaign, he gained international
recognition for successfully treating and
preventing the deadly pneumonic plague
in Harbin, China, in 1911.

Penang, No. 31—The Chinese Deity—TAI PAK KUNG—in a Chingay Procession      British Empire Series

**[461]**
**PENANG, No. 31—THE CHINESE DEITY—
TAI PAK KUNG—IN A CHINGAY PROCESSION**

*Cancellation:* Nil
*Back:* Divided
*Publisher:* British Empire Series

A Chingay procession held in honour of Tai Pak Kung, the Chinese God of Prosperity. A float of the deity is being paraded and watched by a large crowd. Chingay processions involve many highly decorated floats often with maidens seated on them, either in the day or at night, and the display of huge flags carried and tossed skilfully by strong men. This ppc dates from 1924.

**[462]**
**UNTITLED [CHINGAY PROCESSION].**

*Cancellation:* Nil
*Back:* Divided
*Publisher:* Not stated

Another ppc depicting the Chingay procession of 1924 in honour of Tai Pak Kung. The sign on top of the float states: "1924/Prosperity and Good Luck". It was contributed by Kimberley Street (as stated on the fan-shaped panel at the bottom). This float is more European in appearance, and carries a number of dolls, besides a real girl. This real photographic ppc is dated 1924.

**[463]**

UNTITLED [CHINGAY PROCESSION].

*Cancellation:* Ipoh/1930
*Back:* Divided
*Publisher:* Not stated

A real photographic ppc depicting the
1928 Chingay procession in honour of the
Goddess of Mercy, Guanyin, 1928. This
procession was held for four days: 28 and
30 October, and 1 and 3 November. This
ppc shows the first *Ch'ng Peh* (elaborately
decorated car or chariot) carrying
the deity. It is pulled by hundreds of
devotees; many wealthier and prominent
Chinese (with hats and white jackets)
walk before the chariot.

**[464]**

CHINGAY.PROCESSION/1928.PENANG

*Cancellation:* Nil
*Back:* Divided
*Publisher:* Not stated

This is a rare photographic ppc.
Wee Theang Siew (his name is visible
on the banner behind the head of the
chariot)[119] was the President of the Anson
and Logan roads sections. The 1928
Chingay procession was the grandest to
be held, thus a special souvenir booklet
was produced for this occasion.[119]
The procession consisted of about 30
sections, with several *Ch'ng Pehs*. On
each of these sat young girls dressed
as fictitious Chinese and European
characters, and celestial beings. Triangular
flags of different heights and sizes were
prominent throughout, and loud drums,
cymbals and gongs accompanied
the floats.

[465]

UNTITLED [CHINGAY PROCESSION].

*Cancellation:* Nil
*Back:* Divided
*Publisher:* Not stated (private photographer)

The leading *Ch'ng Peh* or elaborately decorated car carrying the Goddess of Mercy (Guanyin). The chariot bearing the Goddess, with its roof of gold, was elaborately decorated within and without, and pulled by devotees.[119]
Date: 1928.

[466]

CHINGAY-PROCESSION/1928. PENANG.

*Cancellation:* Nil
*Back:* Divided
*Publisher:* The Federal Rubber Stamp Co.,/Penang, Ipoh, Kuala Lumpur
& Singapore.

This decorated car became a float called "Britannica"[119] for the 1928 Chingay procession. The three girls atop the float wore jewellery worth $100,000. Four policemen were assigned to walk beside the float to protect it![119]

[467]
CHINGAY PROCESSION/PENANG 1928

*Cancellation:* Nil
*Back:* Divided
*Publisher:* Not stated (private photographer)

The "ever smiling" *Ch'ng Peh* or decorated car contributed by the businesses and residents of Macalister Road, Perak Road and other side roads.[119] Two young girls dressed as fairies are shielded by extended umbrellas. The float illuminations had just been switched on. Date: 1928.

[468]
UNTITLED [CHINGAY PROCESSION].

*Cancellation:* Nil
*Back:* Divided
*Publisher:* The Federal Rubber Stamp Co./Penang, Ipoh, Kuala Lumpur & Singapore.

This 1928 ppc depicts the *Ch'ng Peh* of Carnarvon Street.[119] It is decorated with a large and striking stylised lion head, and is shown passing in front of Universal Pharmacists at the end of Carnarvon Street (near Maxwell Road).

[469]

UNTITLED [CHINGAY PROCESSION].

*Cancellation:* Ipoh/8 MR/1929
*Back:* Divided
*Publisher:* Not stated
(private photographer)

A real photographic ppc dated 1928 of the float entitled "Prosperity"[119] (its name is just visible on the white board at the front); below the board are the letters "P.M.I.A." (Penang Mutual Improvement Association). The 1928 souvenir booklet described the Chingay procession as a "unique event which takes place once in nine years and only in Penang. Although primarily a religious festival to invoke the blessings of the Goddess, its commercial publicity was realised by the merchants."[119]

[470]

UNTITLED [CHINGAY PROCESSION/ GUINNESS STOUT].

*Cancellation:* Nil
*Back:* Divided
*Publisher:* Not stated

The souvenir booklet for the 1928 Chingay procession describes the photograph on this ppc: "A very original note was struck by the giant model of a bull-dog representing the well-known 'Bull Dog' brand of Guinness Stout. The model was most artistically displayed and brilliantly illuminated at night. The four large bottles preceding the bull-dog advertised Gilbey's Invalid and White Port Wines, Meukow Brandy and 'T'-Beer."[119]

[471]

A 44 – MALAY WOMAN/PENANG.

*Cancellation:* Nil
*Back:* Divided
*Publisher:* Nikko Studio, Penang, S.S./Printed in Saxony.

A beautiful portrait in subtle colours depicting a *Jawi Peranakan* woman (she is captioned as Malay). She wears a *baju kebaya*; its collar fastened with gold brooch or *kerongsang*. Date: c. 1910.

[472]

RUBBER TREE,/PENANG

*Cancellation:* Penang/5 JA/1920
*Back:* Divided
*Publisher:* K.M. Mahmed Esoof, Penang./No. 3024

A colour ppc depicting a group of *Jawi Peranakan boys* playing around an Indian rubber tree. This ppc dates from c. 1910.

A 42 – Malay Women – Penang

[473]

### A 42 – MALAY WOMEN – PENANG

*Cancellation:* Nil
*Back:* Divided
*Publisher:* Nikko Studio, Penang. S.S./
Printed in Saxony.

A biview ppc featuring two studio portraits, c. 1910. The lefthand picture shows two women in *baju kurung*, their heads covered with sarongs. The righthand picture shows two ladies in *baju kebaya*. The first census conducted in Penang in 1788 grouped the Chulia (Indian Muslims) together with the Malays. The census cited the place of origin of most migrants to the island as Kedah, but others also came from Province Wellesley, Perlis, Aceh, Calcutta and even Borneo.[107]

No. 79. Native Beauties

Penang
7-8-08

[474]

### No. 79. NATIVE BEAUTIES

*Cancellation:* Written as 7 August 1908;
not cancelled
*Back:* Divided
*Publisher:* A. Kaulfuss, Penang.

This ppc has four views: an Indian Muslim woman (*left*), a Malay man (*top centre*), Malay woman (*right*) and a Javanese man (*bottom centre*). These are posed studio portraits.

**[475]**

NO. 143 MALAY WEDDING PROCESSION.

*Cancellation:* Penang/JU 6/1908
*Back:* Divided
*Publisher:* A. Kaulfuss, Penang.

A colour ppc depicting a Malay wedding procession c. 1908. The ppc shows an elaborate Malay wedding procession with banner, flags and musicians in a coastal town. The wedding party is shaded by a long canopy in the rear. A group of men bring a buffalo as a gift (*centre*).

**[476]**

THE AL HUDA ARABIC SCHOOL. PARTY IN THE BOREA PROCESSION, PENANG, SS

*Cancellation:* Nil
*Back:* Divided
*Publisher:* Not stated

This real photographic ppc captures a *boria* procession by the Al Huda Arabic School, c. 1930. The procession is shown passing in front of the Penang General Hospital. In Malaysia, the *boria* is unique to Penang[111, 112] and is believed to have been introduced by early Indian settlers, particularly Indian Shia Muslims. The word "boria" is of Persian origin and means "mat" in Hindi. A *boria* troupe of "strolling minstrels" traditionally visited homes of wealthy Penang Muslims during the Muslim month of Muharram, and serenaded them till they were paid to leave. The performers wore fancy attire and the songs were eulogistic or comic.[112]

Village Scene. Bayan Lepas.

[477]

**VILLAGE SCENE. BAYAN LEPAS.**

*Cancellation:* Nil
*Back:* Divided
*Publisher:* Co-operative Agency, S.S./ No. 22.

Bayan Lepas (Malay for "the parakeet has flown away") is where the Penang International Airport is currently sited. The photograph in this c. 1910 ppc depicts how the area was then. The attap houses are surrounded by coconut trees. There are two rickshaws in the foreground.

272

Malay House, Penang.

[478]

**MALAY HOUSE, PENANG.**

*Cancellation:* Nil
*Back:* Divided
*Publisher:* No. 35. A. Beach Street, Penang

The idyll of kampong life is captured in this c. 1910 colour ppc. It shows a single-storey attap-roofed house surrounded by coconut and fruit trees.

Fishing Village, Penang.

**[479]**

FISHING VILLAGE, PENANG.

*Cancellation:* 1915
*Back:* Divided
*Publisher:* S.M. Manicum, Penang No. 86

Fishing boats line the beach of this fishing village. When Francis Light landed in Penang in 1786, there were already Malay communities there engaged in fishing. This colour ppc dates from c. 1915.

PADDY CUTTING, PENANG.

**[480]**

PADDY CUTTING, PENANG.

*Cancellation:* Penang/1920
*Back:* Divided
*Publisher:* K.M. Mahmed Esoof, Penang./
No. 3060

This ppc depicts Malay farmers harvesting paddy. Paddy grown on Penang Island and Province Wellesley was mostly planted by Malays, mainly for their own consumption, leaving little for export. The farmer's house in the background is surrounded by coconut trees. This colour ppc is dated c. 1910.

**[481]**

**A 34 – PENANG/INDIAN COOLIES/
BULLOCK CART**

*Cancellation:* Penang/1915
*Back:* Divided
*Publisher:* Nikko Studio, Penang, S.S./
Printed in Saxony.

This two-panel colour ppc, c. 1910,
depicts Indian workers in Penang.
Between the two panels are palm leaves
and lanterns as decorations. Among the
earliest Indian settlers to arrive in Penang
at the time of its founding were Chulias
(Indian Muslims).

**[482]**

**WATER FALL ROAD, PENANG.**

*Cancellation:* Not clear
*Back:* Divided
*Publisher:* K. M. Mahmed Esoof, Penang.
No. 3042

The Nattukottai Chettiar Hindu Temple
(*centre background*) along Waterfall Road.
One of the most famous Hindu temples in
Penang, it is dedicated to Lord Murugan
and epitomises the glory of the Chettiar
community which originated in Tamil
Nadu. The Chettiars here were referred to
as Nattukottai Chettiars, meaning "people
with palatial houses in the countryside",
to distinguish themselves from other
group of Chettiars. They were once a
flourishing community of traders, money
lenders and merchants. Date: c. 1910.

**[483]**

**CHETTY TEMPLE, PENANG**

*Cancellation:* Nil
*Back:* Divided
*Publisher:* Not stated

The caption is printed on the reverse of this c. 1910 ppc. The Chettiar Temple is seen decorated with coconut palm leaves. The origins of this temple date back to 1854.

**[484]**

**NO. 2 – PENANG/INTERIOR OF CHETTY TEMPLE**

*Cancellation:* Singapore/MR 22/1910
*Back:* Divided
*Publisher:* T.C.B. Penang

The Chettiars were a rich class of Indian money lenders, merchants and traders. The lavish interior of the Nattukottai Chettiar Temple reflects this wealth. The temple building was laid out according to a chequered (*chokkatan*) design, and is of fine craftsmanship and decoration.[82] This ppc is dated: c. 1910.

No. 2 – Penang·
Interior of Chetty Temple

[485]
**74 The Silver Cart in the Procession of Hindoo.**

*Cancellation:* Nil
*Back:* Divided
*Publisher:* Not stated

This real photographic ppc, dating from c. 1930, depicts the silver chariot bearing the statue of Lord Murugan being led from Little India towards the Nattukottai Chettiar Temple on Waterfall Road during the Hindu festival of Thaipusam. The festival is held at the end of January or beginning of February, depending on the alignment of the nine planets.

[486]
**No. 220 Chetty Festival, Thaipusam, Penang.**

*Cancellation:* PENANG/1941
*Back:* Divided
*Publisher:* Not stated; printed in England

A real photographic ppc, c. 1940, of the silver chariot carrying the statue of Lord Muruga during Thaipusam. It is outside the Nattukottai Chettiar Temple on Waterfall Road, surrounded by numerous devotees. A number of Europeans watch the celebration.

[487]

HINDU SILVER CAR, PENANG.

*Cancellation:* PENANG/1914
*Back:* Divided
*Publisher:* No. 35. A. Beach Street, Penang

A closer view of the silver chariot that is used to bear the jewelled statue of Lord Muruga (not visible here), c. 1910. The silver chariot was brought to Penang in 1894 from India. Prior to this, the statue was borne on a wooden chariot. The chariot is traditionally drawn by a pair of bulls.

[488]

INDIAN REVOLVING CRADDLE, PENANG.

*Cancellation:* Nil
*Back:* Divided
*Publisher:* Not stated

This mechanical cradle is a rudimentary Ferris wheel. It was commonly used during Indian celebrations, such as Hindu New Year and Deepavali. The caption is printed on the reverse of the ppc. Date: c. 1910.

Native Coolies at Work (Road repairing), Penang

**[489]**
**NATIVE COOLIES AT WORK**
**(ROAD REPAIRING), PENANG**

*Cancellation:* PENANG/1912
*Back:* Divided
*Publisher:* M.J., Penang

A colour ppc. c. 1910, showing a group of Indians brought to Penang to work on road building and repairing. There were Indian settlers in Penang in the years following its founding, many from the merchant class and also convicts whose labour was used for many public works. More Indians were later brought in by the British East India Company to work as labourers, policemen, and sepoys, while others came as traders and civil servants.[120]

COOLIES
IN A RUBBER
ESTATE
PENANG

**[490]**
**COOLIES/IN A RUBBER/ESTATES/PENANG**

*Cancellation:* Nil
*Back:* Divided
*Publisher:* Not stated

Rubber estate workers, c. 1920. Plantation labour during the rubber boom from the 1890s to 1920 comprised mainly of southern Indians who worked as indentured servants.

[491]

**JAPANESE DANCING GIRLS, PENANG**

*Cancellation:* PENANG/5 FE/1912
*Back:* Divided
*Publisher:* M.J., Penang

A colour ppc, c. 1910, of Japanese girls in kimono and carrying fans. Prior to World War II, there were many Japanese prostitutes plying their trade on Argyll Road, Campbell Street and Kimberley Street.

[492]

**NO. 15 – PENANG./THE BURMESE BEAUTIES**

*Cancellation:* Nil
*Back:* Divided
*Publisher:* T.C.B. Penang

Before World War II, the Burmese population in Penang was concentrated in Burmah Road, Moulmein Road and Rangoon Road, as well as Pulau Tikus. Date: c. 1910.

Campbell, Penang

# PHILATELIC HISTORY

A ppc has two sides: the picture, or photograph, side and the address, or message, side. One who collects a ppc for its picture side is known as a deltiologist or cartophilist.

A collector of ppcs for their affixed postage stamps, postal cancellations and other postal markings is a philatelist (stamp collector). One who is both a deltiologist and philatelist would appreciate a used ppc to its fullest.

## Stamp on Picture Side

The postage stamp is meant to be on the address or message side [493-494]. In the early 1900s, it was the trend for the sender to affix the stamp on the picture side [495-496]. Even today, a collector often values this practice. Picture postcards bearing Queen Victoria stamps [495] are uncommon; stamps of King George V and Queen Mary's Silver Jubilee used on ppcs are also not common [496].

## Uncommon Stamps

In 1922, SS stamps were overprinted "Malaya – Borneo Exhibition". However, these stamps were seldom found used on Penang ppcs [497; 499].

Federated Malay States (FMS) stamps, as used on the "Penang Botanical Garden" ppc [498], were used during the period when Kedah's postal service was under Siamese administration (before 1909).

## Uncommon Cancellations

Federated Malay States stamps were sometimes cancelled with the rare "Swiss type" Siamese cancellations [498].

In [500], the stamp is tied by the first E & O Hotel circular date stamp (cds), which was in use for about four months in 1910. Hence, it is a rare cancellation on a cover and even rarer on a ppc.

## Valuation

Generally the value of a ppc is influenced by its age, condition, colouring, scarcity and usage.

How many different ppcs of pre-war Penang are there? Nobody knows for certain but my rough estimation is that from 1898 to 1940 there are about 1,000 to 1,300 ppcs. The best part of collecting ppcs is that no collection is likely to be complete as new ppcs surface on internet auction sites all the time.

In general, a used ppc is worth more than an unused one. A common, unused ppc of Penang is worth between USD 5 to USD 30, while those with rare stamps or cancellations are worth considerably more.

With regard to a used ppc, the scarcity of the postage stamp and its cancellation gives a premium to the ppc. A used Penang ppc with a rare stamp and cancellation may be worth several hundred dollars.

## Conclusion

Picture postcards are sought after by both deltiologists and philatelists. Both hobbies are increasing in popularity in this region due to the rising affluence of the population here. In short, if one collects ppcs for the purpose of investment, one will not be disappointed!

A sepia, multiview photograph depicting various parts of George Town for its centenary celebrations (1857–1957). This photograph is the size of a standard ppc.

281 •

*Opposite*:
Campbell Street, c. 1920. Three-storey shophouses can be seen on the left, while a four-storey building with a roof balcony (*right foreground*) may have been a hotel.

*Below*:
A rare panoramic view of the Penang Harbour, c. 1910, published by the Co-operative Agency. The view stretches from the Government Buildings on the right to Weld Quay on the left.

Panorama of Penang.

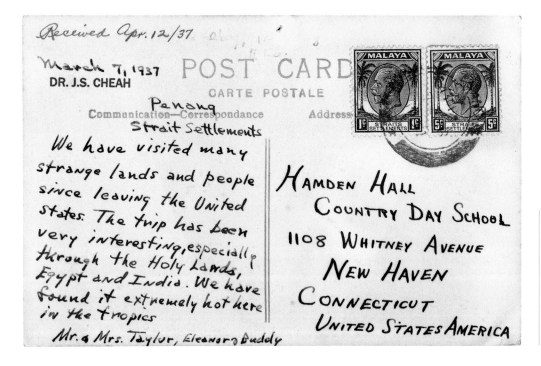

[493]

UNTITLED [VIEWS OF PENANG].

*Cancellation:* PENANG/MR 7/1937
*Back:* Divided
*Publisher:* Not stated

A real photographic ppc with nine
thumbnail views of Penang, ranging
from the Penang Harbour to the Penang
Botanic Gardens.

[494]

REVERSE OF [493].

*Cancellation:* PENANG/MR 7/1937
*Back:* Divided
*Publisher:* Not stated

The address and message side of [493].
This ppc was sent from Penang to the
USA and is franked with King George V
1¢ and 6¢ stamps. The stamps are tied by
the double ring circular date stamps (cds)
"PENANG/MR 7/1937".

**[495]**

**PENANG./JETTY TEMPLE WITH/
THE HOLY COWS.**

*Cancellation:* PENANG/JU 16/1902
*Back:* Undivided
*Publisher:* A. Kaulfuss, Penang/No. 18.

A c. 1900 ppc depicting a Hindu temple.
There are two unusual features on this
ppc. First, the stamp on this ppc is stuck
on the picture side, instead of the usual
practice of fixing it on the address side.
Second, the use of stamps bearing the
image of Queen Victoria on Penang ppcs
is not common.

**[496]**

**NO. 156 BIRD'S EYE VIEW OF
GEORGE TOWN, PENANG.**

*Cancellation:* "PENANG/12 PM/12
        MY/1937"; this cancellation
        is complete, making it of
        premium value
*Back:* Divided
*Publisher:* Not stated; printed in England

A bird's eye view of George Town
from Penang Hill, c. 1930. The use of
King George VI and Queen Elizabeth
coronation (12 May 1937) stamps on
Penang ppcs is not common.

[497]
No. 4 Govt. Building &
Clock Tower, Penang.

*Cancellation:* PENANG/17 MR/1923
*Back:* Divided
*Publisher:* P.L.I. De Silva, E. & O. Hotel.

A Nikko photo of the Government Buildings and the Queen Victoria Memorial Clock Tower. This ppc is franked with SS stamps of 1¢, 2¢, and 8¢, overprinted "Malaya/Borneo/Exhibition" in 1922. These stamps are rarely seen used on a ppc. This ppc is philatelic.

[498]
No. 13 - Penang./Botanical Garden

*Cancellation:* Swiss-type Siamese circular
date stamp/8-12-1910
*Back:* Divided
*Publisher:* T.C.B. Penang/
Printed in Germany

This ppc of the Penang Botanic Gardens, c. 1905, is franked with three Federated Malay States 1¢ stamps tied by Swiss-type Siamese cancellation. This is a rare commercial ppc sent from the Tanah Merah Estate in Kedah to France. The stamps and cancellations are rarely found on Penang ppcs.

Tin Refinery

No. 127 Tinslobs ready for shipping.

[499]

NO. 3 BEACH STREET PENANG

*Cancellation:* PENANG/17 MR/1923

*Back:* Divided

*Publisher:* P.L.I. De Silva, E. & O. Hotel./Photo Nikko/Printed in England

This c. 1910 ppc depicts Beach Street in George Town. It bears two King George V Straits Settlements 1¢ stamps, overprinted "Malaya/Borneo/Exhibition" in 1922. Several other unoverprinted stamps are also used on this ppc. This ppc was contrived by a stamp collector.

[500]

NO. 127 TINSLOBS READY FOR SHIPPING./TIN REFINERY

*Cancellation:* E & O Hotel/16-4-1910

*Back:* Divided

*Publisher:* A. Kaulfuss, Penang./Printed in Germany

This c. 1905 biview ppc is franked with a King George V 1¢ green stamp; the stamp is tied with the rare triple ring cds in violet "E & O Hotel/PENANG" and the manuscript date in ink: "16-4-1910". This cancellation is rare as it was used for only four months in 1910.

# FURTHER READING

1. Cheah Jin Seng. *Malaya: 500 Early Postcards*. Singapore: Editions Didier Millet, 2008.

2. Cheah Jin Seng. *Singapore: 500 Early Postcards*. Singapore: Editions Didier Millet, 2006.

3. Penang State Museum. *Penang: Through old picture postcards*. Penang: The Phoenix Press Sdn Bhd, 1986.

4. Ng, David. *Penang: The city and suburbs in the early twentieth century*. Penang: Georgetown Printers Sdn Bhd, 1986.

5. Khoo Salma Nasution and Malcolm Wade. *Penang: Postcard Collection 1899–1930s*. Penang: Janus Print & Resources, 2003.

6. National Archives of Malaysia and Singapore. *Reminiscences of the Straits Settlements through Postcards*. Singapore: KHL Printing Co. Pte Ltd, 2005.

7. *Penang*. 2011. <http://en.wikipedia.org/wiki/Penang>

8. *Francis Light*. 2011. <http://en.wikipedia.org/wiki/Francis_Light>

9. Wright, Arnold and H.A. Cartwright, eds. *Twentieth Century Impressions of British Malaya: Its History, People, Commerce, Industries and Resources*. London: Lloyd's Greater Britain Publishing Co. Ltd, 1908.

10. Cheah Boon Kheng. "Light on a dark subject". *Glimpses of Old Penang*, ed. Neil Khor Jin Keong. Malaysia: Star Publications Bhd, 2002.

11. *Adelaide's Founder & Surveyor – Colonel William Light, 2011*. <http://www.touradelaide.com/col_william_light/colonel_william_light.html>

12. Goh Ban Lee. "A Tale of Two Cities". *Pulau Pinang* 2(5). Penang: The Phoenix Press Sdn Bhd, 1990.

13. City Council of Penang. *Penang: Past and Present – 1786–1963*. Penang: The Ganesh Printing Works, 1966.

14. Khoo Boo Chia, Curator of Penang State Museum (1976–2006). Personal Communication. 2011.

15. Cheah Jin Seng. *Perak: 300 Early Postcards*. Singapore. Editions Didier Millet, 2009.

16. Cheah Jin Seng. *Selangor: 300 Early Postcards*. Singapore. Editions Didier Millet, 2011.

17. Thorpe, M.J. *Penang Information Guide*. Penang: Pinang Gazette Press Ltd, 1936.

18. Khoo Salma Nasution. *More than Merchants: A history of the German-speaking Community in Penang, 1800s–1940s*. Penang: Areca Books, 2006.

19. *Photomontage*. 2011. <http://en.wikipedia.org/wiki/Photomontage>

20. Kleingrothe, C.J. *Malay Peninsula (Straits Settlements & Federated Malay States)/Original photos by C.J. Kleingrothe, Medan Deli; introduction by John Falconer; captions by Neil Khor, Gretchen Liu*. Kuala Lumpur: Jugra Publications, 2009.

21. Tan Ah Yeang. Personal Communication. 2009–2010.

22. *The Singapore & Straits Directory for 1916*. Singapore: Fraser & Neave Limited, 1916.

23. Committee of Penang Festival '86. *Historical Personalities of Penang*. Penang: The Phoenix Press Sdn Bhd, 1986.

24. *Penang Information Guide*. Penang: K.H. Khaw, 1950.

25. Drabble, J.H. "The expert economy of the Straits Settlements". *The Encyclopedia of Malaysia: Early Modern History (1800–1940)*. Vol. 7, ed. Cheah Boon Kheng. Kuala Lumpur: Archipelago Press, 2001.

26. *Milestones in Growth of Penang Port*. 2011. <http://findarticles.com/p/news-articles/new-straits-times/mi_8016/is_20100329/milest...>

27. Clarke, J.W. "George Town". *Penang: Illustrated Guide*. Penang: The Municipal Council of George Town, 1952.

28. "The Service 66 Years Old". 2011. <http://newspapers.nl.sg/Digitised/Article/straitstimes19590924.2.88.aspx>

29. *Penang Ferry, Yacht & Cruise*. 2011. <http://www.penangonlinedirectory.com/Transportations/Ferry_Yacht%20_%20Cruise_...>

30. Chin Kon Yit, Chen Voon Fee. *Penang Sketchbook*. Singapore: Archipelago Press, 2003.

31. *Norddeutscher Lloyd*. 2011. <http://en.wikipedia.org/wiki/Norddeutscher_Lloyd>

32. S. Durai Raja Singam. *Malayan Street Names*. Ipoh: The Mercantile Press, 1939.

33. *Penang Clan Jetties, Weld Quay*. 2011. <http://travelmalaysiaguide.com/penang-clan-jetties-weld-quay/>

34. *Sungai Pinang*. 2011. <http://www.asiaexplorers.com/malaysia/sungai_pinang.htm>

35. *Welcome to George Town, Penang*. 2011. <http://tourismpenang.net.my/heritage.html>

36. Tang, Julia. "Origins of the State of Penang". *The Encyclopedia of Malaysia: The Rulers of Malaysia*. Vol. 16 Editorial Advisory Board. Tun Abdul Hamid bin Sarji. Kuala Lumpur: Archipelago Press, 2011.

37. *Fort Cornwallis*. 2011. <http://en.wikipedia.org/wiki/Fort_Cornwallis>

38. *Penang Esplanade Walking Tour*. 2011. <http://www.penang-traveltips.com/esplanade-self-guided-tour.htm>

39. *Seafront Grandeur: The Esplanade, the Heart of George Town*. 2011. <http://www.tourismpenang.net.my/heritage_esplanade.html>

40. *Penang Heritage Trail – The Battle of Penang War Memorial (Cenotaph)*. 2011. <http: www.mywisewife.com/penang-heritage-trail-the-battle-of-penang-war-memorial...>

41. "Armistice Day: Penang's War Memorial to be unveiled". *The Straits Times*, Singapore. 8 November 1929, p. 20.

42. Hockton, Keith, Howard Tan. *Penang: An insider guide to its historic homes, buildings, monuments and parks*. Penang: Publisher not stated, 2011.

43. *Souvenir of the Diamond Jubilee Celebrations at Penang*. Penang: Pinang Gazette Press, 1897.

44. The Historical Personalities of Penang Committee. *Historical Personalities of Penang*. Penang: The Phoenix Press Sdn Bhd, 1986.

45. *Penang Heritage: Queen Victoria Memorial Clock Tower*. 2011. <http://www.asiarediscovery.com/malaysia/81-penang-heritage-queen-victoria-memorial-clock-tower>

46. Cheah, Anna. "The Hub of Government". *Glimpses of Old Penang*, ed. Neil Khor Jin Keong. Malaysia: Star Publications Bhd, 2002, p. 10.

47. Loh Wei Leng. "Western Commercial Enterprise in the Age of Empire". *Glimpses of Old Penang*, ed. Neil Khor Jin Keong. Malaysia: Star Publications Bhd, 2002, p. 23.

48. Toh Kok Thye, Dr. Personal Communications. 2011.

49. K.H. Khaw. *Coronation Souvenir*. Penang: Cathay Printers, 1953.

50. *List of streets in George Town, Penang*. 2011. <http://en.wikipedia.org/wiki/List_of_streets_George_Town,_Penang>

51. Proud, Edward B. *The Postal History of Malaya, Vol. 1*. United Kingdom: Proud-Bailey Co. Ltd, 2000.

52. Gibbons, Stanley. *Stamp Catalogue of Brunei, Malaysia & Singapore*. London: Stanley Gibbons Ltd, 2004.

53. *Penang Supreme Court Building*. 2012. <http://www.asiaexplorers.com/malaysia/penang_supreme_court.htm>

54. Wu Lien-Teh, Ng Yok-Hing. *Queen's Scholarships of Malaya (1885–1948)*. Penang: Penang Premier Press Co. Ltd, 1949.

55. *The Free School Magazine* (Editorial). Penang: Unknown publisher, 1920.

56. Lim Teong Aik. "Hutchings School: History". *Hutchings School: 21st Anniversary Souvenir*. Penang: Unknown publisher, 1949.

57. C.S. Wong. *A Gallery of Chinese Kapitans*. Singapore: Government Printing Office, 1964.

58. Sharp, Ilsa. *The E & O Hotel: Pearl of Penang*. Singapore: Marshall Cavendish Editions. 2008.

59. Gardner, Simon, et al. *Heritage Trees of Penang*. Penang: Areca Books, 2011.

60. Bilainkin, George. *Hail Penang!* London: Sampson Low, Marston & Co. Ltd, 1932, p. 209.

61. *Eastern & Oriental Hotel: "E & O" – Penang*. London: Owen Spyer & Co., c. 1930 (year not stated).

62. *Runnymede*. 2012. <http://www.asiaexplorers.com/malaysia/runnymede.htm>

63. Foster, W., Manager of Runnymede Hotel writing to a patron, Captain R. Christiansen, in Bangkok. The postcard is dated 27 October 1924 (collection of author).

64. *Penang Convent Centenary Celebrations, 1852–1952*. Penang: Georgetown Printers, 1952.

65. *Convent Light School*. 2012. <http://www.asiaexplorers.com/malaysia/conventlightstreet.htm>

66. *St. Xavier's Institution*. 2012. <http://en.wikipedia.org/wiki/St._Xavier's_Institution>

67. Parfitt, I.G.J. *S.G.G.S. Magazine* 1(1). Penang: Unknown printer, 1938.

68. *Methodist Boys' School*. 2012. <http://en.wikipedia.org/wiki/Methodist_Boys'_School_(Penang)>

69. *Chung Ling High School*. 2012. <http://en.wikipedia.org/wiki/Chung_Ling_High_School>

70. Thant, T. *A Capture in Ink: The Making of 103 Years of Medical Services*. Penang: Sun Prints Sdn Bhd, 1985.

71. Cheah, JS, Tay G. "The Marei Ika Daigaka (Syonan Medical College) during the Japanese Occupation of Singapore (1942–1945)". *Singapore Medical Journal*, 38 (12): 3540. Singapore: Stamford Press, 2003.

72. *Jerejak*. 2012. <http://en.wikipedia.org/wiki/Jerejak>

73. *Beach Street, George Town*. 2012. <http://www.penang-traveltips.com/beach-street.htm>

74. *Lebuh Bishop*. 2012. <http://www.penang-traveltips.com/bishop-street.htm>

75. Wright, Nadia. "One of Penang's Historical Minorities – The Armenians". *Glimpses of Old Penang*, ed. Malini Dias. Malaysia: Star Publications Bhd, 2002.

76. Chan Suan Choo. *The Pinang Peranakan Mansion*. Penang: Eastern Printers Sdn Bhd, 2011.

77. *History of Lebuh Chulia*. 2012. <http://www.penang-traveltips.com/chulia-street.htm>

78. Khoo Su Nin. "The Acheen Street Community: A Melting Pot of the Malay World". *Pulau Pinang* 2(2). Penang: The Phoenix Press Sdn Bhd, 2000, p. 19.

79. Ong Seng Huat. "The Khoo Clan". *Pulau Pinang* 2(1). Penang: The Phoenix Press Sdn Bhd, 2000, p. 2.

80. *St. George's Church, Penang*. 2012. <http://en.wikipedia.org/wiki/St._George's_Church,_Penang>

81. *Church of the Assumption (Penang)*. 2012. <http://en.wikipedia.org/wiki/Church_of_the_Assumption_(Penang)>

82. Khoo Su Nin. *Streets of George Town, Penang*. Penang: Janus Print & Resources, 1993.

83. *Lebuh Campbell*. 2012. <http://www.penang-traveltips.com/campbell-street.htm>

84. *Welcome to Penang Club Website*. 2012. <http://penangclub.net/portal1/>

85. *Burmah Road, George Town*. 2012. <http://www.penang-traveltips.com/burmah-road.htm>

86. Khor Jin Keong, Neil. *The Penang Turf Club: 140 Years of Racing*. Malaysia: Vivar Printer Sdn Bhd, 2004.

87. Francis, Ric, Colin Ganley. *Penang Trams, Trolley Buses & Railways*. Penang: Areca Books, 2006.

88. *Tribute to Cheah Leong Keah (1875–1941)*. 2012. <http://silverjubileehome.org/silver_founder.html>

89. *Penang Botanic Gardens*. 2012. <http://en.wikipedia.org/wiki/Penang_Botanic_Gardens>

90. Ambiga Devy (ed.). *A Guide to the Penang Botanical Gardens*. Penang: Jutaprint, reprinted 2009.

91. *Penang Hill*. 2012. <http://en.wikipedia.org/wiki/Penang_Hill>

92. "Penang Hill". *Pulau Pinang* 1(4). Penang: The Phoenix Press, 1989.

93. "Bride in Penang in the Sixties". *The Straits Times Annual*. Singapore: The Straits Times Press, 1938.

94. Khor, Margaret. "Penang Hill". *Pulau Pinang* 1(4). Penang: The Phoenix Press, 1989, p. 4.

95. Ahmad Chik and Joan Shori. "Bukit Pinang". *Pulau Pinang* 1(4). Penang: The Phoenix Press Sdn Bhd, 1989, p.14.

96. Lim Kean Siew. "Hill Walks". *Pulau Pinang* 1(4). Penang: The Phoenix Press Sdn Bhd, 1989, p. 22.

97. The Craig Hotel (advertisement). *The Straits Times Annual*. Singapore: The Straits Times Press, 1939, p. 142.

98. *Ayer Itam Village, Penang*. 2012. <http://www.penang-traveltips.com/air-itam-village.htm>

99. Poon Teong. *The Origins: Rules and Regulations of the Kek Lok Si Monastery, Ayer Itam, Penang*. Penang: The Centurion Press, 1907.

100. Lim Pui Huen, Patricia. *Through the Eyes of the King: The Travels of King Chulalongkorn to Malaya*. Singapore: Utopia Press Pte Ltd, 2009.

101. *Lonely Planet review for Kek Lok Si Temple*. 2012. <http://www.lonelyplanet.com/malaysia/peninsular-malaysia-west-coast/…>

102. *Snake Temple*. 2012. <http://en.wikipedia.org/wiki/Snake_Temple>

103. *Seberang Perai*. 2012. <http://en.wikipedia.org/wiki/Seberang_Perai>

104. *Butterworth*. 2012. <http://en.wikipedia.org/wiki/Butterworth,_Penang>

105. Tregonning, K.G. *Straits Tin: A brief account of the first 75 years of The Straits Tin Co. Ltd, 1887–1962*. Singapore: The Straits Times Press (M) Ltd, 1962.

106. "Orang Sebarang: The Gambling Racket in the Province". *The Straits Times Annual*. Singapore: The Straits Times Press, 1936, p. 68.

107. Lewis, Roger Scott. "The First Census, December 1788". *Glimpses of Old Penang*, ed. Neil Khor Jin Keong. Malaysia: Star Publications, 2002.

108. Adams, Margaret. *Penang: Illustrated Guide*. Bolton and London: Tillotsons (Bolton) Ltd, 1952.

109. "Our own correspondent. Prince at Penang." *The Straits Times*, 24 May 1922, p. 9. <http://newspapers.nl.sg/Digitised/Article/straitstimes19220524.2.41.aspx>

110. *Chingay Parade (South East Asia)*. 2012. <http://en.wikipedia.org/wiki/Chingay_Parade_(South_East_Asia)>

111. A. Shukor Rahman. *Flying Colours of Tanjung: The Story of Penang Malays*. Penang: Pintra Printing Sdn Bhd, 2010.

112. Haji Abdul Mubin Sheppard. "The Penang Boria". *Malaya in History* 10(1), ed. Mubin Sheppard. Kuala Lumpur: Printcraft Ltd, 1965, p. 40.

113. Khoo Joo Ee. *The Straits Chinese: A Cultural Legacy*. Amsterdam/Kuala Lumpur: The Pepin Press, 1996.

114. Khor Jin Keong, Neil, ed. *Glimpses of Old Penang*. Selangor: Star Publications (M) Bhd, 2002. p. 133.

115. Ong Siang Song, Sir. "The King's Chinese". *The Straits Times Annual*. Singapore: The Straits Times Press, 1936, p. 38.

116. *Straits Settlements Volunteer Force*. 2012. <http://en.wikipedia.org/wiki/Straits Settlements_Volunteer Force>

117. Cheah Jin Seng. "Opium Addiction in Penang and Malaya (1786–1941)". *To Heal the Sick*, ed. Ong Hean Teik. Penang: The Phoenix Press Sdn Bhd, 2004, p. 23.

118. Wu Lian-Teh. *Plague Fighter*. Cambridge: W. Heffer & Sons Ltd, 1959.

119. *1928 Chingay Procession: Souvenir*. Penang: The Centurion Press Co. Ltd, 1928.

120. *Indians in Penang*. 2012. <http://www.indianmalaysian.com/penang_indians.htm>

121. "Statue of Light back at original spot". *The Star*, 17 August 2003. <http://www.penangmuseum.gov.my/museum/en/museum/blog/returned-its-original-site>

122. *Melaka and George Town, Historic Cities of the Straits of Malacca*. 2012. <http://whc.unesco.org/en/list/1223/>

123. Nordin Husin. *Trade and Society in the Straits of Melaka: Dutch Melaka and English Penang, 1780–1830*. NIAS Press–Singapore University Press, 2006, p. 184.

124. *Taburan Penduduk dan Ciri-ciri Asas Demografi 2010*. Jabatan Perangkaan Malaysia. Putrajaya: Jabatan Perangkaan Malaysia.

125. Loh Wei Leng, Dr. *Penang's Trade and Shipping in The Imperial Age: The 19th Century. The Penang Story – International Conference 2002*. University of Malaya. 2002.

126. Jayati Bhattacharya. *Collaborations and Contestations: The South Asian Commercial Networks in Penang in the Nineteenth and Twentieth Centuries*. Institute of Southeast Asian Studies: Singapore. No date stated.

127. *About St. Xavier's*. 2012. <http://www.sxi.edu.my/index.php?option=com_content&view=article&id=4&Itemid=6>

128. *Our History*. 2012. <http://mbspg.com/cms/aboutus/our-history>

129. *History/Chronology of Leong San Tong Khoo Kongsi*. 2012. <http://www.khookongsi.com.my/>

130. Jones, David, Dr. *Colonial Botanic Gardens and World Heritage: the significance of the Penang 'Waterfall' Botanic Gardens*. School of Architecture, Landscape, Architecture & Urban Design: Adelaide University. Date not stated.

131. *Penang HSBC Building, George Town*. 2012. <http://www.penang-traveltips.com/hsbc-building.htm>

132. *SS Takliwa*. 2012. <http://en.wikipedia.org/wiki/SS_Takliwa>

133. *Penang's vanished spot on the pilgrim route*. 2010. <http://www.igeorgetownpenang.com/features/740-penangs-vanished-spot-on-the-pilgrim-route>

134. *Blue Book For The Year 1914*. Government Printing Office, Singapore: Government Printer. 1915.

135. *Straits Settlements Blue Book For The Year 1938*. Government Printing Office: Singapore. 1940.

136. Lo Man Yuk. "Chinese Names of Streets in Penang". *Journal of the Straits Branch of the Royal Asiatic Society*. Singapore: The American Missions Press, January 1900, p. 212.

137. Nordin Hussin. "A Tale of Two Colonial Port-towns in the Straits of Melaka: Dutch Melaka and English Penang". *Journal of the Malaysian Branch of the Royal Asiatic Society*. Kuala Lumpur: Malaysian Branch of the Royal Asiatic Society, 2002, p. 93.

138. D.S. Jones. "The 'Waterfall' Botanic Garden on Pulau Pinang: The Foundations of the Penang Botanic Gardens 1884–1910". *Journal of the Malaysian Branch of the Royal Asiatic Society*. Kuala Lumpur: Malaysian Branch of the Royal Asiatic Society, 1997, p. 75.

139. Liow Woon Khin, Benny. "Buddhist Temples and Associations in Penang, 1845–1948". *Journal of the Malaysian Branch of the Royal Asiatic Society*. Kuala Lumpur: Malaysian Branch of the Royal Asiatic Society, 1989, Vol. LXII Part 1, p. 57.

## ACKNOWLEDGEMENTS

I would like to extend my heartfelt thanks to:

- Mr Didier Millet, Mr Douglas Amrine, Ms Sng Siok Ai, Mr Martin Cross, Ms Joane Sharmila and Ms Vani for making this book possible.

- Mr Peter How Kian Huat for constant encouragement and technical assistance.

- Dr Toh Kok Thye for the loan of four ppcs.

- Madam Tan Ah Yeang for the loan of two ppcs.

- Professor Cheah Boon Kheng for fact-checking the book.

- The following for providing useful information: Mr Khoo Boo Chia; Mr Koay S.T.; Dr Ong Hean Teik and Dr Toh Kok Thye.

## ABOUT THE AUTHOR

Professor Cheah Jin Seng is a philatelist and deltiologist particularly well-versed in the postal history and deltiology of Malaysia and Singapore. Born in Penang, he is a Fellow of the Royal Philatelic Society of London and a Director of the Singapore Philatelic Museum. A former board member of the National Museum of Singapore, Professor Cheah has written and co-published extensively on the subjects of stamps and postcards in Malaysia and Singapore. He is the author of *Selangor: 300 Early Postcards* (2011), *Perak: 300 Early Postcards* (2009), *Malaya: 500 Early Postcards* (2008) and *Singapore: 500 Early Postcards* (2006), all published by Editions Didier Millet. He also collects Chinese *peranakan* artefacts, old photographs and books related to the medical and local history of Singapore and Malaysia. By profession, he is an Emeritus Consultant at the Department of Medicine, National University Hospital, Singapore, and Professorial Fellow of the National University of Singapore. Professor Cheah is also a Physician and Endocrinologist, having obtained his Bachelor of Medicine and Surgery (Honours) and a Doctorate of Medicine from the National University of Singapore. He is a Fellow of the following institutions: the Royal Australasian College of Physicians, the Royal College of Physicians, Edinburgh, and the Academy of Medicine, Singapore.